STAR-SPANGLED MANNERS

In Which
Miss Manners™
Defends
American Etiquette
(FOR A CHANGE)

JUDITH MARTIN

W. W. NORTON & COMPANY
NEW YORK LONDON

Copyright © 2003 by Judith Martin

For information about permission to reproduce selections from this book, write to
Permissions, W. W. Norton & Company, Inc., 500 Fifth Avenue, New York, NY 10110

The text of this book is composed in Bembo with the display set in Filosofia
Composition by Adrian Kitzinger
Manufacturing by The Haddon Craftsmen, Inc.
Book design by Chris Welch
Illustrations by Michael Wood
Production manager: Amanda Morrison

Library of Congress Cataloging-in-Publication Data
Martin, Judith, 1938–
Star-spangled manners : in which Miss Manners defends American etiquette (for a
change) / by Judith Martin.—1st ed.
p. cm.
ISBN 0-393-04861-6 (hardcover)
1. Etiquette—United States—History. I. Title.
BJ1853 .M298 2002
395' .0973—dc21   2002008352

W. W. Norton & Company, Inc., 500 Fifth Avenue, New York, N.Y. 10110
www.wwnorton.com

W. W. Norton & Company Ltd., Castle House, 75/76 Wells Street, London W1T 3QT

1 2 3 4 5 6 7 8 9 0

*In memory of Pandora Campbell
and for Jeremy Campbell*

Contents

With the author's grateful thanks to David Hendin, Angela von der Lippe, and Kimberley Heatherington

Revolutionary Etiquette
The Formula

HERE IS THE scenario for the heroic struggle to proclaim a new etiquette. Like other historical dramas, it
contains some truth and much blood. Super costumes,
too, but only before the triumph of virtue. It can be set any-
where, and in any time period.

After the noble goals of revolution have been carved into
public stone, the victors' aspirations and bravery lure them on to
an even riskier venture. Dizzy with triumph at having toppled a
government and retooled an economy, revolutionaries begin to
imagine themselves capable of becoming master etiquetteers.
They decide to redesign everyday social behavior for their
countrymen in accordance with the principles for which they
all staked their lives.

So begins the cycle that will typically lead to the post-
revolutionary regime's doom. Hubris strikes again. That it is
expedient to kill a king, rather than to wait for his natural
demise, is something a populace can come to accept, perhaps to
relish. That the people's own customs and costumes are to be

radically changed by edict, rather than being allowed to evolve haphazardly and linger sentimentally beyond their time, is not. Yet messing with the national etiquette is one of the great spoils of revolutionary success.

The vainglorious titles of the vanquished are abolished, and plain, uniclass titles are minted. People will now address one another with simple dignity, as Citizen, for example, or as Comrade.

The clothing styles of the previous regime are seen as hilarious proof of the wearers' foppishness, uselessness, witlessness, and wastefulness, not to mention their callous exploitation of myriad workers whose eyesight, fingertips, and very lives were wasted in producing them. Now that the once-terrifying tyrants have been downgraded to twits, their no-nonsense successors make a show of refusing to demean themselves by wearing (depending on the era) silk knee breeches and wigs, tail coats, dinner jackets, or ties. From now on, dress will be dictated by function, not fashion.

Luxurious possessions lose their glamour when they are revealed to have no intrinsic worth, their only purpose having been to arouse envy and spur competition. As people work together for the common good, rivalry ceases to exist and impractical objects are no longer coveted. Purely decorative art is exposed as a sham, and the cry is heeded to develop art that is universally accessible and ennobling.

The rituals of state are abolished, not only because they represent defunct loyalties but because they are inherently pompous and silly. New ones are promulgated to reflect the rough but communal spirit that opens the era of honesty and decency.

Social customs are discovered to be based on petty deceits and exclusionary practices, whereas a newly cleansed people disdains subterfuge and cliquishness. All such boundaries and niceties are stripped away, and the greatest courtesy is to embrace all and to be unfailingly frank and forthright.

Thus the horrors and hardships of revolution are justified by more than relief from arbitrary injustice and unreasonable taxes. Daily life is bound to improve, now that the uglier sides of human nature have been neutralized by happy circumstances and high-mindedness. The causes of degradation having been removed, people naturally want to treat one another with dignity and consideration.

This blissful state endures as long as the popular government is able to impose it on the newly empowered citizenry by means of terror. The consequences of being denounced to pitiless authorities not only encourage people to practice the new etiquette but keep them alert to lapses from it in others. Interest in who is adhering most strictly and who shows signs of yearning for the old ways runs so high that everyone in the bonded brotherhood enthusiastically turns spy on everyone else to ensure that the rules are not violated. Soon they are all policing and denouncing one another, and even the ruling authorities get into the spirit and start tattling on their peers.

Meanwhile, a general suspicion has been mounting since the entire new regime was observed to be making official and personal use of whatever properties and goods had been left behind by the abolished regime (and yet had escaped its own righteous destruction). Pushed to explain, it declares that it despises all this fancy nonsense, but is heroically sacrificing its own taste to recycle the remnants of the past as an austerity measure; its only motivation is to avoid making immediate replacements so that all available resources can be directed toward relieving the heroic population.

Nevertheless, it begins to appear that the heroic population has something else in mind. It had assumed all along that its own reward for revolution was that it would get to take over the coveted trappings. Eventually, it comes out that just about everyone yearns for the old ways.

True, the revolutionaries had kept themselves going in battle by ridiculing their predecessors, but leisure for sophisticated reflection reveals that those war cries were—merely war cries. When the smoke clears and life resumes its familiar petty struggle, it is impossible to ignore the suspicion that nothing freshly built or instituted can compare with the newly poignant beauty of what was despised and discarded. All those denunciations involved a small misunderstanding. It was not the forms and symbols of the old etiquette that the people resented, time having rendered these graceful and precious. It was the distribution system. Some were receiving undeserved honors and others, undeserved humiliation. This was supposed to be fixed by reversing who was getting which.

So the deserving, meaning the new regime, frankly— although clumsily, through lack of practice—assume the old privileges, even when this puts a damper on the sport of catching one another lapsing from strict observance of their own harshly proclaimed doctrine. When this habit becomes blatant, speeded along by their own relatives' being found to have few inhibitions about appearing exalted, they can no longer pass off the resumed luxury as a manifestation of the previously stated revolutionary policy. This makes them subject to open contempt and ridicule for the double crime of having imposed a new etiquette and having failed to practice it.

In addition, the decorative stuff is not becoming on them. Those who made such an inspiring appearance in battle tatters look suspiciously awkward in their new finery, not having had the training in subtle refinement that is required to handle these goods without making them look stolen. Depending on how rested everyone is after the last revolution, it appears to be time for another change.

As the stranglehold lessens, and the element of fear subsides, whether this takes years or decades, that yearning for the old ways returns with a vengeance. Aristocrats and plutocrats are lionized, descendents of toppled kings are plucked from their shabby lives to have their hands wept upon, and the population is primed for a coup. Anything would be better than listening to that tired rhetoric about The People from badly dressed bullies with brutish manners—even, perhaps especially, strange men who design their own uniforms and pronounce themselves the founders of dynasties. The gaudier the fresh usurpers and uniforms are, the better. Whatever refinements time had etched onto the old customs are no longer discernible, and people accept these cruder versions as a semblance of those better days long ago.

So a new etiquette does triumph, but only as a bowdlerized version of the etiquette-before-last. In time, that, too, is refined, overrefined, and finally pronounced arrogant and laughable. Nostalgia turns its perpetually mournful eye back to the clean and virtuous simplicity of the revolution. . . .

The world has witnessed some spectacular sagas depicting revolutionary mayhem in pursuit of respect. Heroes burst forth from the confines of conventionality. Inspiration burns through fields and factories. Dreary lives turn horrific. Unspeakable cruelty is countered by the unsuspected nobility that arises to defy it. In the finale, glory streams over the land, searing away the suffering.

Then what? Comic villains were toppled, and chilling villains sprang up in their places. The costumes are clumsier and the customs are no more equitable. The best approximation of happiness is to end up with a coalition of colorless rulers who snipe at one another steadily enough to spare the citizens the nuisance of keeping watch while they are busy sniping with their peers. Respect has been dropped from the national agenda, and it is forgotten that in inspiring all that sacrifice, respect had been thought as important as bread.

Perhaps you remember the stylish French version of the drama, featuring not one but two dynastic cycles, the Bourbon and the Napoleonic, or the endless Russian version, which, having once riveted the world with its daring, may yet be droning on for those still paying attention. Budget versions pop up in odd places and run through the cycle so fast that the curious hardly have time to learn to distinguish the warring factions, and hastily assembled humanitarian rescue missions are left stranded and bewildered.

Is it possible to do a version of this with a happy ending?

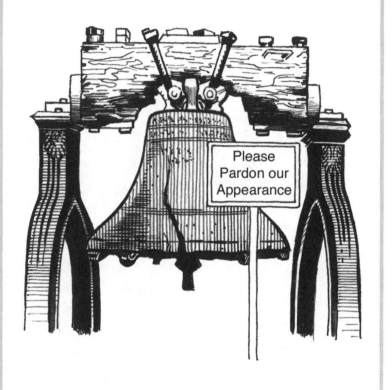

Please
Pardon our
Appearance

Chapter 1

The Pitch

Equality and Dignity, Once and for All

ARE THERE NO revolutionaries who can get this right? What would it take to make people realize that although a decent standard of behavior is worth fighting for, it requires an ongoing struggle and the consent of the governed?

It would take leadership that was serious about etiquette, respectful of tradition, determined to make reasonable changes for the benefit of all rather than only to aggrandize itself, and willing to apply a light touch in administering these. It would take a population committed to fairness in theory even if it has trouble with the practice, and reasonably open to improving its ways.

Etiquette as theater

It is invaluable for the people who attempt this to have a sense of theater. Etiquette governs the words and signs by which people shape their thoughts and intentions to make them palatable to others, instead of spewing them out at will, and it is the business of the theater to know how to use outward manifestations to proper effect. On stage, words, looks, and gesture are used to reveal, whereas in life, even the best of citizens will occasionally need to employ them to conceal, but anyone who wants to promote human harmony has to understand the language of behavior.

They should be receptive to different approaches to scripting their lives, and willing to keep rewriting in the determination to achieve the desired effect. They should have the ambition to go after whatever roles they want to play, confident that talent and work will succeed (although knowing the right people never hurts), and to be able to contribute to an ensemble. They should know how to use design and gesture to capture attention and dramatize a message. They should be able to participate in dazzling displays that produce a sense of identity and delight. They also need to realize that selling the product is part of the job.

The people suited to do this, who cherish the ideals of fairness and are expert entertainers, turn out to be the citizens of the United States. Ours is an immigrant population that was self-selected from around the world for the desire to be treated fairly, the imagination to sketch a new life, and the determination to pursue it. It is the proponents of egalitarian behavior and their descendants who have been developing the new world etiquette.

It is something of a hoot that this task falls to Americans, whose manners have been universally ridiculed as both backwater and brash, who are racked with self-doubts about mastering even the etiquette of taking their daily bread, who voice their yearning for civility while justifying a rash of new rages. All the same, we have had an enormous and beneficial influence on the way people everywhere behave. We have streamlined state ceremony and cautioned pompous courts to court popularity. We have modernized dress and modes of address, narrowing the range of usage so as to minimize the differences between the weak and the powerful. Right now, we are busy catching people at such traditional sources of amusement as belittling women, berating the poor, and smoking, and telling them to be ashamed of themselves.

Etiquette at war

We can do this because our revolution did have a happy ending. We followed the formula—rhetoric, revolution, ridicule, reform —but managed to omit its last element, the counterrevolution. We were thus saved from repeated carnage, although not spared from tepid reruns of the emotional and stylistic cycle.

During our revolution, we kept up our spirits by laughing at the enemy's gaudy uniforms and mincing ways. Afterward, our forefathers considered themselves charged with the business of designing a form of etiquette that would be philosophically consistent with the new country's ideals. They agreed on the principles and fought over the particulars, and we have been at it from that day to this.

We have always had dissenters and backsliders aplenty. From the beginning, we have had our own self-anointed aristocrats, who, lacking pedigrees featuring ancient warriors and plunderers, pride themselves on immigrant-ancestors as ranked by the date—never mind the reason—that they fled the countries where they were known. We also have vigilant forces to keep the hoity-toity in line, although the weapon used to spread fear has never been the guillotine or the gulag, only the sharp edge of American satire.

We have had generational etiquette conflicts that turned bitter, and ethnic, racial, and geographical ones that turned monstrous. Our Civil War was fueled by opposing ideals of manners:

the graceful in contrast to the forthright, to put it generously; or, as characterized by one side, the civilized as opposed to the savage, and as characterized by the other side, the decadent as opposed to the dignified. In our own era, when that war's more immediate causes have become moot and the economy keeps shifting the population around so that northern and southern affiliations exist more through adoption than birth, the animosity arising from those conflicting styles of manners is still running high, mostly among the losers.

Clashing styles

We keep up the other conflicts as well. Peaceful etiquette development is propelled by the fact that in times of convoluted customs, people yearn for directness, while in times of bare behavior, they long for charm and order. We are in the latter period now. After decades of advocating total communication unhampered by tact, a no-frills demeanor uncluttered by such grace notes as honorifics and precedence systems, and self-assertion unrestrained by consideration for family, social, and community harmony, our public discourse is dominated by a call for civility.

The force pushing these swings is obscured from general understanding, however, because all people always believe themselves to be behaving naturally (as whatever rules they have grown up with seem, through habit, to be natural). No one admits to countenancing artificiality, which all would consider tantamount to condemning themselves as frauds. Therefore, people who are unhappy with the general social tone, for whichever excess it happens to be practicing at the time, always cast the manners they advocate as honest and sincere, in contrast to the hypocrisy and selfishness of the manners they observe.

In periods, such as the Victorian, when etiquette had grown highly complicated, the charge of artificiality brought by their Edwardian children seemed obvious, although that smart young set considered themselves exceedingly clever to discover and decry their elders' delicacy. In the alternating loose periods, such as our own, believing that this is still the problem requires the argument that the present bluntness is nevertheless artificial because humanity is, in its natural state, caring, considerate, and charitable, and these qualities, if allowed to flourish unrestrained, will produce effortlessly polite behavior without the nuisance of obeying rules. Therefore, it is reasoned, the rude behavior we endure is actually the result of human nature being warped, through society's pervasive lies or demanding conditions or unnecessary suffering or, worst of all, its repressive attitudes toward sex. (That society represses sex is also a truism of every period, however licentious and overpopulated.)

American etiquette's solid foundation

Despite all this commotion, and despite the result that every era both uses and protests rules, the original American principles of manners brandished after our revolution have never been overthrown. All that happens is regular ricocheting from predictability to creativity, and back from chaos to constriction; evolutionary changes paralleling social and technological developments; and, as a constant, everyone denouncing everyone else's behavior. The miracle is that we manage these without undermining the basic American commitment to the Etiquette of Equality.

Although—or perhaps because—our forefathers never managed to agree on specifics, much less codify (and laughably less enforce) a body of rules for daily behavior, American manners have pretty much developed along the guidelines these gentlemen did explicitly set out. Changes that look like upheavals keep occurring, but these are associated with changes in the philosophy and circumstances of the society, not a total rejection of the original premise. Alternating desires for more openness or for more orderliness have not destroyed that. (Great errors and widespread lapses in living up to our standard are common, as they are in all cultures, but if a standard were judged in terms of the people who fail to meet it, we should have to conclude that the existence of criminals demonstrates that the legal system is useless.)

Even Americans who revile etiquette—a stand that passes for idealism in back-to-human-nature periods such as the late twentieth century's, from which stray adherents linger among us—declare that they do so in the cause of equal respect for and treatment of all. This is the very tenet on which American etiquette is based.

The curiosity of having compassionate people attack a system that mandates and codifies consideration for others is doubly odd when the etiquette-bashers are Americans, whose national etiquette refuses to dignify anything resembling class distinctions. It arises from the common error of assuming that etiquette exists only in regard to formal situations, particularly those involving irritatingly stiff clothes and costly but mysterious table implements. Those who condemn all of etiquette on that account fail to examine their own conventions, which may favor painfully body-piercing jewelry or require the skill of subduing hot, dripping food using only paper and plastic; illogically, these are exempted from their definitions of etiquette regarding clothing and food. Thus they are able to come to the misguided conclusion that a predilection for costly discomfort renders etiquette oppressive to the poor and that tossing it will be no great sacrifice on the part of the comfort-loving crusader.

Protecting the powerless

The opposite is true: A major etiquette system is needed if the powerless are to be protected in support of the American principle of protecting minorities. By requiring the strong to restrain themselves in their behavior toward the weak—and they are bound not only by the ordinary rules but by a special supplement in the form of that counterintuitive rule known as noblesse oblige—it skewers the Darwinian system that would otherwise prevail.

Pushing people around because you are powerful enough to get away with it is, by definition, rude. Societies that condone or even institutionalize such practices do not even try to pretend these are polite. Instead, they define the victims as being not fully human, and therefore outside of the society's system of etiquette protection.

This is a notorious historical failing, of which our greatest patriots were guilty, and which subsequent generations have striven to correct. Yet forms of it survive. The unrepentant use this exclusionary rationale to sustain the illusion of being ladies or gentlemen no matter how harshly they treat their employees or children. Many modern moralists also favor an exclusionary definition, because it enables them to humiliate people who disagree with their ideals without damaging their conviction that they are benefactors of humanity.

No matter who uses the might-makes-right system, powerful

individuals or powerful majorities, it is a violation of our etiquette principle requiring equal respect for all. That goes not only for racists, misogynists, and people who are just plain nasty but for crusaders for virtue and the distinguished authors of that sacred principle of equal etiquette for all.

A paralegal system

For all its pesky restrictions, etiquette is an unheralded champion of liberty. Nowhere is that more evident than in America: A society that loves freedom enough to want to protect rudeness itself against legal action paradoxically cannot manage to do this without pledging obedience to the authority of etiquette. Mere exhortations to be tolerant rarely have discernible results. There has to be a complete etiquette system with clearly defined rules regulating trivial actions.

Etiquette-bashers will agree that the depth of a society's devotion to freedom can be measured by the extent to which it tolerates offputting behavior. Can one insult its leaders with impunity? Stomp on its flag? Make ugly faces and revolting gestures to important people? Wear vulgar clothes in public? Flaunt, if not actually expose, what our forefathers were taught to refer to delicately as "any part of the body not usually discovered"? Shout awful things at crowds? Drive everyone crazy with disgust and indignation? The United States takes pride in limiting its legal system to ban only behavior that is actually dangerous, as these and other forms of irritating behavior ordinarily are not.

As far as we know, however, the intention was not to create a society that was perfectly free and perfectly unbearable. It was taken for granted that custom and social pressure, if not our vaunted sense of fairness, would be powerful deterrents to keep people from routinely exercising their freedom without regard to how ugly this might make life for their fellow citizens—and ultimately for themselves, since these free and angry citizens would be no more inclined to accept casual indignities than are they.

Reasonable people recognize that although maximum freedom is desirable, there must be some restraint placed on behavior if life is to be lived more or less in peace—even if the usual proposal for reconciling these goals is not quite workable. Would-be etiquetteers are always suggesting, in effect, that the restraint be represented by severe restrictions slapped on people who are annoying them, while the sacred commitment to absolute freedom be represented by a lack of restrictions on their own actions, not only because they mean well but because the people whom they upset deserve the worst. This accounts for why, when we are all able to agree that we desperately want civility, we have not been able to achieve it, even though doing so would require nothing more than—just doing so.

The weapon of opinion

Fairness aside, how are these advocates of civility going to make other people (who are probably also loudly advocating civility) behave? Absent the ability to fine, jail, or execute offenders, etiquette has no tough answer to that cheeky question, "Yeah, and who's going to make me?"

The power of social disapproval is in bad repute. When it is not dismissed as ineffective, it is condemned as intrusive, if not unjust. It may be that the greatest proof of the effectiveness of social disapproval is its demonstrated ability to turn on itself. It has made a social crime out of being "judgmental." What, except a fear of social disapproval, could make people eager to deny, with a touch of pride, that they exercise their judgment?

This is not to suggest that Americans no longer pass judgment on one another. Anyone who believes that tolerance has reached that amazing point should try lighting a cigarette, even in a place where it is legally permissible, or declining to take off his tie and jacket when urged to make himself comfortable. What the apparent ban on judgment is understood to mean is that the areas have changed in which disapproving of one's fellow citizens is socially permissible. Sexual habits and criminal history: off limits. Body weight and consumer choices: fair game.

Incentives to obey

Nevertheless, the moral authority of etiquette has been all but vanquished by the cult of self-interest. Promoters of politeness are pathetically reduced to pleading for it as yet another way of pursuing personal gain. Not daring to suggest that one should behave well because it is the right thing to do, they promote it as yet another ploy to achieve material success or as a safety measure to prevent violent retaliation.

That such promises constitute something of a fraud has not escaped public notice. There is some truth in the declaration that charm helps people overcharge, and that suaveness can tame rage, but anyone can see that counterexamples abound. It is not unusual for ruthless people to triumph, supercilious people to profit, and kindly people to be their victims. If immediate practical consequences were the only reason to refrain from rudeness, the case can be—and constantly is—made that immediate selfish considerations urge practicing it.

The long-range practical consequences are not used as an

incentive to obey etiquette, presumably because they are thought to exceed the contemporary attention span. In contrast to the immediate danger of angering drivers, future public retaliation seems to strike too randomly and generally to make purchasing protection through politeness worthwhile. Regardless, such consequences do catch up with the situations. When enough people have secured an advantage for themselves by dropping all pretense of respecting the sensibilities of others, those others claim that they have no choice but to practice such behavior themselves. The advantage is nullified, and the atmosphere becomes so contaminated that eruptions of fury are a common phenomenon.

A profession's reputation

A modern illustration of Short-Term Interests v. Long-Term Interests can be found in the evolution of behavior deemed appropriate and effective in the legal profession, in regard to its interest in being considered trustworthy. In its earlier stage as a mere service job, lawyering was not especially highly regarded, but in the twentieth century, when law developed a tradition requiring courtly behavior on the part of direct adversaries, it acquired enormous public esteem as the domain of gentlemen. Then someone discovered that gentlemen could only put up pathetic defenses against attack dogs. Those unhampered by professional etiquette saw those exposed gentlemanly necks and bared their teeth.

However eloquently traditional leaders of the profession deplored this deterioration of standards, they naturally went with the winners, the object, after all, being to win. As a result, brutal methods achieved victory not only in legal cases but also in competition for positions, even within the old gentlemanly firms. Viciousness replaced courtliness, and those who would not switch styles lost out.

Soon there were few etiquette-bound gentlemen left to be snarled away, only attack dogs (by this time of both sexes, as the change coincided with the rise of women in the profession) snarling at other attack dogs. The edge offered by rudeness disappeared as suddenly as it had arisen, and adversaries were again equally matched, but at a cruder level.

Eventually, there were two related results that even yet confound the legal profession. The first was that legal contests became mired in petty wrangling, to the extent that these are consuming time and money, not to mention the apparatus of the justice system, at frightening rates. If lawyers are able to accept the diminished intellectual challenge in the switch from argument to shouting match while profiting from the accelerated billing, it is because they failed to foresee the second, inevitable, long-range result. Sacrificed politeness, combined with burgeoning revenue, soon placed the legal profession in the public esteem at a level hardly above that of thugs.

Some may count lawyer-bashing as a small price for a large income, but that would be another instance of shortsightedness. In the long run, reaction is taking the form not only of lawyer jokes but of exploration, development, and use of alternative services. One may argue that a litigious society cannot afford to scorn its lawyers, but the society is no less health conscious, and the medical profession, with its combination of rudeness (in this case, arrogance toward clients) and prosperity, has also suffered in practical ways from public anger. Lawyers and doctors have much to learn from rock stars about making conceitedness glamorous and from headwaiters about making intimidation effective.

Setting new lows

Other such downward cycles, where the rude succeed and therefore attract imitators, have been spiraling throughout the various subdivisions of working and domestic life. As they reach their unpleasant conclusions, everyone's quality of life deteriorates. That, along with boredom with behavioral minimalism as a style, now makes the cause pressing. Casual but constant noncompliance with etiquette has filled public space with insult and invective, and poisoned professional and personal relationships with criticalness and callousness. Rule-dependent activities, such as sports contests, college classes, and legislative sessions, have erupted into melees that hinder them from fulfilling their own missions. Anti-etiquette forces have made defiance of rules—any rules, not only ones perceived as unjust—seem heroic.

The theory that harmony was to be achieved by approximating a childlike state, eliminating inhibitions that might interfere between impulse and action, turned out to be less of a success than advertised. It failed to allow for the appearance of childlike results, such as people freely bashing one another for no better reason than that they were cranky.

A premature obituary

Cumulatively, this has taken its toll, and the result was the sudden announcement, everywhere, of the demise of American etiquette. This is an hysterical exaggeration. It ignores the fact that while the surface was eroding, the foundations of American etiquette were undergoing an urgently needed renovation.

Within living memory, wholesale insults to vast categories of human beings were a standard feature of ordinary conversation and public discourse. Anyone belonging to, or simply respectful of, a race, creed, gender, sexual orientation, disability, or other target who did not make a show of being amused by this received a more personalized, second insult for being a humorless poor sport. One-way etiquette based on power, where politeness is expected by those who do not accord it to others, was the rule in otherwise respectable households and workplaces, where those in a position to get away with it demanded deference they did not reciprocate.

Judgment has now been passed on such practices, and social disapproval has driven them underground. This did not occur without cost. If some people were to invent pejorative terms such as "sexual harassment" for what other people called "just a bit of fun," everyone would take up the practice and engage in retaliatory proclamations of injury. The pejorative term "political correctness" was adapted to express disapproval of the enlargement of etiquette to cover all people, in spite of this being a principle to which all Americans claim to subscribe. It was made plausible by being argued almost exclusively by means of cases where malicious intent had been falsely attributed to obviously innocent remarks and behavior. Thus, well-meaning people who only meant to condemn prickliness and slander found themselves in the peculiar position of defending the expression of bigotry.

The dilemma of freedom

Meanwhile, an even more insidious tactic was being worked by people from all parts of the political spectrum. Fed up with the petty annoyances with which they were constantly pelted in a society shaking itself free of the bonds of etiquette, they began turning to the legal system to slap down whatever peeved them, from smoking cigarettes to burning flags. The idea that the law should take over the domain of etiquette fired up both those who rejoiced to have a smirking reply to that question "Who's going to make me?" and those who seized the chance to challenge any rule, no matter how innocuous, that had escaped reclassification.

In each case, everybody concerned was squawking about the sacred right of freedom. If they hadn't pretty much fought one another to a standstill, they might have chipped away at the etiquette system enough to compromise everyone's freedom. A nation without etiquette would soon seek to govern trivial transgressions with the heavy hand of the law.

Fortunately, there is no such thing as a nation without etiquette. No street gang or day care center or fast food court can get along without its own etiquette, much less a nation. How would anyone know who is cool, how to celebrate birthdays, or when it's safe to sit down at someone else's table?

Making the legal system so ferocious and thorough that it ran through private property making people take their dirty feet off the sofas would not be enough. Etiquette does more than act as a paralegal system to root out annoyance before it blossoms into crime. It defines a community by providing the language of rituals and symbols with which members identify their commonality while busily sizing up one another individually.

A system of symbols

The ability of everyone in a society to understand its symbols instantly—as well as those of any of its myriad of subdivisions he or she happens to frequent—gives life a degree of predictability. Without having to think about it, and usually while adamantly denying that they are doing it at all, people go right on examining appearance and gesture for the answers to such questions as "Are you new in town?" and "Am I going to get into trouble for telling you how this business should be run?" and "Are you available?" (That last refers—among other things—to the sales clerk whose studied posture and refusal to gaze up has signaled that help is not going to be available, despite there being no other customers in the store.)

It doesn't seem right or sensible that the length of a person's hair, for example, should convey information about his or her politics, friendly or hostile intentions, romantic habits or line of work—especially since hairstyles quickly change and the symbolic vocabulary could be reversed overnight. Fortunately, it is not supposed to be sensible; this is symbolism, and symbols are, by definition, arbitrary. Everybody knows what is meant at any given time—which is why it did 1960s teenagers no good to argue that George Washington wore a sort of ponytail, too—and everyone uses the system to send and receive information. At the century's opening, the youthful chief executive officer of America Online appeared wearing a suit and tie at the announcement that his company was buying Time-Warner, whose middle-aged chief executive officer stood next to him in an open, tie-less shirt. It caused nationwide amusement to catch them attempting to co-opt each other's symbols, the younger man dressed as an older East Coast executive in a long-established branch of the communications business, the older one, as a youthful boss surging ahead in the newest aspect of the business.

Anyone could see that the younger man won, and not just because he represented the buyer. His clothing symbolism was Grown-Up in Charge, while the older man's smacked of the leisure of retirement, if not the concession that elders were now supposed to take their clues from youth. A year later, the older executive was still tie-less—but now shackled with an identification badge—at the announcement of his actual retirement, while his own younger successor at AOL Time-Warner assumed that position impeccably dressed in the grown-up get-up of suit and tie.

Culture's emotional hold

Because symbols give a society its identity, they are charged with emotion. So are rules from another branch of etiquette that governs from the small, daily ones, such as eating, to the special religious, civic, and ceremonial ones, such as always seem to involve overeating. War prisoners, from the Civil War to World War II's concentration camps, speak of the possession of an eating implement as a prized symbol helping remind them of their humanity.

Failing to respect the symbolic power of apparently casual customs is asking for it. Examples of socially dangerous behavior are: not mustering enthusiasm for the local food delicacy (which amounts to career self-destruction in anyone running for political office), violating your high school's sense of propriety about dress (the one held by the students—violating the one set by the school is socially rewarding), wearing a baseball cap at a baseball game while the National Anthem is being played, and suggesting a disconnection between a bride's being handed from her father's protection to her husband's in cases where the union has already been blessed with children.

In the very act of spurning tradition, people demonstrate their attachment to it. It is common for young adults establishing their own households to refuse to follow the minor rituals they knew as children, such as the patterns by which their own families celebrate Thanksgiving or Christmas. Fair enough, but then why do they always announce dissent by declaring, "I want to make my own traditions"? Not, "I'm going to do things differently;" not "I want to do it my way."

A desire for their "own traditions," as opposed to just their own practices, is well known to those interested in advising them how to proceed, who trumpet the come-on of "Create your own tradition!" What this means is that people who reject the rituals they inherit are far from rejecting the concept of inherited tradition. They just want to be the designers, and harbor the illusion that their traditions will be followed into the future, presumably because theirs are better designed, and because their children will be more appreciative of parental efforts and tastes than they are.

From rudeness to revolution

Every day, we have illustrated for us the paradox that it is the very people who violate and condemn the system of expected behavior codified in etiquette who are most outraged when it is violated by others. The vengefully destructive driver claims to be justified because his victim failed to yield or drove maddeningly slowly, violating points of traffic etiquette. The murderer who seems to have committed a senseless crime (the name we give to violence not motivated by love or money) explains that his victim had shown him disrespect, an etiquette violation that has, for centuries, inspired capital punishment at the point of swords or pistols.

All this was happening in the last decade, a period in which etiquette had first been declared long dead, and then declared recently deceased. Even if we were not undergoing a period of hyper-etiquette activity, this would be nonsensical. Try as one might, no society and no individual succeeds in eschewing etiquette. However exciting a prospect, it is impossible. One can follow the prevailing rules or violate them, one can exhibit good manners or bad, but if there is such a thing as natural behavior, one would have had to live in total isolation to exhibit it.

Etiquette systems of one kind or another govern all social intercourse, formal and informal, which is why faulty ones are able to do so much damage. A system that denies the innate human need for dignity to specific categories of people, typically the poor and the enslaved, fosters incendiary resentment.

It follows that how people are routinely treated in situations that are not significant enough to be regulated by law is no small factor in political history. That brutal manners can be more enraging than brutality itself was depicted by Charles Dickens in *A Tale of Two Cities,* in the scene where stunned bystanders exhibit only paralyzed shock at the marquis whose carriage has killed a proletariat baby. It is only when the carriage owner, Monsieur the Marquis, insults them, verbally and through the contemptuous gesture of dispensing a tip as if to compensate the loss, that they are moved to strike back. This illustrated a lesson that England had at last learned from long keeping a wary eye on the neighboring turmoil. Fear of revolution finally taught a profligate aristocracy to go to the extreme measure of practicing circumspect manners in public. It culminated in the early Victorians' feigning unenviable morality so convincingly that the entire era maintains that reputation to this day.

So it is not much of an exaggeration to declare that etiquette dissatisfaction helps cause revolutions. All right, it is not the

chief cause; but the immediate provocations are well documented, while this anthropological angle is overlooked. If etiquette based on equality cannot cure rudeness, using any other
base institutionalizes rudeness against some segment of the society that is not going to like it.

People are driven to desperate measures over conditions that
make their daily lives miserable, most obviously ones that touch
upon their bodily needs or fears. However, we also know that
matters of the soul, such as religion, nationalism, cultural tradition, and idealism, can arouse equally great passion and self-
sacrifice among those who might otherwise lead physically
comfortable lives. Etiquette, the superficial manifestation of our
deepest concepts about how human beings should treat one
another, with special attention to how everyone else should
treat us personally—our fundamental sense of manners—
touches upon both.

*Enraged
honor*

Rudeness does not make daily life unbearable the way hunger does, but enduring daily
humiliation and abrasiveness often comes to
seem intolerable. One cannot shrug off as
exceptional cases that contemporary epi-
demic of rages that we now recognize as inciting behavior
wildly out of proportion to its causes: road rage, parking rage,
airplane rage, real estate rage, surfing rage, neighborhood rage,
queuing rage, and so on.

Admittedly, we have an expectation problem here, if not a
sanity problem. These explosions are occasioned by minor setbacks everyone knows to expect—a driver's stealing a parking
place, a flight being overbooked, a real estate transaction falling
through, a surfing beach being overcrowded, a neighborhood

being annoyed by a barking dog or an uncut lawn, a line having its strict order by arrival time violated because someone saves a place or breaks in or another counter opens and people run for it.

What turns general irritation into personalized rage is a sense, however disproportionate, that the trifling transaction has deeply violated an individual's honor. It is an outrage to be treated in such a fashion; to allow insult to go unpunished is to surrender a fundamental sense of humanity. The next step (on the quick route over the brink) is a quest for revenge at any cost. Strange reasoning may be required to turn a weather-induced traffic delay into a personal insult tendered by a member of the flight crew, or a competitive bid in the real estate market into a personal insult from the seller, buyer, agent, or the lot of them. Nevertheless, this is done every day.

American influence

For all that, American etiquette, like other American forms of culture—one might say entertainment, one perhaps being a subdivision of the other—has become the most influential force of its kind in the world. However haughtily foreigners may resent and resist it, they cannot ultimately prevent themselves, or at any rate their children, from succumbing to it.

American ways are practiced, the excesses along with the basic principles, to some extent just about everywhere that repressive regimes are not intensely occupied with the effort to suppress them. The English and the Japanese, to name two nations with immense pride in their own highly developed systems of etiquette, have been transformed by them. It is not just a belated shift toward modernism that, as recently as the mid-twentieth century, shattered the English disdain of people who are "in trade" and the Japanese disapproval of "romantic" marriages. The dignity of honest labor and sacredness of marital love are two pillars of American belief in the sovereignty of the individual, and American etiquette provides both the respectability and the patterns of behavior, not to mention the blue jeans and tulle wedding veils, that enabled other countries to adopt them.

Foreign prejudices

Yet from the beginning of its history, America has drawn universal sneers for the crudeness of its etiquette, as it does to this day. Originally, this may have been because foreigners holding low opinions of their émigrés (it is not usually the people who are successful and admired at home who pack up and move away) believed they saw their prejudices confirmed. They may have despised these people for their religion or their poverty, but such contempt takes the form of taunts at the ways people dress, eat, speak, and conduct themselves.

As immigrant populations weeded and transformed the customs they brought to America, absorbed versions of one another's similarly altered customs, adopted new rules suggested and occasionally practiced by their leaders, and found themselves developing ones in order to adapt to their new lives, American etiquette moved from its ideals into recognizably distinct forms.

Nevertheless, the countries that had lost citizens to America long remained in ignorance of the existence of American etiquette as such, of either the formal nature being proclaimed or the informal nature being spread by practice. They therefore concluded that Americans were trying to practice the etiquette of their countries of origin, but not managing to get it right: not succeeding in acting act like them, the poor slobs.

This is notably stated in comparisons of American manners with European manners, although each continent has its version of how America mangles its own, hence correct, manners. The English, especially, have long had the habit of judging Americans as failed Englishmen, in manners and language. The chief spokesperson of this view remains Frances Trollope, whose *Domestic Manners of the Americans*, published in England in 1832 after she spent three years in America, is still used as an instrument for sneering at the American behavior she observed for not meeting the English ideal she imagined.

Mrs. Trollope had a great many small but withering complaints. On her scrappy travels, she encountered Americans who casually ate with their knives and lacked inhibitions about chatting up strangers. This was doubtless true, as refinements were scarce, but as an observer of etiquette, she might have provided some context.

The misunderstood fork

For centuries, the English had resisted the fork in favor of the knife (and the ever-ready hand), and in Mrs. Trollope's lifetime, there were still English country aristocrats who prided themselves on eating with their knives as their distinguished ancestors had done. Ignorance of the history of etiquette ought to be a disqualification for making retroactive interpretations of manners. For example, King Henry VIII is seared into the public mind as grabbing food with his fingers and tossing bones over his shoulder. Indeed he did, but not, as is now believed, as a manifestation of his gross appetite, analogous to the method he is thought to have used in grabbing and discarding wives. The less satisfying fact is that he was using correct table manners of his time and of some time to come. That embodiment of French finickiness, King Louis XIV, who posted ever-changing court etiquette rules on "tickets" (which cleverly kept attendant nobles in a state of etiquette panic that distracted them from political plotting), thus giving us the meaning of "etiquette" that we use today, could be seen eating in the same rough style a century later.

Considering that the fork had been introduced into England in the early seventeenth century (some four hundred years after it had arrived in Italy from Byzantium) and that it took the English an additional two hundred years to get used to using it, it hardly seems the instrument of choice with which to attack American etiquette. Forks also began appearing at American tables at the same time, although certainly not routinely. On both sides of the Atlantic Ocean, those few who did use forks put down their knives or spoons when doing so and held their forks in the right hand. When general usage of forks spread, Americans continued this traditional etiquette that early European fork users had begun, while in Europe, the fork was merely added, as a pusher, in combination with the knife or spoon, which was still firmly gripped in the right hand. Thus in the divergence between the modern European and American methods of eating, the American is actually the older European tradition.

Mrs. Trollope's complaints

Mrs. Trollope's complaint about Americans' openness to strangers was not only misguided but uncharitable, considering how much she drew on this trait to make her way in a strange country. The Internet has now made conversation with strangers universally commonplace, but in rough terrain sparsely populated by newcomers, it was a necessity not known in densely packed cities, where a more desperate longing is for privacy. As one of those ruined visitors who came to America to make her fortune—although one who arrived with an attitude—Mrs. Trollope needed the guidance of people to whom she lacked proper introductions, even to achieve her rather splashy failure. (Her downfall was to invent the shopping mall before its time. She set up a huge, flashily festooned mercantile building offering a variety of geegaws for sale, but the good citizens of Cincinnati failed to understand what would be entertaining about spending the day there, buying useless goods they could find cheaper elsewhere.) American business greed was another object of her scorn. The fortune she made off, if not in, America through her book would not have been possible had Americans reacted to her curiosity with the stoniness developed as a necessary shield by people crowded into an island kingdom.

The Trollope and de Tocqueville views of equality

What she did understand was that her real quarrel with American etiquette, with its cheeky self-satisfaction, proud servants, and bristling patriotism, was in fact a quarrel with equality. As she realized, people whose constant thought is that they are just as good as everyone else (while they notice that some of those everybody elses are more fortunate than they) are hardly concentrating on deferring to the feelings of those who fancy themselves to be of a higher order. Modern admiration of Mrs. Trollope's opposition to slavery might be tempered by her declaration that a working class with a sense of being anyone's equal was a

worse evil than slavery, and that an advantage of abolition
would be to humble such people and reinstitute an approximation of the class system.

As Mrs. Trollope was back in Europe polishing off her dis-
missive conclusions about America, another European was sailing to America to look at the effect of democracy on America.
Alexis de Tocqueville also examined, among other things, the
relationship between equality and etiquette. He was more pre-
scient than Mrs. Trollope, who held on to the idea that Americans might come to their senses and realize that egalitarianism is
not worth enduring that insufferable familiarity from one's
obvious inferiors, but then his interpretations of American
manners were also different.

Count de Tocqueville was familiar with how complex etiquette can become in an aristocratic society and how prickly its
members get when they know the exact degree of deference to
which it entitles them and live in suspicion of being short-
changed. He saw a mild-tempered America, free from constant
vigilance against insult because no one expected or owed obeisance, so there were no such accounts to be kept. The general
inattention to details of etiquette was neutralized, he believed,
by a strong desire to live in harmony that put people in the
habit of showing consideration to others.

Accusations and illusions

Americans have since proven that we do
not need to renounce equality to be irritable,
and now that the final frontier has been
reached and gentrified, the old frontier
friendliness recognizes fewer boundaries of
privacy than ever—as anyone can attest who has received unso-
licited health or child-rearing instruction from passing strangers.

Unruffled tempers and care to preserve a pleasant atmosphere are not what Americans report about their fellow citizens. What the citizens are doing instead is shouting at one another in the streets, while the politicians keep promising to bring back civility. So far this has mostly resulted in politicians' shouting accusations of incivility at one another.

The illusion that manners may be perfect elsewhere is as common as the illusion that they were perfect in another era. If we look around the world, we see sports fans careening out of control, women being insulted as a matter of daily routine by those who claim to be their protectors, children being harshly stifled, and meticulously tailored men using their rolled-up umbrellas to take taxis away from the tourists who hailed them first.

Foreigners might observe that although they may have courtesy lapses, these all stem from the infiltration of American etiquette on a system that was working until we came along. We might observe that although we may have courtesy lapses, these stem only from the practice, not the theory, and that we just need to get the word out. We might also observe (since nationalistic arguments are rarely characterized by logical accountability) that the etiquette of egalitarianism is always in flux because it responds to the will of the people; and that American liberty precludes enforcing a uniform standard of behavior other than the minimal decencies that are matters of morals, rather than manners, and thus fall under the rule of law rather than of etiquette.

Home-grown criticism

Contemporary criticism of American etiquette is not likely to condemn its source in egalitarianism except through the trail of arguments that free manners are indicative of immorality, and that they need to be safeguarded by authoritarianism. Purely surface criticism abounds, as it does within and among all cultures in response to the weaknesses and changes in the routine practice of any prevailing etiquette. If there is a fillip to criticism of American behavior, perhaps it is not so much envy of America's prosperity and resentment of its power, as is commonly assumed, but the relative safety of indulging in condemning this, as opposed to attacking touchier nations, because we do it ourselves.

We do it to an extraordinary extent. Unaware of the history of American etiquette (or of any etiquette, or of the fact that there is such a thing as the history of etiquette), many Americans take the America-bashers' word for it that foreigners in general and the English and French in particular observe a permanent standard that we fail to meet. Some laboriously teach themselves to eat in the new, cruder, European style with the thought that being European, it must be older and more sophisticated than our own method. Mrs. Trollope's prejudices are cited to this day by Americans condemning our heritage of etiquette advances wisely crafted by our own pantheon of heroes.

Yet for all the American self-criticism and romance with foreign ways, most of us probably feel that as American behavior is the outward manifestation of the American commitment to equality and liberty, it must therefore be the system that the enlightened freely choose for themselves. This is why wild-eyed charges that America is using force or wealth to undermine the traditional etiquette of other peoples in preparation for a massive cultural takeover are considered laughable.

Movies
and
manners

Abroad, the great weight of American influence is commonly attributed to the triumph of capitalism and perhaps its most cunning manifestations, the Hollywood movie and television soap opera. We may argue about whether violence on film inspires violence in life, but nobody denies that the American concept of the manners it takes to be debonair or to be tough is derived from the movies and television. So it makes sense to presume that the worldwide distribution of American film is responsible for the spread of American clothing codes, American nomenclature, American modes of address, American gestures, American ceremonies, American courtship patterns, and American professional routines. Foreigners who use and/or deplore American T-shirts, slang, ubiquitous first names, dating, and lack of deference to elders and bosses trace all this directly to the American movie.

This explanation may be begging the question. If our entrepreneurial success is connected with our approach to work, our movies are a manifestation of our approach to manners. This does not mean that our movies serve to illustrate our etiquette; far from it. Much of what American movies show is considered bad manners by our own general standard. Although Americans are given to demanding that the entertainment industry do the job of instructing the citizenry in etiquette (and all other desirable forms of behavior, including tolerance, safety, health, and patriotism), on the grounds that it has the easiest time getting everyone's attention and also that it owes something back because of its great riches, this is not feasible for several reasons:

Proper behavior is not the most entertaining spectacle in the world to watch. Drama requires conflict. Stories in which immorality is inevitably punished would be prissy enough without adding the simplistic notion that manners are perfectly matched with morals, and thus depriving us of such interesting characters as the charming villain and the insufferable do-gooder. Finally—perhaps because of the pressure or the dramatic counterproductivity or the traditional artistic contempt for artificiality in others—the industry has shown no particular talent for the subject. Operas, films, plays, and television dramas that work prodigiously to recreate the costumes and settings of a particular historical period or of privileged segments of modern society are content to make uneducated guesses when it comes to reproducing the etiquette.

Manners and movies

Turn the manners and movies connection around, however, and it works. Inventing and perpetually tinkering with our national etiquette has made us good at drama. Americans are all seasoned scriptwriters and performers, not in show business, but in life; most of us also dabble in costume, makeup, set design, and publicity, and all of us are critics.

Through necessity and inclination, our country's founders had set out to produce a new etiquette for the new nation. They had plenty of source material in the form of customs brought from various parts of the old world, some already outdated, some garbled in memory, some never quite mastered, some adapted to local conditions, some combined into hybrids. They used much of it, so the American surface had a recognizable look to Europeans—but they tossed out the script.

In the countries they knew, the citizens of different classes were born into their roles and story lines. They expected to stay in the same place and station in life, and their work and family life were predictable. People being what they are, there were plenty of upheavals making escape possible or expedient, and not a few adventurers refusing to comply with such expectations—and America loomed as a solution and a destination in many of these cases. The point was that the expectation existed.

Here, everything was supposed to be up for grabs. People being what they are, most took their patterns for life from what they saw around them. The point was that the expectation was otherwise.

People came from afar and moved around. They could easily change their names and their histories. Family precedent and community pressure notwithstanding, they were expected to contribute to creating their own personae, line of work, marriages, associates, fortunes, and way of life. The way fresh slates are issued so freely now that it is considered mean-spirited to mention misdeeds ("Yes, he was an embezzler, but that was three years ago and he's paid his debt to society." . . . "He no longer advocates lynching, so you can't judge his record by that") is connected with the historical American faith in retakes.

Once that creative spirit is loosed, there is no aspect of the drama that isn't considered a candidate for change: characters, dialogue, sets, costumes, and the special effects of ceremonies. In everyday life, the forms these take are called etiquette. A certain number of particulars had to be designed to get the nation going, but its shapers' genius was in laying that foundation of equality and dignity for all, without insisting upon wiping out the past or designing the future. They played with the rules themselves; they were Americans. They granted others the liberty to do so, too. And so we became a nation of etiquetteers.

Chapter 2

The Producers

The Founding Fathers Invent a Civilized America

I N THE COLONIAL era, etiquette was a subject no right-thinking and/or God-fearing person could ignore. Manners and morals, which philosophers and theologians had been pondering in tandem since ancient times, had not yet been forcibly unlinked by modernity, with its high-minded attempt to glamorize morals by trashing manners. Anyone who thought about virtue, or was enjoined to do so from the pulpit or lectern, had to tally acts of rudeness and politeness, not just sins and benevolences, in keeping accounts. The clever combination of good intentions and good excuses not having been invented, actual behavior mattered.

Conflating manners and morals closed off the possibility that a good person could be impolite, so harsh punishments were administered for the sort of activities everyone still enjoys both doing and condemning others for doing, such as flirting and gossiping. No slack was cut for etiquette violations that might stem from qualities we would generally consider forgivable, perhaps even endearing, such as foolishness, high spirits, and/or

youthfulness. Children, being given to such illegal tricks as
making funny faces and seeming more knowledgeable than
their parents, were considered especially hard cases.

The manners-morals equation was also supposed to close off
the possibility that a bad person could behave politely enough
to pass for good, there being no generous quibbling about condemning the deed rather than the person. Countless examples
to the contrary did nothing to erase the shock that made keeping one's sins decently out of public sight and knowledge, commonly given the ugly name of hypocrisy, the most shocking sin
of all. That has been an enduring legacy, even in these forgiving
times when we easily dismiss the sin only to pursue retribution
for the cover-up. Although the more imaginative forms of public self-abasement and humiliation, such as dunce caps and
stocks, fell into disuse, the principle survives of making embarrassment an essential part of punishment, as well as a popular
spectator sport.

*Ancestors
at
play*

All this solemn attention to etiquette
among the colonials retrospectively inspired
the peculiar notion that they must actually
have behaved themselves. On the contrary,
any society's body of laws or rules provides a
thorough description, written in the nega-
tive imperative, of the choice methods by which its people
drive one another crazy. Produce a list of laws and rules from
any unknown society, and you will have a good description of
how they passed the time. There are no rules against things no
one is tempted to do, and without a rich variety of bad behavior, there would have been no reason for authorities to work
themselves into such a dither. Instances of Puritanical drunken-

ness and lewdness were widespread enough to have sufficed to keep their law enforcement agents and vigilantes in a lively state, even if an impressive number of other forms of fun or carelessness had not been put on the proscribed roster. Condemning sin should never be confused with eschewing it.

Meanwhile, in the Mother Country, Georgians were no less interested in etiquette (or less devoted to drunkenness and lewdness), although they may have been focusing on etiquette in ways that were not conspicuously right-thinking or God-fearing. Mr. Richard Brinsley Sheridan and his ilk were working the joke of etiquette being the great life-study of sissies and smoothies. Debauchery carried out by means of haughty attention to form is an eternally irresistible subject, and the highest English circles supplied a wealth of rollicking examples of fops whose affectations led them to sneer at honest folk and rotters whose politeness enabled them to slide past guardian parents to reach their prey.

Politicians at work

At that, the frankly frivolous or, in the case of royalty, the truly profligate were judged less harshly than any public servant who committed the sin of acknowledging that etiquette—aside from whether one considers it a duty or a hobby—can be an effective social tool. Moralists may have been exhausting themselves trying to persuade everyone else to behave well whether they felt like it or not—the concept of being true to one's feelings, as a higher form of morality than being good to others, was far in the future—but when statesmen advised taking advantage of the disconnection between surface behavior and blunt inclination in order to be effective, they were likely to be dismissed as toadies or tarred with the name of Machiavelli (as if he didn't have enough troubles when his government career ended), still being invoked generations later as the devil incarnate.

Nevertheless, politicians in every era and under every form of government understand the need to be studied, rather than spontaneous, in their behavior. How could anyone whose lifework depends on making himself or his patron persuasive and popular—or at least passable enough not to be in constant mortal danger from the populace—not have as keen an interest in etiquette as in rhetoric? Some can't help admitting that they use such tools to repackage themselves because they prize the skill and forget that it makes society at large nervous and suspicious. Additionally, they are prone to figuring, against everything that political history and experience has taught them, that no one outside their circles will find out what they are really thinking or doing.

Architects of the new etiquette

Lord Chesterfield's *Letters to His Son*, in which that gentleman let his illegitimate son in on the secret that ingratiating manners assist both statesmanship and seduction, was published at about the time that American patriots were fed up with cajoling the English and were using muskets instead. Yet when our most prominent leaders took up arms, they did not put down etiquette. On the contrary, many of them already had experience fooling around with etiquette rules, and were eager to take on the responsibility of reforming English etiquette, which was more at odds with American ideal than was English law.

The job was nothing less than to translate the emerging nation's ideals into state ritual, ceremony, and, through example and precedent if not by fiat, daily behavior. Benjamin Franklin,

Thomas Jefferson, and George Washington, in particular, were predisposed to become architects of the new etiquette. All three of them had been dabbling in the field separately for decades. There would be no question of farming the task out to protocol officers while the major thinkers were content to wait to be told where to stand and when, if ever, to move in or out of one another's way.

Nowadays it stuns Americans to hear that these three national figures were seriously interested in etiquette. Iconoclasts may take this revelation as confirmation that General Washington was a snob, Mr. Jefferson a hypocrite, and Dr. Franklin willing to go to any length for a laugh. Admirers venture the defense that it was surely not the formality of etiquette rules with which they were concerned, but the principles of society or the organizational structure of government. That too, but they were interested in the etiquette of everyday life, including such specifics as dress, conversation, and hospitality, and they wrote about etiquette under its proper name, advocating and advancing a large body of rules. Amazingly, each managed to escape the onus that any sign of interest in the subject put on their contemporaries, as well as on their political predecessors and successors.

Dr. Franklin's etiquette

In Dr. Franklin's case, the comic routine does not obscure the fact that the subject matter was one of his lifelong interests. Before taking up statesmanship, he was well established as one of the drollest people ever to advise others to do as he said rather than as he did. As he wrote in *Poor Richard's Almanac*, a brilliant mixture of morals with manners, and courtesy with careerism:

"Eat to please thyself, but dress to please others." (This is the man who triumphantly shocked Paris by flouting the official dress code.)

"Hear no evil of a Friend, nor speak any of an enemy." (He was the darling of the greatest salons of all time with his delicious conversation, and it was not entirely limited to abstract topics or, when he discussed individuals, discreet and charitable observations.)

"He that lives carnally, won't live eternally." (Never mind).

Dr. Franklin was the only one of the lot whose writings on etiquette are still read for pleasure, as opposed to history homework. He was a matchless professional.

General Washington's etiquette

General Washington is mistakenly credited with having been a child prodigy at etiquette, quite aside from the goody-goody behavior of legend, because a list of one hundred and ten rules of etiquette exists in his teenage handwriting. Far from being his own work, these rules—mixed with not only morals and career advice but such basic injunctions as waiting until no one is looking before killing any vermin that happen to be inhabiting one's clothing—had been written by French Jesuits, and he learned them from a well-used schoolbook translation. For all we know, the youthful Washington may have been assigned to copy out these rules as punishment for breaking them. The more deferential theory is that the young gentleman was merely practicing his penmanship and naturally chose suitably refined material with which he was in perfect agreement.

In adult life, George Washington took to issuing his own etiquette rules. Many were in connection with the presidency, where he had the inescapable job of setting precedent, knowing that whatever he did would radiate authority. Others—such as his decrees that he would sit down to dinner at the appointed hour without waiting for tardy guests, and that he would retire at his preferred bedtime regardless of the inclination of any of his guests to keep right on partying—address problems that any citizen might have, although perhaps lack the nerve to settle so decisively in the host's favor.

General Washington's graciousness and his flaring temper were equally well known. When he was not driven to swearing mightily or stomping in anger on his own hat, he paid such fastidious attention to matters of form and daily ritual, both in the military and on the plantation, as to keep those around him on the alert to avoid offending his particular sense of the fitting. Abigail Adams must have chosen her words carefully when she described him as having "a dignity which forbids familiarity, mixed with an easy affability which creates love and reverence." Her husband was perhaps less politic, but certainly more succinct, when he referred to his former boss and predecessor as Old Muttonhead.

Mr. Jefferson's etiquette

Mr. Jefferson's interest in the etiquette system of legislatures known as parliamentary procedure dated to his student days at the College of William and Mary, when he starting taking notes on the subject. Although as president he was to become the great (and notoriously unsuccessful) advocate for laissez-faire etiquette, he harbored no such liberality toward legislative bodies. Serving in the Maryland Legislature, the Virginia House of Burgesses and House of Delegates, the Continental Congress, and presiding over the United

States Senate did much to confirm his lack of faith in the etiquette capacity of legislators. Left to their own sense of decorum, he found, the people's chosen representatives could be counted upon to trample the rights of the weaker among them and the reputation of the institutions in which they had the honor to serve.

When he departed the legislative scene to become president in 1801, the material he had compiled from various sources and been using to preside over the Senate was published under his name as *A Manual of Parliamentary Practice*. It came out in pocket-sized edition, at his insistence: He cherished the hope that a copy would find its way into each senatorial pocket, and that those gentlemen would turn to it, rather than to insult and violence, when in need of guidance in methods of attending to the public's business.

Mr. Jefferson's extensive legislative experience had put him particularly on guard against vulgarity and boredom (both causing it and coping with it—although he recognized that the latter could overreach human limits). As reading rules always gives one a vivid picture of the situation the rulemaker hopes to control, here are some salient ones from his section on Order in Debate:

No one is to speak impertinently or beside the question, superfluously, or tediously.

No person is to use indecent language against the proceedings of the house . . .

No person in speaking, is to mention a member then present by his name; but to describe him by his seat in the house, or who spoke last, or on the other side of the question, &c., nor to digress from the matter to fall upon the person, by speaking, reviling, nipping, or unmannerly words against a particular member. The consequences of a measure may be reprobated in strong terms; but to arraign the motives of those who propose or advocate it, is a personality, and against order. . . .

No member shall speak to another, or otherwise interrupt the business of the Senate, or read any printed paper while the Journals or public papers are reading, or when any member is speaking in any debate.

No one is to disturb another in his speech by hissing, coughing, spitting, speaking or whispering to another nor to stand up or interrupt him, nor to pass between the Speaker and the speaking member, nor to go across the house or to walk up and down it, or to take books or papers from the table, or write there.

Nevertheless, if a member finds that it is not the inclination of the House to hear him, and that by conversation or any other noise they endeavour to drown his voice, it is his most prudent way to submit to the pleasure of the House, and sit down; for it scarcely ever happens that they are guilty of this piece of ill manners without sufficient reason, or inattentive to a member who says anything worth their hearing.

Oh, and take off that stupid baseball (or tricornered) cap: "No member is to come into the house with his head covered, nor to remove from one place to another with his hat on, nor is to put on his hat in coming in, or removing until he be set down in his place."

Tourists or television viewers familiar with the live, as opposed to officially recorded, proceedings of the United States Congress may be interested to hear that these rules, while no longer used by the Senate, are still among those used (in the sense of being acknowledged and consulted, perhaps more than actually being observed) to govern the United States House of Representatives.

That Mr. Jefferson and other giants of the Enlightenment put their faith in etiquette rules rather than trusting to moral character to prompt public servants to behave themselves is striking, even allowing for the fact that "character," in regard to politicians, had not yet been defined to mean "sex." Well into our own cynical times, a contrary fantasy persists, evidence from modern family life notwithstanding: that if people get to know one another, they will get to like one another, and if they like one another, they will treat one another courteously.

Therefore, the current solution to that disreputable congressional behavior that Mr. Jefferson deplored is the vacationlike congressional retreat, where legislators, accompanied by their families, indulge in some recreational ruling-class solidarity before returning to Washington to resume business as usual with reviling, nipping, and unmannerly words. It should be noted that when they flout parliamentary rules, members of Congress could justify this on a premise similar to that of the retreat: that one must act from the heart toward others, reflecting, rather than disguising, how one really feels about them.

Etiquette enforcement

Unlike your general run of Utopians and other designers of A Better World for Everyone, the original American etiquetteers were figuring on human nature's remaining pretty much what they had observed it to be, rather than being uplifted by their visions to previously unscaled heights of selflessness. So while checks and balances were being built into the structure of government, checks on grandeur and harshness were being built into its etiquette.

As the gentlemen of that time well knew, monarchies were not the only forms of society in which too much official interest in nonlethal behavior could make life a burden to ordinary folk. Colonial settlements that had been founded on one kind of liberty or another, achieved at great human cost, had a talent for institutionalizing innovative forms of petty tyranny. Etiquette regulation that scrutinized the most ordinary human impulses (such as the sort of swearing in which General Washington indulged) and attempted to enforce compliance by the most appalling forms of social shame (social disapproval or shame being etiquette's chief form of punishment), or by the even less subtle sanctions available under the rule of law, was widely practiced. The price for being sassy or silly could equal that with which these people would have been charged in the old country for full-blown heresy. Although it was the Puritans who captured historical credit for criminalizing such universal human indulgences as overdressing, dirty dancing, and sleeping in on Sunday, etiquette policing was widespread throughout the colonies.

Yearning for tolerance does not necessarily inspire people to grant it to others. Neither does distaste for a hierarchical system where one has been assigned to the bottom layer necessarily prejudice people against hierarchies when they have a chance to be on the top.

Offers from Puritan aristocrats to transplant themselves to the Massachusetts Bay Colony with their noble status and powers intact were declined with thanks by those who got there first, but this did not prevent the latter from ranking their own

inhabitants by social status. Since there were no nightclubs
where the chic needed to be separated from the masses, these
lists were used to assign seating for church congregations and
standing for Harvard students. The South was no more laid
back. Early members of the Virginia House of Burgesses
included some former indentured servants, along with the
many who claimed aristocratic ties to the old world, but that
distinction was lost as they all metamorphosed into the First
Families of Virginia.

*American
moderation*

With bad examples to guide them from all
directions, not least in their own midst, the
Founding Fathers, along with other Founding Relatives, eyed one another warily and
began hammering out an American proto-
col. Purging official life of daily reminders of condemned ways
of doing things was the comparatively easy part, at least as far as
ideology was concerned. Those who favored recreating the
forms they had risked dying to eliminate were simply voted,
argued, or ridiculed down. If people wanted to worship George
Washington as kingly, if not divine, or strut about calling themselves the new republic's aristocracy, they could do so to their
hearts' content, as there would be no tribunals to restrict the
people's freedom to be foolish. However, they would be on
their own. Counterrevolutionary etiquette was not going to be
sanctioned by federal law.

Nor was a zealous brand of revolutionary etiquette. While
some were dreaming of new forms of grandeur, others advocated
a strictly no-frills etiquette in which, for example, even the
barest, most universally applied courtesy titles would be condemned. (It was not until the twentieth century that they got

their wish. Attempts to modernize female honorifics by reverting to an old form that politely failed to distinguish between the married and the unmarried resulted in so much anger and confusion that it became easier to dispense with all such grace notes for anyone. Oddly, both those who denounced the use of Ms. and those who insisted upon it mistakenly thought it to be new, whereas Ms. had served as an abbreviation for the—then respectable—title of Mistress as long as have Mrs. and Miss.)

It may or may not have been true that an early American attempt to exchange American titles for the French Revolution's soon faltered on the question of whether the female equivalent of Citizen would be Citess or Civess. In any case, refusing to legislate this small but emotionally charged issue surely contributed to the success of the new country. The Ms.-Mrs. controversy rages on, but the government wisely refuses to become involved.

Protocol issues

The harder part of the Founders' etiquette assignment was to decide how the elected representatives of a free people should behave and be treated, considering that they would occupy a special position among, yet enjoy no higher status than, their fellow citizens. This was not a paradox that could be resolved, but it did call for specific decisions about matters on which many (in the spirit of the new freedom) held violent opinions and demanded a say.

What would be the chief executive's title, and how should he be addressed directly? What should he be called, if anything special, after his term of office?

What about his wife, who takes his rank by courtesy but has none of her own?

How much deference should be shown him by other federal and state officials, who have their own dignity to uphold?

How can ceremonial functions be designed so as to be impressive without attributing undue majesty to those participating and giving them counterrevolutionary swelled heads?

How accessible should the chief executive be to the general public, with its overwhelming volume of pressing grievances and petitions?

How accessible should he be to society, with its overwhelming volume of invitations?

What should he wear?

No, wait, that last item was not put out to public debate. Clothing is perhaps even more obviously loaded with symbolism than any of those other topics, but delicacy demands that some matters be left to the discretion of the individual. Sure enough, there is evidence that just about every president the country has had, has understood the importance of the wardrobe question and given it serious attention. General Washington favored velvets and silks, yet wore homespun brown cloth (and plain silver shoe buckles) to his first inauguration. Others' attempts to dress up without looking stuck up, or to dress down without appearing to be dumbing down, have met with less success: Richard Nixon's business suit worn on the beach was ridiculed as pompous; James Earl Carter's cardigan sweater worn for televised talks was ridiculed as undignified, although his bearing his comfy nickname on official occasions was already a commonplace. Now that even the color of a tie is analyzed as a factor in presidential elections, the candidates have surrendered their taste to wardrobe consultants (although without a notable improvement in public approval).

Meanwhile, the national tradition of poking fun at the president for expecting to be allowed any dignity was under way. Other architects of government had discovered the general merriment to be had from playing with the idea of what to call the head of state and government. Entries included:

His Elective Majesty—fancied by the next person who might have held it, John Adams.

His High Mightiness—shot down by a senatorial crack that while this might suit President Washington, a man of high physical stature, how would it look on—naming no names, but conceivably dousing Mr. Adams's chortles—a "puny" man who might succeed him?

His Magistracy—presuming that a consensus could be reached about which of its syllables should be stressed.

His Supremacy, His Supreme Mightiness, His Highness, His Serene Highness, and numerous variations along the lines of, but stopping just short of, Superman.

His Highness the President of the United Sates of America and Protector of their Liberties—submitted (surprise, surprise) by a committee, namely the Joint Congressional Committee on titles, which took a month to come up with it.

The shortest suggestion—a previously owned and still-used title that, had it not been disqualified on political grounds, might have served the purpose of terminally galling the chief enemy of the new state—by an odd coincidence, the first American chief of state could be, in title if not in fact, simply—King George.

These proposals were all based on what was floating around at the time, and as James Madison told Congress,

If we have recourse to the fertile fields of luxuriant fancy, and deck out an airy being of our own creation, it is a great chance but its fantastic properties would render the empty phantom ridiculous and absurd. If we borrow, the servile imitation will be odious, not to say ridiculous also; we must copy from the pompous sovereigns of the East, or follow the inferior potentates of Europe; in either case, the splendid tinsel or gorgeous robe would disgrace the manly shoulders of our chief.

Meaning: Guys, we'd be making fools of ourselves.

So in the end, republican simplicity won out, along with the practical consideration that "President of the United States of America" had already been handwritten into the Constitution. Fears that were voiced, and not only by John Adams, that it might be too common a title were promptly confirmed by a Rhode Island innkeeper who is believed to have replied to the announcement that the president was about to honor her establishment, "The President must go on to the next tavern." She had assumed it was the mere president of Rhode Island College. (This would make her the originator—and the college renamed as Brown University the subject—of the well-known Harvard-hubris joke, "The President is in Washington to see Mr. Wilson.")

The President of the United States was to be addressed as plain "Mr. President," and Mrs. Washington, for one, is said to have scrupulously done so. She herself was frequently called Lady Washington, a term that soon fell into oblivion (if one doesn't count Claudia Johnson's being nicknamed Lady Bird, and thus giving rise to a British guffaw about why Lord Bird so freely countenanced her public travels with Lyndon Johnson). Dolley Madison was supposed to have been quite at ease with being called Her Majesty. Such terms as Lady Presidentess or Mrs. Presidentess appeared now and then, sometimes in adulation of the lady in question, and sometimes in derision, as when Edith Wilson was thought to be running the government for her incapacitated husband. Finally, the problem of how to reconcile the presidential hostess's exalted courtesy rank with her true lack of rank other than as a private citizen resulted in quasi-official sanction being given to a title, "First Lady," that, as Jacqueline Kennedy pointed out without being able to stop people from using it in reference to her, makes the president's wife sound like a saddle horse. This not only stuck, but stuck us with whole stables full of such apparent winners as First Daughter, First Brother, and First Dog.

After his term of office, the president himself would be a mere private citizen, a change that Count de Toqueville saw as a swift and amazing descent into anonymity but that Dr. Franklin characterized as a step up: "In free governments the riders are the servants and the people their superiors and sovereigns. For the former therefore to return among the latter is not to degrade them but to promote them."

Harry S. Truman, who was fond of this Franklin quote, was the penultimate president to act accordingly. After he and his successor made the prescribed modest return to private life, the country collected a gaggle of former presidents all calling themselves and one another "Mr. President" at the same time. The etiquette rule that requires reserving that title for the incumbent and a former president's reverting to the last title he held that was not unique, such as governor or general, was followed by former presidents General Washington through General Eisenhower. It is still on the protocol books, where it languishes unheeded by the public and the Messrs. President themselves.

The stylistic dilemma

After all that work, a protocol-pooped first government turned over to the president the stylistically impossible task of appearing as both humble and exalted; a federal authority respectful of, but not subservient to, state authority; an unpretentious citizen thinking himself no better than his meanest countryman yet a figure of enormous dignity, respected, if not venerated, by all. Even the inaugural proceedings, the ceremony to raise to the country's highest honor someone who was expected to make it clear that he wasn't taking it too personally, was left to the president's own design, with only the oath of office specified.

George Washington had a gift for the double role. After he was safely dead, John Adams described him as one of the "great masters of the theatrical exhibitions of politics. Washington understood this art very well, and we may say of him if he was not the greatest President, he was the best actor of Presidency we have ever had" (up to that point, of course, although he would most certainly still be a contender).

He was capable of the most charming deference and humility, said to have bowed to a slave and offered apologies for provoking someone who had knocked him down. He could also do a deep-freeze that rebuffed and punished on the spot any liberties attempted against the dignity of his position. Gouverneur Morris was said to have once won a bet that he could greet him with a genial slap on the shoulder; did so—and then declared that the victory was not worth suffering the cold stare it produced.

The only person who seems to have bested General Washington at this was Alexander Hamilton, who was among those who had egged on Gouverneur Morris but who, when serving as General Washington's aide-de-camp, was himself dressed down by him for the disrespect of keeping his superior waiting. Colonel Hamilton had a strong excuse, in that he had been detained by the Marquis de Lafayette, but he toughed it out by stalking off, and not only refusing to accept the apology the general sent him but refusing to continue in his immediate service. Later, at a happier stage of their working relationship, Alexander Hamilton was one of the people to whom the first president appealed for protocol advice. Indeed, the former may be said to have sacrificed his life for etiquette, having deliberately aimed his pistol clear of his dueling opponent, Aaron Burr, who observed no such reciprocal delicacy.

Ostensibly, George Washington was not defending his personal honor in these etiquette skirmishes. Dueling aside, such scenes were undertaken as symbolic trials of the dignity of his and others' hitherto untested official positions. They were largely understood as such, this being a time when everyone was skittishly aware of the importance of large and small evidence of the country's viability among nations.

Stylistic power struggles

The precedence of federal government over state government, and incidentally of elected position over wealth (a powerful factor in weighing social heist in the colonies, as where is it not?), was settled by a massive snub he delivered, during a presidential tour, to John Hancock, governor of Massachusetts and one of the country's richest citizens. The governor literally left the visiting president out in the cold with the argument that as he, the governor, was in his home state, any visitor should wait upon him. This did not go over, even with Bostonians, whose turf he was standing upon both literally and figuratively, and who inherited the greeting honors in his absence. With his own constituency rattled and President Washington canceling dinner rather than yield, Governor Hancock quickly changed the grounds of his nonwelcome to a plea of illness, and was reduced to the pitiful ploy of bolstering his claim by having himself carried into the presidential presence on a litter.

Heavy symbolism was required to demonstrate that although the president would visit the Senate to deliver formal remarks, he had precedence there as well. President Washington would make the trip riding in solitary splendor in his state carriage, occupy an elevated, thronelike chair with its own crimson canopy, which was kept for such occasions, and depart after his message with no more than a bow. Safely home, he would await a further show of senatorial deference in the form of a full congressional procession to his residence, which is what it took for the legislature to deliver its replies.

On occasions where there was no challenge to his supremacy, the president gave his modest side free play. He is on record as having declined the suggestion of a crown, although one was never formally offered; a salary, although he used an expense account, perhaps rather liberally; and an elaborate funeral, although his death plunged most of the country into extensive (although not unanimous) mourning. He and Mrs. Washington believed in "simplicity of dress and everything which can tend to support propriety of character without partaking of the follies of luxury and ostentation," he claimed.

His ceremonial style was a mixture of pageantry and plainness. A triumphal tour, undertaken in a cream-colored coach drawn by six white horses and then a bunting-covered barge manned by thirteen masters of vessels in white uniforms, brought him from Mount Vernon to New York for his first inauguration, with flowers being thrown at his feet and a laurel wreath surreptitiously rigged in the arch under which he passed so that it landed as a surprise on his head.

Inside that head, however, there seems to have been a dread of how long he might be expected to keep up that sort of thing. Ten days after the inauguration, he was pleading with Vice President Adams, Alexander Hamilton, and John Jay for help in setting limits on playing the public's darling.

In a tone of dismay, he asked

Demanding access

whether a line of conduct, equally distant from an association with all kinds of company on the one hand and from a total seclusion from Society on the other, ought to be adopted ... whether, after a little time, one day in every week will not be sufficient for receiving visits of Compliment ... whether it would tend to prompt impertinent applications & involve disagreeable consequences to have it known, that the President will, every Morning at 8 Oclock, be at leisure to give Audiences to persons who might have business with him ... whether, when it shall have been understood that the President is not to give general entertainment in the Manner the Presidents of Congress have formerly done, it will be practicable to draw such a line of discrimination in regard to persons, as that Six, eight or ten official characters (including in the rotation the members of both Houses of congress)

may be invited informally or otherwise to dine with him on
the days fixed for receiving Company, without exciting
clamours in the rest of the Community . . . Whether it would
be satisfactory to the Public for the President to make about
four great entertainments in a year . . . [or whether there
would be] danger of diverting too much of the Presidents
time from business or of producing the evils which it was
intended to avoid by his living more recluse than the
Presidts. of Congress have heretofore lived . . .

and so on.

The vice-president assured him that "the system of the President will gradually develop itself in practice, without any formal
communication to the Legislature or publication from the
press" and recommended what came to be a major presidential
tool, the anonymously favorable press leak: "Paragraphs in the
public prints may, however, appear from time to time, without
any formal authority that may lead and reconcile the public
mind."

Well might the president have worried, nonetheless. Legions
of guests, invited and uninvited, had been entertained at Mount
Vernon, and its owner, although he claimed the right to keep
his own hours, had seemed helpless to get rid of them. In addition to his duty as a landowner to aide the passing traveler in an
era without motels and rest stops, there was his attraction as a
national hero. Although he acknowledged the legitimacy of
"any sober or orderly person's gratifying their curiosity in
viewing the buildings, gardens &ct," he had complained that the
place "may be compared to a well resorted tavern, as scarcely
any strangers who are going from north to south or from south
to north do not spend a day or two at it."

Now he was the official leader of the entire nation, and at this time, when people expected access to their leader, they meant access. According to B. Randolph Keim's *Hand-book of Official and Social Etiquette and Public Ceremonials at Washington*, one of the more respectable such nineteenth-century works, "the people generally were unaccustomed to the conventionalities of high official station, and often waived all ceremony in pursuit of their personal ends. It is said that the President's House [in New York] was thronged at all hours of the day and night, and that frequently the crowd pressed into the private apartments of Mrs. Washington before she had arranged her toilette, and on several occasions the President himself complained, before she had arisen from her bed."

Limiting access

Surprise bedroom visits aside, President and Lady Washington, between them, managed to pare down their social appearances to receptions on Tuesdays, tea parties on Fridays, and official dinners on Thursdays, making it clear that while he was available for business, visits would not be welcome at other times. He established a rule that the president never accepts invitations and never has to pay any calls at all, even return calls (unless he happens to feel like it), thus ridding himself of a time-consuming chore when personal calls did the job of checking around now handled by telephone calls and e-mail. He discouraged fanfare, squelching an aide who announced his presence at his first levee with a great flourish by a chilling statement, "Well, you have taken me in once, but by God, you will never take me in a second time!"

As he settled into the presidency, this did not stop his being criticized for wanting to show himself off. The citizenry was beginning a tradition of suspecting its presidents, and especially their wives, of using state ceremony to indulge their personal taste for social grandeur. To this day, we foist the highest state entertaining on the president's wife so that we can sneer at her for caring too much about parties. The national celebration of George Washington's sixty-first birthday, along with "the absurdities of levees & every species of royal pomp and parade," was denounced by a newspaper as a sign of his monarchial leanings. You elect a man president, even a man who has explicitly denied any interest in being a king and who says he equates the election victory with a death sentence, and the next thing you know he shows signs of hoping one day to be immortalized by a grateful populace rushing out to buy furniture on the Monday nearest to his birthday.

Mr. Jefferson's style

The next of the great etiquetteers to assume the office was Thomas Jefferson, genius in so many fields and unwilling to give up in this one. (John Adams, whose family background of minor tradesmen had placed him in a pre-equality social position inferior to that of the landowning Founders, once admitted to having no gift for manners, although he touted gentlemanliness in a way that led people to question his claim to it.) Unlike General Washington, whose prickliness and grandeur made his gestures of humility awesome, Mr. Jefferson, the etiquette radical of the lot, essayed a stylistically consistent humility that struck many as ostentatious.

The grubbiness of Mr. Jefferson's presidential inauguration, at which he wore humble clothes and clopped along, first on horseback and then walking, was later found to be the accidental result of his son-in-law's bungled attempt to get an expensive new coach and a velvet suit delivered to him in time. It was nevertheless all of a piece with what he called the "Revolution of 1800," his plan for stamping out any remnants of imperial-appearing etiquette and substituting an entirely republican one. By example and by edict, he was back in the etiquette business.

After suavely enjoying Parisian society, Mr. Jefferson had practiced being the target of no-privilege etiquette at Conrad's boarding house in Washington, where he lived during his vice-presidency. His place at table was the very lowest and coldest seat, according to his friend Margaret Bayard Smith, and when one fellow boarder, the wife of a Kentucky senator, pleaded with the others, who included members of Congress, that they show respect for his age if not for his rank, she was refused on the same egalitarian grounds that the elder statesman espoused. The breaking point came on the day of his inauguration, when the lady herself, her democratic zeal strained beyond endurance, offered her own place at table, which Mr. Jefferson smilingly declined.

*Pêle Mêle
Etiquette*

Adapting boarding house etiquette for the White House, he directed that no one, whether domestic or foreign so-called dignitary, be endowed with extra dignity on the basis of rank. He wrote a Memorandum on Rules of Etiquette, also known as Pêle Mêle Etiquette, in which he directed his cabinet to abolish any semblance of order in diplomatic, national, or private gatherings:

I.   In order to bring the members of society together in the first instance, the custom of the country has established that residents shall pay the first visit to strangers,

and, among strangers, first comers to late comers, foreign and domestic; the character of stranger ceasing
after the first visits. To this rule there is a single exception. Foreign ministers, from the necessity of making
themselves known, pay the first visit to the ministers of
the nation, which is returned.

II.   When brought together in society, all are perfectly
equal, whether foreign or domestic, titled or untitled, in
or out of office.

All other observances are but exemplifications of these two
principles.

I.   1st.   The families of foreign ministers, arriving at the
seat of government, receive the first visit from
those of the national ministers, as from all other
residents.

2nd.   Members of the Legislature and of the Judiciary,
independent of their offices, have a right as
strangers to receive the first visit.

II.   1st.   No title being admitted here, those of foreigners
give no precedence.

2nd.   Differences of grade among diplomatic members,
gives no precedence.

3rd.   At public ceremonies, to which the government
invites the presence of foreign ministers and their
families. A convenient seat or station will be provided for them, with any other strangers invited
and the families of the national ministers, each
taking place as they arrive, without any precedence.

4th.   To maintain the principle of equality, or of pêle
mêle, and prevent the growth of precedence out
of courtesy, the members of the Executive will

practice at their own houses, and recommend an adherence to the ancient usage of the country, of gentlemen in mass giving precedence to the ladies in mass, in passing from one apartment where they are assembled into another.

This is surely anti-elitism at its most refined. The idea that no one person should ever be recognized as superior to anyone else—that not only should birth and wealth be disregarded as indicators, but also ability and achievement—keeps surfacing in America, and here was the optimal test of whether it could be made to work.

It had been proposed by someone who was impeccably disinterested, as he occupied the highest position in the land. Far from having been catapulted onto this pinnacle from humble origins, an experience that has been known to leave wariness about lurking etiquette expectations, he possessed the knowledge, training, and experience of a gentleman. By any ranking system of personal qualities—erudition, culture, talent, success, eloquence, even looks—he would have been spectacularly safe.

Furthermore, Mr. Jefferson knew a thing or two about designing revolutionary social systems. This one was on a miniature scale, in a situation over which he had total control, or so it would appear. If there were any person who could have pulled it off, it was he, and if there were any circumstances under which it could be favorably launched, it was then. It is hardly in the interest of diplomats, or anyone else likely to be entertained by the president, to antagonize the august host by balking at his dinner party arrangements, however eccentric.

Yet they did. The whole business turned out to be a fiasco

and an embarrassment. Pêle mêle was the equivalent of the hostess of a formal dinner party saying airily, "Oh, just sit any-where," except that in such cases, the guests only tend to hang back feeling foolish, whereas at Mr. Jefferson's White House dinners, they rushed forth in fits that made the legislature look demure by comparison. Some voted with their elbows to take what they believed to be their symbolic or personal due, others with their feet to escape. The dinners featured imported delica-cies and rare wines, the domestic staff was said to be larger than the entire staff of the Department of State, the host was an attractive and highly cultivated widower, as thoughtful of others as he was intelligent—but the new etiquette was producing miffed matrons who threatened boycotts and even more indig-nant diplomats who threatened war.

The result of this experiment shows that perfect egalitarian-ism is as elusive as perfect communism later turned out to be. In the Jeffersonian White House it was not only the presumed ability to believe that all others are as good as oneself that was overtaxed. Working relationships were rendered chaotic by the pretense that there were no distinctions between people with authority and those at their command. Responding with equal attention to a grandee who has been sent to represent his king and the grandee's valet who is sent to fetch gloves not only fails to charm the official and frightens his servant but sabotages any chance of accomplishing business.

The populist style

Nevertheless, the theory is so seductive to the American heart that it keeps being tried in one form or another. In the modern busi-ness world, the fiction that the workplace is a democracy is maintained by the universal use of first names and exhortations from bosses to speak up freely. This is a charade people cherish, although it never fails to jar the naïve that the veneer can be ripped off in an instant by those jovial open-door bosses when they want to avail themselves of the power they actually possess.

We do not accuse Mr. Jefferson of playing to the populace outside his dining room, but one might have supposed that at least the American public, which is notoriously impatient with protocol and unsympathetic to—if not gleeful at—cries emanating from the outraged egos of the privileged, would have been charmed. Not a bit of it. Mr. Jefferson's show of humility, which extended to informal, if not slovenly, dress, was frequently interpreted as being intentionally insulting.

That the populist approach could be scorned by the population was demonstrated at the first inauguration of Andrew Jackson, where etiquette license granted to a jovial and supportive crowd turned them into rioters who trashed the White House and had to be lured out of it with vats of punch placed on the lawn. Another such scene characterized the second inaugural celebration of Abraham Lincoln, when the rush to the buffet table set off a scene of looting that required soldiers, as well as police, to quell. Although there were those who characterized all this as good fun—Walt Whitman was enchanted—or as proof of the vulgarity of the masses, general opinion ran against the presidents for their inability to rule their own admiring guests.

This is because scoffing at toffs is only half the story of the American attitude. It is true that when a president makes a special effort to emphasize the dignity of the office, he is ridiculed and resented for his arrogance and accused of monarchial ambi-

tions. It is equally true, however, that a president who empha-
sizes his ordinariness is ridiculed and resented by the American
people for his lack of dignity and accused of unworthiness.
There is not much room between asking "Just who does he
think he is?" and "If he's so ordinary, why should we look up to
him?"

This is a contradiction with which these gentlemen's successors are familiar. Purposefully proletarian presidents seem to
alternate with those who aspire to mildly aristocratic bearing,
each seeking to avoid the criticism that dogged his predecessor.
Oddly, the few who have erred on the side of idiosyncratic styl-
ishness—Franklin Roosevelt, John Kennedy, Ronald Reagan—
have been fondly hailed by the masses as, of all things, royalty.

Why should this matter to anyone except those with careers
or money staked on the outcome of an election? For that matter, why, before there was any such evidence, did questions of
demeanor seem so important to those inside the Beltway (centuries before there was a Beltway and when the seat of government wouldn't have been inside it if there were)?

The civilized American

As John Adams said first, and others have
said with increasing frequency since, politics
is, among other things, an acting job. In the
case of the Founding Fathers, it was not only
a question of personifying what America
stood for but inventing the civilized Ameri-
can. General Washington and Mr. Jefferson presented opposite
archetypes, although they were both so versed in the most
refined etiquette of their time that there doesn't seem, at this
historic distance, to be that much difference between them. We
have now witnessed more crudely drawn versions of the benev-

olent but aloof natural leader and of the man of the people whose simple directness refuses to be clothed in ceremony.

We have yet to see a better fusion of the two approaches than accomplished by Benjamin Franklin who, lacking the background advantages of the other two and the platform of the presidency, played to world acclaim the role of the deceptively plain American whose sophistication made rubes of princes. "C'est là le Grand Franklin!" the Parisians shouted in the streets as he made his way to the most fashionable salons, in his casual clothes, to be fawned over by elegant beauties. Among the archetypal American roles, versions of this still play better abroad than mutual agreement on European superiority, but no one has ever done it with greater success than Dr. Franklin.

But everyone gets to try. For presidents as for private citizens, how to behave as an American was left to each individual. Despite their own predilection for tinkering with rules and styles, the producers of an American etiquette wisely settled the most pressing state questions, leaving freedom for filling in the rest and room for change. Thoughtfully, they left explanations of the basic direction they expected it to take, and examples of how this could be dramatized.

Chapter 3

The Concept

All Men Are Created Equal

I T IS NO accident that Americans have an aptitude for show business. Every immigrant family had someone who had walked out on whatever was playing at home. These individuals had flipped through the particular scripts they had inherited and the scenarios they could foresee, and decided that they could do better. They had been cast as peasants, heretics, criminals, cannon fodder, debtors, nuisances, failures, trouble-makers, fallen women, portionless younger sons, and/or scum, and they quit rather than play their assigned parts.

Then they got busy doing rewrite. Daring and creative as they seemed to be, the treatments they turned out tended to be vividly reactive but not realistically visionary. Depending on the manner in which each had suffered, the motivation was never again to endure religious persecution, poverty, political persecu-tion, starvation, ethnic persecution, injustice (or, in the case of criminals, justice), wars, droughts, famines, taxes, tyranny, or thwarted love affairs. The projected first American story line was that risks, adventures, and hardships, buoyed by faith in God and oneself, would lead to such grand but vague endings as peace, freedom, and plenty. Later that last item was upgraded to untold wealth.

This describes an action drama rather than a manners one. When a grievance fires up the imagination and nerve to reject prevailing conditions and set out for the unknown, rather than to rebuild on the spot with existing social materials, the story is sketched only up until the point of arrival. The question of what sort of behavior the adventurers should avoid repeating in the new haven so as not to re-create the ills being escaped is overlooked or dismissed as obvious. Compared to the excitement of overcoming political and geographical obstacles, working out the logistics of happily-ever-after is a bore.

Thus the manners genre gets stuck with depicting only comfortably static societies where the fashion-conscious develop amusing quirks and tricks in order to tweak one another awake, and the thrill of a plunge into the unknown is represented by marriage. This narrow definition of manners as a way of making the rudiments of life unnecessarily expensive and complicated in order to provide the rich with an inflated sense of superiority has diverted rigorous thought from a condition essential to the success of community life.

The language of behavior

Realize it or not, everyone uses manners, just as everyone uses language. There are numerous languages, and they all change over time and circumstances; people may speak badly or well, they may understand one another imperfectly or not at all; they may use formal language on some occasions and specialized slang or shop talk on others, but there is no human interaction without language, and there is virtually none without manners, the language of behavior. Recognition of this is what impels reformer movements to invent etiquette codes.

Individuals generally figure that they can just do without. Inattentive to evidence in their own families that etiquette is malleable enough to follow changes in generations, they cannot imagine its adjusting to greater upheavals. They therefore conclude, and frequently announce, that etiquette itself is defunct. Even now, people who say they want to change manners do not actually contemplate change. Instead of proposing exchanging a rule they dislike for one they like better, they propose simply to drop it, along with the principle underlying the rule. Rejecting the ladies-first system of precedence in cases where something more than first-come, first-served is needed did not, for example, result in a more reasonable system of precedence, such as deference to age or necessity, but to an etiquette vacuum in which the most logical system of precedence flourishes: the strong pushing the weak out of the way. Despite experiencing the evolution of etiquette, as some aspects of it fall into disuse and others are refined and updated in accordance with social and personal changes, people believe the choice to be limited to practicing, or refusing to practice, the only possible rules, by which they mean the rules of their childhoods.

They much prefer the second option. So when they want to rid themselves of the old etiquette along with the old form of society that practiced it, they fail to recognize that they need a replacement etiquette, just as escaping one form of government makes it necessary for them to live under another form. Disastrous as it is to mandate a radical change in etiquette, ignoring the cultural pull that remains even when the culture itself has been rejected, it is worse to believe that it is optional to have any system of etiquette. Rudeness that remains unchecked by people who surrender at the first charge that they are being old-fashioned can undermine any society. There is no such thing as an etiquette-free zone. People still have to figure out how to behave, and what they do during a state of etiquette anarchy is not pretty.

Etiquette anarchy

When individuals are left to improvise their manners, they naturally act in their own immediate interests, rather than giving fair consideration to the conflicting interests that must be balanced in order to create a harmonious community. Typically, nowadays, people will declare that it is no longer necessary to do anything they consider a nuisance, such as answering invitations, which interferes with the delightful spontaneity of deciding what one feels like doing at the moment, or writing letters of thanks when there is nothing more to be gained as the presents are already in hand. Society has evolved beyond such expectations, they explain, although it does not seem to have evolved beyond their expectation of being on the receiving end of invitations and presents.

This creates some tension between them and their desperate hosts and irate benefactors. Mind you, those people are their relatives and friends. Add the anger produced by vast numbers of strangers recognizing no obligation toward one another in the way of yielding lanes or parking spaces, and you soon have a state of social warfare.

The idea that one can restore peace by encouraging people to develop warm feelings inside, rather than by imposing rules and social pressure on them from the outside, is surely belied by rampant rudeness among families and friends. If love alone made people behave considerately toward one another there would be no divorce. Nevertheless, that is the tack that is taken among idealistic people who think so well of human nature that they believe conflicting interests to be the unfortunate result of misunderstandings that need only be aired to evaporate.

America has a long history of idealistic communities trying out this idea. They end in acrimony because the one skill the members usually know less about than farming is developing a system of etiquette. Worse, they see idealism and isolation as excuses to abandon practicing the etiquette of the outside society. As one Transcendentalist who managed not to be carried away by the Brook Farm romance put it, "I could better eat with one who did not respect the truth or the laws, than with a sloven and unpresentable person. Moral qualities rule the world, but at a short distance. . . ." Phew. This concession was made by Ralph Waldo Emerson, the moral (and manners) philosopher.

It takes determined manners theorists to produce workable change. This is especially true for a society that harbors the notion of social equality, which, although it has made a number of historical appearances, never seems to develop without a struggle. There is something about the concept—that everyone else is as worthy as oneself, and that the people whom one envies are not fundamentally different—that is eminently resistible.

Cultural baggage

In fact, no immigrant arrives in an etiquette-free condition. Although the avowed purpose of emigrating is to jettison whatever was weighing one down, which ought to result in traveling light, immigrants always show up loaded with cultural baggage. Because the illusion of inevitability surrounds the behavior to which people are accustomed, they keep it in mind as a standard even when the impetus for embarking is to flee that hated social structure. It remains an influence whether it influences them inadvertently to continue to follow it, or to make sure they do everything in the opposite way, or actively to work to preserve it, only with the important adjustment that they personally intend to play better roles.

That last possibility, in which the immigrants would get to be the ones who harass people for holding different beliefs, or who live lives of refined leisure on land that others work, is always a popular choice. It was in that spirit that the earliest immigrants brought their hierarchal ideas of manners with them, figuring that as they hacked away at the new territory to re-create what familiar comfort they could, they would use the familiar etiquette that seemed natural to them to rebuild what seemed the normal social order. For some, the attraction was the opportunity to become enforcers of the faith, instead of heretics; for others, the hope to become pampered aristocrats instead of the lackeys who made their ease possible.

The difficulty would be to recruit people to take the parts on the lowest level of the hierarchy, equivalent to the slots that they had vacated in the old country. The trouble was that everyone else who had had some choice about coming to America had the same plan. The very examples of the people who thought themselves superior served to prove that anyone could rise. The rhetoric of the successful had the effect of inspiring others with ambition, rather than with awe. Brutal force and lesser forms of pressure could supply the labor, but not produce a class that would remain more or less peacefully, and at least apparently reliably, subjugated.

That the colonials hoped to create through etiquette, by establishing rigid social markers, backing them up with religion, and enforcing them by law. Such drastic measures were needed if there was any hope of putting down people who, like the rule-makers, were fixed on the idea of a better life. The immigrant population ranged from the God-fearing to the police-fearing, but it was homogeneous compared to the social range left behind. For different reasons, the solvent-upper and hopeless-lower classes had stayed home. Colonial officials were of petty distinction by home standards, well-born adventurers had no personal advantages over upstarts when it came to taming the wilderness, and indentured servants, unlike slaves, were free to harbor uppity notions while working off the barriers to prosperity.

Furthermore, the familiar social markers were missing. There was no peerage. There was so much land that acquiring some was no indication of respectability or accountability. Whatever background credentials people could claim from the Old World could be held in suspicion, but they were nearly impossible to check. Roughly speaking, the new population achieved de facto equality. Something obviously had to be done.

That is how it happened that the big etiquette issue among them was, indeed, equality. As in: It Could Happen Here. As

John Randolph, Mr. Jefferson's cousin and political opponent, put it, "I am an aristocrat. I love liberty. I hate equality."

In the North, the etiquette of inequality was promulgated in a desperate effort to create instantly obvious distinctions among the chief groups: manual laborers, modest people of business, and those who worked in the professions. Matters of dress, behavior, and speech for each were under government control, although not particularly successfully.

However, the basic idea did succeed. Social distinction based on jobs has not only continued to prevail throughout America but now, centuries later, has found its way to the Old World. In European society, doctors, lawyers, and clergy had been considered a sort of upper servant class whose barely perceptible claims to greater dignity had to be nourished with an occasional cup of tea in the parlor, just as if they were genuine gentry who prided themselves on doing nothing useful. The real division had been between those who worked at all, and those who could manage, whether in luxury or in debt, without having to do so.

The onus against being "in trade" hung on in England for nearly three hundred years, while American philosophers were extolling the uplifting effects of manual labor. Ralph Waldo Emerson declared that it gave him "such an exhilaration and health, that I discover that I have been defrauding myself all this time in letting others do for me what I should have done with my own hands." Ultimately, however, the noble American work ethic triumphed to the point where young royals scrambled to put themselves out for hire and the Eleventh Earl of Sandwich proudly announced that his family was going into the sandwich delivery business. All those years before, European aristocrats had been amused and bewildered by the attempts of Americans to explain what, other than money, was the social difference between those who reckoned themselves an American aristocracy and those whom they excluded. Weren't they all busy chasing after gain, whereas a true gentleman would only be chasing after game?

At the time, ordinary Americans were just as bewildered and a lot less amused. The empowered colonials were regulating everything they could to impress upon farmers and other small-timers the difference between them. Specialized etiquette knowledge is commonly used to establish boundaries, and theirs was as strict as any high school clique's in demanding deference and establishing special privileges for its version of an upper class. Massachusetts state law forbade "men and women of meane [sic] condition" (it was mean to have a net worth of less than 200 pounds) from "wearing Gold or Silver lace, or Buttons, or points at their knees, or to walk in great Boots, or Women of the same rank to wear Silk or Tiffany [the gauzy fabric, not the shop] hoods, or scarfes." Officials such as Governor Joseph Dudley were as touchy as street toughs, constantly checking whether they were being shown enough respect. If one whom they considered to be of their own kind erred, he would be spared the harsh and humiliating punishments reserved for commoner criminals.

An unusual feature was that etiquette for the privileged was not designed for enjoyment. Other governments elsewhere had imposed sumptuary laws and other restraints on indulgence in luxury, but the purpose was to reserve the best for the most powerful, whether to make others envious, or to keep down the level of envious competition among them so that they could be all the more heavily taxed. In America, with its emphasis on religion, the church was backing the government's social stratification as a sign of humility, but nevertheless pounding away all the more at the rich on the issue of self-control. "The most essential Ruyles of Good Manners are to be found among the Laws of our Lord JESUS CHRIST," Cotton Mather thundered at them in church, where the seating was allotted by social class. So the pleasure, such as it was, consisted of being acknowledged as socially superior rather than having a good time, rather like the pride taken by a modern restaurant customer being shown to a "good" table at a restaurant with indifferent food.

There was little security in such status, because members of a class that distinguishes itself by its behavior lose their membership if they lapse. An earl is still an earl when he is drunk as a lord, as it were, but an American who makes one thoroughly false move is no longer a lady or gentleman. Nor can he spare his descendants the trouble of making their own way, whatever starting advantages he may give them. This is in keeping with later American principles of individual merit and effort, not to mention American taxes, but it makes a mockery of claims to any sort of class system, as opposed to economic stratification alone.

The peskiest problem, for those with aristocratic fancies, was that those people of mean condition were not enthusiastic about playing along. A consequence of systematically preventing the masses from behaving like their self-identified betters was to turn many of them into the etiquette-equivalent of scofflaws. Unable to recognize those betters as the equivalent of the classes traditionally owed deference, and thwarted from imitating their look as a step toward achieving their status, they were notoriously prone to turn cheeky. Humble and obedient in this world, rewarded in the next, might be the official Puritan line, but historically, it had a short run.

Southern inequality

In the South, the difference between slaves and slave owners (of whom there were remarkably fewer who could afford to be such than the numbers who defended the system because they aspired to be) hardly needed to be flagged. In any case, it would not have been in the interests of the powerful to open the question of which of those two groups had the more refined manners.

What occurred, instead, was a peculiar example of the cultural melding that was to characterize American etiquette: While holding to the conceit that American behavior was based entirely upon British traditions, Americans were, in fact, unknowingly picking up attitudes and customs from one another's home countries. This mixture of influences is one of the two major factors in American etiquette, the other being the revolutionary decision to condemn hierarchal distinctions.

Those who constituted the upper economic classes of the south believed themselves to be living a version of the British outpost life, an emotional affiliation that was to draw them reciprocal British sympathy during the Civil War. If a handful had actually experienced upper-class British life (and were in America on government assignment, in hopes of making a fortune to take back—or because they were no longer welcome at home), the difference was soon lost between them and those who had not but who were quick studies, both financially and socially.

More subtly, so much so that they failed to notice it them-selves, southerners were learning to practice African manners. It is not from the British that what came to be known as southern graciousness was developed, with its open, easygoing style, its familial use of honorifics, and its "y'all come see us" hospitality. The higher the southern family's pretensions, the more likely the children were to be receiving daily etiquette instruction from someone whose strict sense of the fitting came from her own cultural background—the house slave who occupied the position known as Mammy. Charles Dickens was among those who noticed that southern ladies spoke like their black nurses.

Some house slaves had been of high social class in Africa, as the slave trade had recognized no distinctions, and the fact that virtually all other people had come to America out of dissatis-faction with their lot at home obviously did not apply to those who were brought by force. The aristocracies of other countries were therefore more likely to be represented among them than among the general population, and the background of a slave might be seriously above that of his or her owner.

British visitors were quick to pick up on this, although with-out making the connection between the aristocratic manner they were astonished to observe in house slaves and the likely explanation of its being these people's heritage. Instead, the kindly inclined, such as Fanny Kemble, attributed the courtli-ness she observed in Africans to "a natural turn for good man-ners." A later visitor, Lady Emmeline Stuart-Wortley, called it "Chesterfieldian manners," but if those came naturally, Lord Chesterfield would not have to have been at such pains to teach them to his natural son.

The tasteless made sport of the incongruity between the Africans' dignity and their state of enslavement, and supposed that their behavior was an exaggerated form of what they observed in their masters. That in itself was an exaggerated form of the reaction that foreigners have long held to refined manners among any Americans: that they couldn't possibly be their own.

Mark Twain, who was given to egging on Mrs. Trollope and her ilk, nevertheless took an original approach. He credited foreign influences for virtues that Americans believed to be of their own devising, and for all that was worst in southern manners. In particular, he targeted the number one promulgator of mythological revival, to whose imagination many a supposedly ancient tradition (and much of the romantic Highland culture) can be traced, Sir Walter Scott.

In *Life on the Mississippi*, Mark Twain wrote:

*The
Sir Walter
disease*

Against the crimes of the French Revolution and of Bonaparte may be set two compensating benefactions: the Revolution broke the chains of the *ancien régime* and of the Church, and made of a nation of abject slaves a nation of freemen; and Bonaparte instituted the setting of merit above birth, and also so completely stripped the divinity from royalty, that whereas crowned heads in Europe were gods before, they are only men, since, and can never be gods again, but only figure-heads, and answerable for their acts like common clay. Such benefactions as these compensate the temporary harm which Bonaparte and the Revolution did, and leave the world in debt to them for these great and permanent services to liberty, humanity, and progress.

Then comes Sir Walter Scott with his enchantments, and by his single might checks this wave of progress, and even turns it back, sets the world in love with dreams and phantoms; with decayed and swinish forms of religion; with decayed and degraded systems of government; with the sillinesses and emptinesses, sham grandeurs, sham gauds, and sham chivalries of a brainless and worthless long-vanished society. He did measureless harm; more real and lasting harm, perhaps, than any other individual that ever wrote.

Most of the world has now outlived good part of these harms, though by no means all of them; but in our South they flourish pretty forcefully still. Not so forcefully as half a generation ago, perhaps, but still forcefully. There, the genuine and wholesome civilization of the nineteenth century is curiously confused and commingled with the Walter Scott Middle-Age sham civilization and so you have practical, common-sense progressive ideas, and progressive works, mixed up with the duel, the inflated speech, and the jejune romanticism of an absurd past that is dead, and out of charity ought to be buried.

But for the Sir Walter disease, the character of the Southerner—or Southron, according to Sir Walter's starchier way of phrasing it—would be wholly modern, in place of modern and medieval mixed, and the South would be fully a generation further advanced than it is. It was Sir Walter that made every gentleman in the South a Major or a Colonel, or a General or a judge, before the war; and it was he, also, that made these gentlemen value these bogus decorations. For it was he that created rank and caste down there, and also reverence for rank and caste, and pride and pleasure in them. Enough is laid on slavery, without fathering upon it these creations and contributions of Sir Walter.

This would mean that the fantasy of traditional American southern manners is based on a Scottish writer's fantasy based on a centuries-old fantasy about a fantastic society. That would make it perfectly in keeping with the postmodern method in use today, where people pick what they are pleased to call "customs" from different cultures (their own or others') and imaginations (their own or others') and defend them as sacred.

Yet all this has coalesced into an American historical mythology that has amazing staying power. Stripped of such inconvenient aspects as their peasant or criminal origins and their moral fervor and moral failures, types from societies roughly based on our past still serve as models of manners to emulate or avoid. The stern and self-denying Puritan lives on, not only in the useful capacity of demon responsible for all sexual dissatisfaction, but in the concept of a New England aristocracy loosely conferred on all who attend its schools and take on its deceptively shabby style. So, too, the southern lady and gentleman are vivid among us as the ultimate examples of cultured graciousness or of cunningly ingratiating decadence. Into these types, later versions—the nineteenth-century self-made industrialist and the tortured and delicate twentieth-century poet—have merged with Proustian ease.

The declaration of etiquette

Basic American manners, the fundamental structure on which these various stylistic oddities would be nailed, was built with a small amount of material extracted from the Declaration of Independence. This may not be the obvious place one might think of looking for etiquette guidance, but it contained an inspirational catch-phrase that stuck: "All men are created equal."

This is the sole written instruction on the subject bequeathed to us by the Founders that we seem to feel we need. ("Pursuit of happiness" stuck, too, but hardly as etiquette guidance.) With it, the hierarchal heritage was discredited. By no means did that disappear, in attitudes or in practice, but it became indefensible. All purely American etiquette can be said to derive from this statement, just as Herman Melville asserts, in *Moby-Dick*, that all law derives from the principles of the whaling code: "A Fast Fish belongs to the party fast to it" and "A Loose-Fish is fair game for anybody who can soonest catch it."

"All men are created equal" is not even the complete sentence. It was never intended to carry the vague meaning we assign to it. Every word of it has been under fierce contention throughout American history. The definitions we agree to superimpose on it keep having to be revised, because we keep reinterpreting the principle on which it is based. Thus it is the perfect instruction from the front office to a creative people assigned to write their own etiquette scripts: noble, vague, and flexible.

The phrase is on every citizen's lips, for use in a bewildering array of situations. We are just as proud of it as if we knew what we meant by it.

Before it was yanked out of its context in the Declaration of Independence, it referred to the philosophical concept of the natural rights of man, rather than to our inalienable right to jockey for social position and display an attitude at work. Applied to etiquette, we believe it has to do with respect. Like kindergartners who know they are supposed to share, we know we are supposed to treat everyone with equal respect, but have a hard time bringing ourselves to do it. It is amazing how quickly after independence this ideal was transformed into the ever-popular assertion, "I'm just as good as anyone else," and its more pugnacious refrain, "Who do you think you are?"

"All men are created equal": If we examine each word (counting the compound verb as one), we get three shifting definitions and one baffling one; and when we put them back in order, we see at least as many possible interpretations, each capable of discharging a righteous argument and heralding a different vision of society.

All . . .

The subject of this phrase determines who is covered. Etiquette being a social system, the rules presumably apply only to and toward human beings. (Making insulting remarks to a television set is not an act of rudeness, for example, although making remarks to the movie screen and thereby annoying people who are trying to watch is.) Yet could that "all" really mean—everybody? Isn't there any human being or group for whom we can show a little invigorating disrespect, or, put more gently, whom we can reasonably identify as occupying a place where we can expect them to look up to us without any particular effort on our part?

The people who signed on to that phrase certainly did not intend "all" to mean *everybody*. Slaves and Indians failed to make the cut. Prisoners could not and cannot claim an inalienable right to liberty. In other etiquette systems with which the revolutionaries were familiar, and in practices then current in America, some people could expect politeness without practicing it themselves, and others were constrained to practice it without receiving any. To claim to include all human beings was a bold innovation, and we have been working on living up to it ever since.

. . . men . . . In contrast, "men," as we know from the subsequent rendering of those rights into law, did mean men, not women, much less the most recently created human beings, also known as children. So we begin with confusion, knowing that "all" is not meant literally but that "men" is. Equality, and by extension respect, was to be accorded only to men, but not to all men.

In terms of legal standing, both "all" and "men" have, through painful struggle, expanded over the centuries. Considering the emotional turmoil over the inclusion of women in the category of those Americans who would be fully equal to the ones setting the terms, the linguistic part was easily solved by a clever trick. Until recently, the words "men" and "man" had been used in two senses, one ("man's struggle against Nature," "man and his environment") assuming that women were included in the definition, and the other ("men's club," "men's underwear") assuming, equally blandly, that they were not. Retroactively, we now choose the inclusive definition, even as that is disappearing from common usage.

We keep playing around with the definition of a child, not only changing the number of years a person must attain before qualifying for equality under the law, but using different ages simultaneously, according to what he or she happens to be doing or attempting. Maturity is generally acknowledged more speedily when it comes to being tried for murder than in registering to vote, or when it comes to consenting to marry than in consenting to copulate.

For social, rather than legal, reasons, the hierarchal system based on age is faltering. Although making distinctions based on age does violate the concept of total equality, what could be fairer? With any luck, age happens to everyone. According greater respect to greater age is the system most likely to give everyone a fair turn at high status, not to mention its being a nice little consolation for the loss of supple skin and a memory for names.

Not enough of a consolation, apparently. When the young balk at granting respect or authority except on the basis of their personal evaluation of the individual, American adults tend to agree. Once again, those who stand to benefit from inequality are responsible for suppressing it. In the youth-conscious American culture of the last fifty years, respect based on age is treated as an insult; the courtesy that age demands is that everyone pretend to mistake its age. "You make me feel old" is the puzzling accusation of those who obviously are toward those who are obviously trying to be polite to them. This campaign has been hugely successful, so the affronts of being offered a seat on public transportation or addressed deferentially with honorific and surname are no longer likely to occur.

From being considered outright parental property to be disposed of at will, children have achieved rights both in gaining protection and in exercising independence that some (some lawyers, that is, but probably all children) argue need extensive expansion still. Meanwhile, the concept of animal rights has appeared as a movement to extend "all men" to mean all creatures.

This is certainly not to suggest that the rights accorded by a society developing a system of law whose guiding principle is equality, and the respect accorded by the same society developing an etiquette system whose guiding principle is based on equality, are going to come out the same. In many cases, prevailing etiquette lagged disgracefully behind when it came to showing respect for people after they did achieve legal equality. Social and professional exclusion and open insults, as well as taunting under the guise of joking, continued to be generally countenanced. Small marks of respect, such as being addressed by surname and title or not being kept standing when others are seated, were still routinely withheld. It appears that allegiance to fairness alone does not activate the social recognition of equality, which has to be jump-started by fear. Almost every immigrant group was treated with open rudeness until amassing enough political power to make that dangerous.

This unfortunate legacy, hardly an example of courtesy, is largely responsible (along with silver forks and selfish brides) for giving etiquette a bad reputation. Rude behavior, no matter how widespread and conventionally accepted, cannot be classified as manners, any more than immoral laws can be called justice. In both cases, they must be changed when society comes to realize that they violate the principles that the system exists to ensure.

It is not that courtesy, generosity, and gallantry were never practiced, only that they were not mandated. When people are not qualified to be a reciprocal part of the etiquette system, being good to them may be considered a virtue, but it is also easily accepted that being harsh or cruel to them can be a virtue, of the "for their own good" variety. Within the system, no such leeway is allowed. Honor is at stake if one gentleman so much as looks cross-eyed at another, and it must be avenged.

. . . are created . . .

The predicate would seem to be fraught with controversy. "Are created" clearly is intended to refer to the Creator, not a concept everyone accepts on faith, as it were—not even a concept that everyone of faith accepts on faith. It is now understood to refer to humans' individual arrival on the scene without particular reference to God, or to the mystery of how individuals of our overwhelming subtlety and competence appeared from the inhibited loins of our immediate, less gifted forbearers, which is too difficult a concept to fathom.

That is not, however, the sticking point. Uncharacteristically leaving the creation allusion to be heard as literal, poetic, or any combination thereof, we have found other material in these words to inspire clashes and crusades. How equally can we be said to have been created if some are born richer, healthier, or more advantageously placed than others? How can society nullify this initial violation of its principle? Even if we do start out the same, will it last? Is this something society or individuals should be responsible for maintaining? Can the order be reset if it gets messed up?

These questions did not arise when it was accepted that God was directly responsible for setting the starting conditions and checking periodically to make sure that subsequent fortunes of individuals matched their merits. For centuries, that first assumption was an especially popular and self-evident argument among those born rich, as was the second among those who achieved success.

Now Americans of good will do not espouse any version of the concept that conditions of birth should affect the respect an individual deserves. It seems strange that historic figures whose other beliefs we venerate should have overlooked this, and some moderns do not consider that having lived in less enlightened times is a sufficient excuse when applied to people who otherwise devoted themselves to identifying and improving the conditions around them.

One of the last general beliefs about unequal creation to be discarded was the condemnation of illegitimate children for the sins—not of their fathers, so much as of their mothers. This social stigma lasted well beyond the emergence of a fervent belief in the innocence of children, itself possibly a corollary of the concept of equality at creation. Finally, the only argument for maintaining the stigma had become the sacrifice of the individual for the good of the community, in that targeting the innocent child of unmarried parents protected as yet unconceived innocent children who would be likely to be born lacking a father's protection if social disapproval of illegitimacy disappeared. That such did turn out to be the result did not mitigate the American distaste for the unfairness it involved.

Nevertheless, social tinkering is our heritage, and expansion of the social conscience has now assigned society the task of compensating for the unequal conditions under which huge numbers of people are created. This has become the country's most emotionally charged issue. General agreement that we must break the cycle by which poor people live in poor neighborhoods where their children go to poor schools so that a poor education condemns them to poor employment prospects which condemns them to live in poor neighborhoods, and so on, is stymied on the question of where in the cycle the break should occur. At any point that a break is attempted, another version of the equality argument opposes it: That helping the poor to live in better neighborhoods, or making special improvements to their own schools, or getting their children into better schools, or giving them employment advantages—that each of these denies equality to those who receive no such help.

The fallback method has been to lower the general level so as to deny advantages to those who have them, even innate personal advantages. "Elitism" is the term of condemnation used by those who charge society with compensating for the unequal distribution at creation of intelligence and artistic taste (although not of athletic ability or financial acumen) by holding those who do posses them to commoner standards.

. . . equal

Now comes that impossible word, "equal." No matter how inclusive the system, no matter how compensatory the society, we do not all come out alike. Should we ignore that fact and act as if we were?

Politeness cannot survive without ignoring facts, and yet the talent for doing so as a courtesy is in dangerously low supply. Under the mistaken notion that others want to know everything that passes through their heads or races through their emotions, many people no longer disguise having had a boring time at a party, feeling disappointed by a present, or being overcome with amazement when they notice that a person is tall or fat or uses a wheelchair.

If we had the self-control to pull off behaving as if everyone

were, in fact equal, would we want to do so? Presuming patriotic devotion to equality, as manifested in our legal system,
would we also want to have it as a feature of our etiquette system and accord everyone an equal level of respect? Circumstances of birth aside, this would involve eliminating the factors
of position, age, and achievement, and, indeed, the hierarchal
claims of each of these has been eroded in the interests of maintaining the equality with which we are supposed to have been
created. Mr. Jefferson's failed experiment in refusing to recognize the differences in professional rank has not discouraged
others from trying.

The pêle mêle workplace

We are even now in the middle of a massive effort to use etiquette to deny a formal
workplace structure that everyone knows
exists but agrees to hide because of its inher-
ent inequality. The intent was to replace a system in which people of low rank were stripped of their dignity by being treated
as children. The most obvious example of this was that they
would be addressed by their given names while being expected
to use formal address to the higher-ups. As this was a common
way of treating women and black people regardless of their
positions or the formality of the circumstances—notably in
courtroom and other official proceedings—and both groups
tended to be relegated to menial jobs, the difficulty, sometimes
impossibility, of rising was reinforced in every trivial exchange.

In keeping with the new pattern of leveling courtesies by
removing them from those who have them, rather than granting them to those who don't, bosses who were cornered by
charges of injustice began demanding to be addressed by their
first names. Far from resisting being reduced to childlike status,

a generation intent on flaunting its youthfulness regardless of actual age was pleased. Furthermore, this coincided with the entry of prophylactic popular psychotherapy into the workplace as a technique for increasing productivity.

Sessions in which personal confessions and frankly stated feelings became job requirements deliberately did away with the remaining business manners as a barrier to the desired intimacy. When professional behavior was thus jettisoned, it was replaced by the manners of friendship. Not long ago, private correspondence would have been hidden from supervisors, partying would have been limited to theme-decorated coffee breaks marking the holidays, employees' children would be present only in photographs pinned to their parents' work stations. Now leisure-time clothing, parties in the office, and openly acknowledged computer games and personal e-mail, although they may have been instituted to compensate for long hours, contribute to the fiction that work is incidental to camaraderie.

The ability to slip into a professional role, ignoring one's personal identity, is all but lost. It is no longer just the person who is supposed to be waiting on your restaurant table who takes the opportunity to belie the impersonal rule and tell you something about himself, but also the person who is supposed to be performing your wedding ceremony who starts reminiscing about his own wedding, and the formal speaker who opens by confiding the difficulty he had in deciding what he should say. In some cases, these asides might come from the same impulse small children have when they shout their names from behind their Halloween costumes and announce that they are not really ghosts. A deeper motivation seems to be connected with the equality issue. It is a method of asserting that one is more important than one's job would suggest and entitled to be treated as a social acquaintance rather than someone providing a service.

This is matched by a corresponding inability to recognize that anyone else is appearing in a professional capacity, and that therefore no notice should be taken of that person's personal attributes. How many years is it taking men to learn that the same compliments and gallantry that would be welcome in private life may be dramatically unwelcome on the job? Even those with no untoward designs on their female colleagues appear to be having trouble with the concept that using social manners on them, even ingratiating ones, reduces the woman's work contributions to providing a diversion, as both men and women may happily provide for each other in social life.

That gender should not be a factor at all in workplace manners, distinctions being legitimately made only in regard to the individual's rank and job description, is a difficult enough concept when the workplace also serves as a major source of romantic contacts. When, in addition, bosses behave as if they are at the same level as their employees and colleagues behave as if they were thrown together by affection, it is hardly surprising that workers are easily fooled or forgetful.

In less potentially explosive ways, workers constantly fall victim to this false pantomime of friendship that obscures the realities of the impersonal workplace. Office parties are a notorious trap for those who are fooled by the surface amenities into believing that the normal cold assessment of employees' behavior has been suspended, and their carefree behavior will be greeted by supervisors and rivals with the same enjoyment as it would be by friends, any excesses on their part being met with fond forgiveness. Another shock awaits people at the end of their jobs or careers. The honorably retired worker, no less than one who was fired, is embittered to find how quickly office friendships dissolve into embarrassed excuses. It turns out that with the exception of separate friendships that have been nurtured in the traditional way, any illusion of office friendship vanishes in an instant.

Marketplace manners, in which people crisply assess and act upon the professional advantages of any opportunities that become available to them, are still openly practiced, however. They may be observed in any gathering of what we still call private life—the party at which guests are angling to make business contacts, the dinner where guests are told to bring food, contribute to a cause, or even pay their own way, the wedding, birthday, graduation, or anniversary celebration that is used to solicit funds or specific goods, and where the cost of the refreshments is calculated against the return in presents.

It is not that the workplace lacks crassness. However, its custom is that the demand for social funds be lightly disguised as group sociability. There may be constant collections of cash to buy presents, but colleagues do not give or request cash as presents, as relatives and friends increasingly do. The fiction of equality may extend to including the boss among those for whom money is collected, or employees' agreeing to take over the sponsorship of workplace ceremonies, such as promotion or retirement parties.

In the end, the friends-and-family charade at work remains because inequality of rank is so offensive to the American notion of fairness that it must be disguised, even by the very people who could better protect their interests by acknowledging it.

*What
we
believe*

Perhaps the most charming interpretation of equality as expressed in everyday manners is the notion that under fair conditions, we would all achieve comparable levels of success. It is akin to the notion that we are immortal, and therefore illness and death are failures of personal habits or attitudes, or of botched medical treatment or stymied (or underfunded) research that can some day be overcome.

Whether these concepts are true is unimportant; they are essential because they inspire all that is best in American society, from modest attributions of triumph to luck and hard work to widespread dedication to bettering conditions. What else do we have to go on?

Well, we have our fundamental paradoxes, in which we all believe:

We are all equal, and anyone can rise to great heights.

We always behave naturally and can reinvent ourselves any way we choose.

We honor our heritage and invent our own personal traditions.

We operate strictly on merit, and nobody is better than anyone else.

We have the right to behave as we please, and to make others stop behaving obnoxiously.

We are all friends and nobody owes anything to anyone else.

We admire youth and deplore children other than our own, but sometimes them as well.

We believe that education is the key to success and exposure
   to civilization is corrupting.

We are proud of our democratic process and distrust politicians.

Chapter 4

The Plot

Citizen Meets Success

A s a preview, "The streets are paved with gold" turned out to be misleading. Flashily excerpted scenes often are. So did other coming attractions for The American Dream:

> "Free of fear and want, we will devote all our thoughts to God."
>
> "They'll never find us there."
>
> "Our children will grow up safe from wicked influences."
>
> "Your husband will never find us there."
>
> "Never again will we have to endure prejudice or oppression."
>
> "No one there ever goes hungry."
>
> "We will be the masters there."
>
> "Our American relatives must be rich, and how happy they will be to see us all."

When the picture became clear, the newcomers, having been

self-selected for the imagination to envision change, set right to work on The American Dream 2. Rather than being stuck on the discovery that conditions were not as advertised, and lacking the luxury of being bored enough to find their reality-show travails a sufficient amusement, they devised new plots. These also pursued the themes of moral, social, and economic mobility becoming achievable through geographical mobility, but as scenery and local color were added, the methods and goals began to shift.

*Old
World
folk tales*

One must concede that these new plots were not absolutely new. Rags to riches, the deeds of heroic wanderers, good guys versus bad guys, and the power of true love to conquer any obstacle are all ancient stories. Every culture has its lore that supplies subjects for public sculpture and schoolchildren's essays while delivering its curriculum on manners and morals. We are all only too familiar with those modest folk who achieved glory by killing dragons, feeding mysterious strangers, and answering riddles. It is through such lessons that the joy of marrying upward is taught—to boys, who are advised to take foolhardy risks, and to girls, who are alerted that sweet humility is the key to the jaded hearts of the hereditary ruling class (although girls who pay close attention might notice the scrupulously inserted caveat that model behavior only works if accompanied by extreme good looks).

Immigrants brought along their inherited tales, but more as sentimental bric-a-brac for the hearth than guidance on how to behave outdoors. No stretch of the imagination made these resemble human experience within living memory, so they were not likely to have been freshly illustrated even in their lands of origin. Here, it was not their being heavily staffed with royalty that made them seem out of place; indeed, American children are even now presumed to maintain a keen interest in the marital prospects of princesses. What made the old stories look faded in the new space was that they hardly favored individual enterprise over laudable but sedentary virtues, and that success by either method amounted to winning over the favor of the powerful.

American folk tales

New ones were necessary to set behavioral guides for the present, as well as aspirations for the future. What story you are in, and how it is projected to advance, must be known to determine how you should look, behave, and treat others.

In the American revisions featuring contemporary settings of settlements and wilderness, frontiers and farms, slums and boulevards, daring counted more than humility. Wild twists of fortune did not seem like forlorn wishfulness arising from remote mythology but actual possibilities, illustrated through contemporary rumor. What freshly infused them with life, so that they resonated not only in America but, eventually, wherever else in the world they spread, was faith in dramatic change.

The illusion that life never changes except for the worse (prime example: the younger generation is never as respectful and obedient as the older generation ruefully remembers being forced to be), and that therefore it never will, requires short lifespans and severely limited access to what we now call news. Centuries featuring spectacular geographical or technological discoveries or philosophical and economic revolutions rattle that notion. Then the timid foresee the end of the world, while the bold foresee the end of all human troubles.

America, with its successive upheavals based on exploration, war, political reform, war, industrialization, war, social reform, and war, was an audience receptive to exhortations to wrest rewards from change that might be received skeptically elsewhere.

The likelihood of starting with nothing and achieving fortune, position, and/or honor?

The confidence that we will always win because we fight for what is always right?

The belief that love is an unstoppable force?

The conviction that it is never too late to start again?

We count on all this. It was not until the country became rich and powerful that a petulant pessimism slackened these beliefs. Even then, moral indignation about self-perpetuating poverty, corrupt politicians, romantic betrayal, and wrongful national policies presupposes that a higher standard is obtainable. There is no point in protesting wrongs to those who lack the conscience to care. The apparent bitterness that characterized the pity politics of recent decades is belied by its confidence that calling attention to unfairness will shame people into redressing it. And so it is in private life. Dewy-eyed third marriages and fortunes garnered after bankruptcy keep the general optimistic blaze rekindled.

American folklore extolling virtue, success, fairness, adventure, and love has, over the years, adapted to a variety of moods and conditions. Neither cynicism nor lewdness has succeeded in quashing its basically hopeful tone, possibly only because the storytelling convention demands a satisfactory resolution. Although these plots are now identified with film because they are regularly distributed through our entertainment industry, they were long before featured in American literature, plays, and amateur, story-packaged instruction. Political plots can fire people up for short periods, but it is narrative plots that keep the warmth stoked, and the glow from our daydreams can be glimpsed around the world.

Rags to Riches

Gold in the streets (or its natural cousin, Gold in Them Thar Hills) is hardly a Pilgrim cry. Earlier arrivers had hearkened to it, but they tended to pocket what they found and go home. Yet from the beginning, the quick (favorable) reversal of fortune has been a basic American plot, associated with a variety of means, from the ingenious to the rapacious, and of emotions, from inspiration to indignation. Its premise is not so much that everyone will get rich as that everyone should try and that those who succeed are, by a nice little tautology, the very ones who patently deserve to be successful. There are various versions of this plot line, depending on the prevailing idea of what it takes to be deserving, besides starting out poor and ending up rich.

The classic version began as the humble and hopeful idea that the land should at least have the grace to support the righteous. In the wilderness, riches, to explorers and settlers alike, meant that before there could be any literal or metaphorical hope for gold, America was obliged to yield at least survival-level bounty. When that was humbly begged as a favor from God, He came through, however appalling were the setbacks whose divine purpose the faithful were hard-pressed to fathom.

There was assumed to be a strong connection between achievement and moral worthiness, mitigated, in cases of what appeared to be misjudgments, by human sympathy for suffering on the part of the relatively innocent and by religious faith in ultimate justice.

Once some of the godly had amassed more than the sustenance for which they had petitioned and promised eternal thanks, they began to presume to figure out the divine system. Since God was evidently not planning to distribute earthly rewards to everyone in equal shares, those who got the best deal concluded that they were clearly His personal favorites. To believe otherwise would smack of the impious notion that God made mistakes.

Such twice-blessed Americans did not apply this theology retroactively to the blessedness of the rich and powerful who had oppressed them or their forebears in the old country. Nor did that idea come up when revolutionary Americans began to cast doubt on the proposition that God, by a similar method, anointed kings. In America, at any rate, He operated on the merit system, and the proof of merit was having managed to raise oneself to riches. Since those who rise have to start out lower, work was pretty much unavoidable, and riches inspire reverence, examples abounded.

The smug and heavy-handed manner in which these religious colonies read the distribution of God's earthly rewards as justification for mimicking the old class system was muted by the inhibitions of the same creed. The consequence of believing that God does not look favorably on the lazy or the luxurious was to rule out enjoying leisure once one had the means. However much they valued their advantages, the pious did not shrink from this implication. In the American story, virtue was expected to remain actively striving, thus quashing the chief attraction of belonging to the upper classes, hitherto and elsewhere also known as the leisure classes.

The rich already had the aristocratic principle of noblesse oblige to dampen their fun. Tethering advantages to responsibilities toward the disadvantaged is a venerable tenet of manners that seeks to control the natural response to wealth and power, which is to have a high old time pushing people around and showing off. It had produced an etiquette intended to mitigate class exploitation, just as it produced the etiquette of chivalry in an attempt to mitigate the degradation of women. These historical contributions, which are forgotten to the extent that etiquette is now identified with the very evils of snobbery and misogyny that it fights, may not have had equalizing results. Still, the mere fact that the legitimacy of the principles of noblesse oblige and chivalry were acknowledged by the powerful is evidence of etiquette's long-time campaign against the misuses that inequality inspires.

The American twist went amazingly further. It dared to suggest that curtailing the pleasures that success could produce was not enough: One should pretty much forgo them in order to keep right on working, as an end in itself, behaving and living as if the goal of success had never been reached. Because of the grim frugality by which this credo was sometimes characterized, it received scant credit for being so much finer a concept than the aristocratic cult of uselessness, with all its flouting and flaunting. For some, it also provided a more interesting life.

True, the virtue of eschewing luxury and lasciviousness did not come to characterize the culture, in spite of a weakened attempt at frugal-chic that lingered a while among the colonists' descendants. It just gave the Puritans a permanent bad name. Europeans who measured their pedigrees by the number of generations they were removed from the working ancestor who had established the family's fortunes could afford also to pride themselves on being removed from the work of spending that money to display the family grandeur. Having had major shopping done on their behalf in the past, they could sneer at those who were forced to do their own. Successful Americans often mimic this superiority to the nouveaux riches, but at their own risk. If they don't buy and build their own accoutrements, they are not likely to have many. Anyway, it is a waste of time for Americans who inherit great riches to mythologize their useful ancestors, not only because the old tycoons were too well documented to pass for refined, but because we actually prefer their type to that of their silver spoon descendants.

The dichotomy between those who admire energetic enterprise and those who idealize static splendor continued throughout America's social history. Victorian and Edwardian literature and humor played on their coexistence in families, typically between the self-made man and his gently born son-in-law, each of whom finds the other a practical or social asset but despises him as a social or practical liability. Even then, there was slippage toward the American manner, not only on the part of disillusioned American heiresses who had married into aristocratic poverty but on the part of European noblemen dazzled by the daring spirit that these young ladies had inherited from those supposedly vulgar American parents. Disdain for striving had not taken into account the possibility that dynamic people might be not only richer but more exciting than static ones.

Neo-Puritanism

Whether Americans used their gains to purchase foreign crests, expensive rural simplicity at home, or drugs wherever they could find them, those who defected from the basic Puritan work ideal when they could afford to do so would seem to belie its hold. Yet here it is, back full-force in American life.

Just a generation ago, some citizens were celebrating and others were lamenting the rise of unabashed hedonism. Moral restraints were said to be strained, if not snapped. Sensation seeking had seemingly swept away forever the plodding pleasures of labor and domesticity.

Of course this happened mostly in the national mythology. Millions of people continued to go quietly to work and home as usual. All the same, the alarm had consequences. The immediate one was that some of those millions began wondering why they were the only people missing out on this huge and exciting change, and the rest began worrying that their children might not miss out on it. Soon it was no longer only social rebels or pioneers who were acting upon such newly flipped axioms as: promiscuity is good for health, divorce is better for children than a home unwarmed by parental romance, tight pants and tiny skirts are comfortable, the work of the world is boring, and, not least, etiquette is bad for human relationships and should be replaced by self-assertiveness and uncensored communication.

In the natural course of events, augmented by some bad scares from disease and terrorism, these pronouncements are being gingerly reexamined. As more people complain of panacea failure, a phalanx of social explainers is able to produce studies to prove that whatever everybody is complaining about reflects a social problem. (Fortunately, professional turnover is usually rapid enough to prevent the same people whose studies proved that maladjusted children suffer from a surfeit of maternal attention, for example, from having to produce studies proving that maladjusted children suffer from a deficit of maternal attention.) The astonishing part is that the most striking reversal was accomplished almost spontaneously, without the tedious process of bolstering the obvious with insignificant statistics—and that it turned out to be, frankly acknowledged as such, hardly short of that much-ridiculed Puritanism.

All that agonizing about a pleasure-addled society lolling around refusing to earn its keep, all that bragging about rejecting materialism and the stifling demands of the workplace—and suddenly young people were voluntarily plunging into business and consumerism. Because there were no longer clearly separated working plans for men and women, the number of strivers almost doubled.

Not that the original players would have recognized their replacements. The articulation of virtue had been dropped, not only because of the separation of church and economy but because it became acceptable to notice that godly virtues and business virtues do not always converge (a situation some enterprising religious organizations are striving to correct). Nevertheless, the fervor of modern devotees of the work ethic would surely shock their progenitors out of the traditional lament that nobody who came later appreciates how disgracefully easier life has become.

At least they didn't work on Sunday, even if they scrupled not to enjoy the day. Now stores and chores dominate the weekends and evenings of laborers. The longest working hours and least hope of relief from the call of duty burden the very people who can most easily afford to purchase their ease. As being overworked became a point of pride with the rich, the less privileged have been quick to insinuate that they, too, are allowed no respite. It has become a conventional form of flattery to tell people, "I know how busy you must be."

Technological miracles have enabled the call of duty to reach workers everywhere and at every time—in the bosom of the family, in the bosoms of others, at mealtime, at sport, on holiday—and, for that matter, in the very act of attending services of worship. The few who dare to dispute that the summons to attend to business takes precedence over the other realms of life are marginalized as unsuccessful.

The domestic workplace

That this happened in the same period that people were being urged to break loose from the constraints of politeness at home, thus bringing on a dramatic increase in open domestic hostility, was probably not a coincidence. At both places, the change was prompted by advocacy for informality, naturalness, and frankness, but the phony assumption of social manners at work may have created a more pleasant environment than the crudeness and lack of consideration for others known as being oneself at home.

To be sure, the modern workplace with its leisure-time clothes and parties for personal celebrations and holidays (of which every Friday is one) would strike any self-respecting Puritan as the picture of sloth. This is not the case if one understands that the other realm of life, the domestic world that comprised family, society, culture, philanthropy, and all the other nonprofit activities that are supposed to make life worth supporting through labor, has been crowded almost out of existence. Those superficial concessions are not supplements to leisure but substitutions. The workplace has accommodated itself to accept remnants of the formerly vital and vaunted domestic realm not only out of pity for its beleaguered workforce but because home is still compelling enough to distract workers' attention and to lure them away from overtime or from work itself.

The defectors are mostly women, because women used to run that realm when the realm of business was run by men. Domestic life has always had the greater lip-service prestige—family and friends being said to be all that matters, and earning money to be meaningful only in their service—and zero real prestige, because it doesn't bring in any money. Therefore, when the household doors stood open to let women out in the streets in search of gold, which remains the quintessential American heroic task, it was not thought necessary to replace them in those negligible jobs they had been performing. That, in addition to replacing the incomes that men had been constrained to supply for their wives and children before the normalization of divorce and illegitimacy, was left up to individual women to manage as best they could.

Those who refused to leave the vast personal world unattended, or who felt bad about doing so, or who frazzled themselves trying to do both jobs at once, were initially cited as examples of women's unfitness for the working world. Men had managed both having jobs and having families and friends; why couldn't women?

Eventually, people began to notice that the reason that men had been able to manage both is that they didn't. The world of labor for hire, with its imperious time demands, could be tailored for a worker who merely dipped into a personal life without managing its tasks and responsibilities only because he had a wife managing that. Once that revelation was out, it could be noticed that this method of subcontracting personal life, along with its admitted attractions of emotional bonding with children and friends, was not optimal for men, either. In some fashion, everyone needs to make a living and everyone needs to have a personal life, and a lifetime spent doing only one of these, no matter how successfully, is ultimately unsatisfying.

Cooperative partnerships in which a couple managed both realms were known to exist. The notion of colleagues as family—"one big happy family" was the phrase businesses used to tout themselves in times that were less cynical about both—might be traced to pioneering, farming, and mom-and-pop stores, where families were co-workers. Small business ventures by immigrants are often organized this way up until the children have been educated to the American ideal of making their own way in their own way.

Nevertheless, the two parts of life have different goals—the family's being to sustain all members through good times and bad, the business's being to sustain itself commercially using whoever is useful at the time—and therefore require different manners. Loyalty, tolerance, and a permanent interest in the development and contentedness of each individual characterize successful family life; the dispassionate selection and use of qualified workers characterize successful business life.

To switch approaches and manage both requires enormous

dexterity, and the consequences of applying the wrong one to the wrong realm are severe. A family that deserts its unproductive members or disowns its uncooperative ones is as much of a failure as a business that puts all these relatives on the payroll.

At times, it has been considered feasible business practice to mimic family behavior with promotion paths, compassion for difficulties, and job security. Now that ruthless practices have frankly acknowledged the impersonal nature of business, efforts to make the workplace seem like home, from welcoming employees' pets to the office to sending out their laundry, appear as optional perquisites. None of this, not even such basic efforts as parental leave or day care, has solved the dilemma of managing the domestic realm in a workplace designed for married men. That solution awaits a revolution as stunning as the industrial revolution, which divided life's two great realms, the professional and the personal, between the genders, and thus misplaced vast numbers of women and men and cheated them all of a full life. We have yet to discover that virtually all women and all men want to be able to occupy both realms, and making them pretend their co-workers are their families and friends isn't going to do it.

We have been in this untenable situation now for more than a generation with no more serious solutions being proposed than adding more stopgap measures to the workplace, or returning to the gender division system. At least the latter worked, it is being said, skipping over the fact that it never worked for women if they expected, as did their male colleagues, to have families.

Respect for work has been revived at the expense of respect for any other aspect of life. The neo-Puritan work ethic, complete with its promise of rewards in the world yet to come (interpreted in the high corporate world to mean storing up luxuries to enjoy in a cushy retirement that, like heaven itself, one hopes to stave off), now occupies center stage. Valuing people for their efforts and achievements, and thus expecting everyone to lead a useful life, even those who can well afford to be useless, is one of America's greatest contributions to the world. It is only the detail of how to accomplish this without sacrificing the values of personal life that we haven't managed.

Rags to Riches: The Remake

Meanwhile, other versions of rags to riches, less venerable but nonetheless fixed in the American tradition, are also enjoying long runs. These address the flaw in the work ethic, namely work.

Envisioning streets paved with gold naturally postdated the Pilgrims, as it presupposed the existence of streets, although the idea was previously held by marauding explorers. The natural bounty of the mainland was never so yielding as to lend itself to the sort of food-dropping-into-the-mouth fantasies that came to be focused on Polynesia. Those who mistakenly acted on the implication that riches would be available for the easy picking found they had to get busy if they hoped to eat. Free or cheap land still had to be tilled. Even the great Gold Rush required wielding heavy tools.

Those for whom the good life is not necessarily the godly life and the thought of hard labor is unnecessarily harsh yearned for alternative methods. The two most popular American plot lines about getting to riches from rags without running oneself ragged are illustrated by relatively modern and oddly similar stories. Both take place in soda fountains, and both are convincingly disputed. In one, cleverness is substituted for the sterner virtues, and in the other, cuteness.

The soda fountain legends

The earlier one might be termed The Legend of the Coca-Cola Bottle. This refers to the (counterfactual) story that in the 1880s, when Coca-Cola was made at soda fountains by pouring syrup made from cocoa, kola nuts, and secret ingredients into a glass and adding carbonated water, a clever person offered the druggist who had concocted it a secret that would make his drink into a fountain of fortune. The deal was to be that if this secret proved useless, there would be no charge, but if the druggist wanted to adopt it, he would have to pay (the figure in question depending on what whoever relates the story considers to be an outrageous sum). The secret turned out to be two words—"Bottle it"—and the fee had to be paid or the druggist would have had to keep stirring.

The other story is The Legend of Schwab's Drugstore. The plot is that one day in 1936, a teenager playing hooky from Hollywood High was sipping an ice cream soda at Schwab's fountain when another customer realized that there was something about the girl, mostly having to do with her sweater, that qualified her to become a major motion picture actress; and the next thing young Lana Turner knew, she was one. Later, the same sudden promotion from customer to movie star was said (by Mr. Schwab, who by this time was doing a brisk business in aspiring actors) to have happened at Schwab's to Ava Gardner, Robert Taylor, and others.

The effect of this on the soda fountain business can only be compared to the effect of bottling Coca-Cola. The effect of both on the American work ethic was even more dramatic.

In point of fact, the idea of bottling Coca-Cola was put forward in a conventional way by regular businessmen to the person who had acquired the syrup rights after its inventor, and the bottling business was a joint venture among them. Miss Turner maintained in her autobiography that her discovery was not made at Schwab's, that she was not wearing a sweater, and that she was drinking not an ice cream soda but a Coke.

No matter—both stories became an inspirational part of American folklore, taking their place with the traditional plot of achieving success through virtue and hard work, which had enjoyed a revitalized credence and popularity in the nineteenth century through the novels of Horatio Alger, junior.

The bottling story embodied the idea that a flash of cleverness was equal, and more likely superior, to the tedium of work as a method of achieving huge success. One idea, whether it had to do with better-mousetrap practicality or Hula Hoop frivolity, would be enough, if brazenly promoted, to set a person up for life. The dot-com boom of this turn-of-the-century was a renewed demonstration bolstering faith in this, both on the part of those who paid fortunes for clever ideas and those who made the fortunes—and then lost them, if they violated the basic premise of one-effort-is-enough by slipping back into work ethic habits to strive for even more.

In the Schwab's story, producing an idea is not required. There is a piquancy in the circumstance that the subject was not only doing nothing (not counting whatever effort went into straw action) at the time she was selected to receive fame and fortune. She was actually doing less than nothing, in the sense that she was truant from her required job of attending school. She was not even putting in the thought and effort of figuring out what she wanted to do and then hanging out where she thought it was likely to happen, as did the legions who hoped to copy her success.

Nor could she have done anything, as the basis of her selection (accepting her claim that she was not wearing a tight sweater) was indefinable and unlearnable. Personality, flair, a certain look—whatever went into "star quality," it was unrelated to the traditional skills of being an actor, however useful those might prove to be after the breakthrough.

Being rewarded for being cute or being clever seems to relate to our ideal of equality, in that it can happen to anyone. The stories of tycoons and movie stars who rose from humble backgrounds appeal to us more than those about second-generation successes in either area. We may be fascinated with following family dynasties, but we expect them to come to a bad end to validate the merit system.

Although the cute and the clever may not have worked for their success, we expect them to do so afterward. Their job, like that of a constitutional monarch, is to embody the national character, whatever we think that is at the time. Fortunately for them, we no longer expect paragons, having become disillusioned with the ones we thought we had, to the point where we would rather they didn't pretend. Anyway, we need sins to keep the story interesting. We only require them to be goodhearted and, above all, entertaining. It is a better system than employing monarchs, because ours show us that although everybody doesn't find gold in the streets, the person who does could be anybody.

Good Guys v. Bad Guys

Americans have a penchant for showdowns between good and evil. It provides us with opportunities to play heroes, and that is a role to which we, as a nation and as individuals, feel peculiarly suited. Such struggles may be conducted elsewhere with more passion, ferocity, and endurance, but we are good at taking positions on a myriad of topics, large and small, that had not previously been considered controversial, and challenging those villains who fail to catch on. If we did not stake out new ideological territory, this would be too much like the summer camp game of arbitrary "color wars." This is not beneath us, exactly, but it is not dignified, either.

The truism, new to historians but old to observers of human nature, that the good guys are the ones telling the story, works in our favor as experienced spinners of morals and spin. That does not, however, fully account for the confidence we bring to our casting demand. We believe that we can demonstrate that our claim goes beyond that universal disposition to think well of oneself, which has been known to inspire the most heinous criminals and cruel societies with the fervor to convince themselves and, not infrequently, others of their nobility. We may yield to no one in righteous self-admiration, but we believe we can prove our goodness objectively—and not just by the ecumenical method of brandishing an endorsement from God.

Heroic job qualifications

First there is our history of declaring that it was not our own inferiority but the injustice of the various countries from which we emigrated that kept us down, and of having demonstrated that we could, indeed, do better.

Then there is our ideology, that mix of freedoms and marketing strategies that we are convinced everyone else envies; we have seen this mimicked by enough other societies to support that conviction.

Next, there is the living proof of our own constant bickering, which provides a show both of our magnanimity for tolerating internal dissent and of our power in being able to withstand it.

Finally, there is our devotion to self-improvement, giving us a defense against charges of arrogance and support for our consumerist faith that the newest version of anything must necessarily be an improvement on the old.

Good Guys v. Bad Guys allows just about everyone to try out for the heroic part, even those who had previously been typecast as villains. In religion and in the American mind (as opposed to American life, where vagrants are considered as suspicious as elsewhere), the mysterious stranger is presumed likely to rescue everyone before disappearing in a cloud of heroism. Part of our heritage of immigration is the expectation of being taken at face value, never mind what they used to say about us before we left. What we say about them is that they were bad, we are good, and that's why we left.

So originally, there was no problem finding bad guys to fight. They were the ones who ruled the old countries, and the ones who challenged our ruling the new one. At a comfortable distance from our triumphs over both, we have taken all but the newest sources of immigrants and trouble back into our sentimental embrace, as if our clashes with the former had been sport among good friends and with the latter, some regrettable bullying we have now outgrown.

During wars, elections, and social movements, sides are easily delineated. It is during the quieter periods, when we still have to cast the part of enemies in order to have something for comparison and blame, that we are at our worst. During peacetime, people make do with home-grown enemies—various groups and types, their own relatives, neighbors, and other handy individuals. A typical collection would include the latest wave of immigrants (pictured as predators), plutocrats (pictured wearing evening clothes during the day), bosses, men, women, gays, the religious, the irreligious, the elderly, the younger generation, parents, in-laws, spouses, and, best of all, ex-spouses.

Peacetime enemies

As etiquette-based protests knocked some of these off the lists, replacements appeared that would seem to contradict American self-righteousness. These included various branches of our own government, government itself, particular American businesses, business itself, our various figures of authority, and authority itself. What preserves our good opinion in such conflicts is the belief that a mysterious element called The People remains pure, although it must be on the alert against elements that ignore its principles and wishes. Thus, democracy and free speech allow us to elect the holders of political office and, at the same time, entertain a group prejudice against elected politicians.

Good causes/bad behavior

The concept of duty may have become tainted since it came to include duty foremost toward oneself, but duty toward others survives, even if often interpreted as being in inverse relationship to the connection—

far-away strangers first, family last. We are idealists who stand ready to fight for right, although sometimes we may be quicker to charge than to figure out which way to go.

This can be more than the confusion caused by changing world alignments. Even allowing for the range of loyalists, dissenters, partisans, reformers, protesters, loyal opposition, bigots, grumps, and crazies on the domestic front, any clash should seem coherent from one vantage point or another. Yet things got increasingly muddled to the point where it has been difficult to discern good from bad. One of our archetypal crusaders is the person who has changed sides and then offers, as a special qualification of leadership, his having been duped by the side (Communism being a prime example) he now vehemently opposes. It appears to be a free-for-all in which, the question of virtue aside, it is not even clear which are the lesser evils that should be distinguished from the greater.

Much of this comes from a disconnection of cause from methods, on the assumption that virtue in one cancels the need for any in the other. We often feel a strong sense of commitment, but it is not always clear who needs to be committed. Road rage and the rages that quickly developed behind it are fueled by something approximating righteous indignation against willful incompetence; they attack this by methods that, in turn, bring the maddeningly inefficient activity to a complete halt. Idealists routinely employ public humiliation (screaming at passersby to make examples of them) and private embarrassment (shaming donors to make them give more) in the hope of improving the lot of humanity. On the assumption that you catch more flies by sticking it to them, good causes have gone into partnership with bad manners.

A very different source of confusion is goodness itself, in the form of sophisticated concepts that undermine the definition of Good Guy. Besides the spurt in crassness, there has also been growth in kindness, fairness, modesty, humility, empathy, generosity, and tolerance in the latter twentieth century, which ought to have purified the conflict. War reparations, whether arising from humanitarianism or a global economic system that made it impractical to sustain enemy nations, and curtailed victories made lagging forgiveness seem like poor sportsmanship. Television produces a clear view of war, with its carnage splattering all sides, literally and metaphorically, and revealing that war is always brutal, no matter who conducts it, and suffering is always pathetic, no matter how much it is provoked. Poverty is no longer hidden, and the crowing of the rich that fortune is fairly accorded on the basis of personal merit has been jeered and shamed into silence. The civil rights movement tore the accepted façade from racism, and provided a pattern by which other prejudices were unmasked and socially condemned.

Bad guys/pathetic behavior

Meanwhile, under the onslaught of social science, the ranks of the homegrown bad guys were also being thinned. With various soft disciplines firing off their explanations of human behavior, the concept of free will as a factor lay bleeding, along with that of responsibility of people for their own actions. Undesirable behavior came to be viewed as part of a chain reaction that turned victims into perpetrators. Until America was under direct attack, the idea that evil might exist had been confined to comic books. Crime itself acquired a new euphemism, "a cry for help," and fastidious people became careful to pair any expression of sympathy for crime victims and their mothers with an equal concern for the criminals and their mothers, although this is somewhat muted as a result of yelps from the injured innocent.

We still do give recognition to victims, but it is a matter of scale. The name of hero is bestowed on those who fall victim to our national enemies equally with those who subdue them. Being victimized by society is honorable enough to have become competitive. A whole new version of Good Guys v. Bad Guys opened up, in which the Bad Guys were the previous winners and the Good Guys were those who had lost. This is a high-minded approach, because it depends on both sides agreeing that spoils should be voluntarily forsworn in the case of victories that can be shown to be immoral.

Yet a disarming sympathy has disarmed the individual's own moral mechanism, the conscience. Feeling guilty, which had been the self-administered punishment for doing wrong, was redefined as a virus that attacked the good and the bad indiscriminately. Feelings of worth, which had been the self-administered reward for doing right, turned into self-esteem, a tonic to be administered to the bad to make them good. As therapy became sport and entertainment, it was revealed, through greater, sometimes public, exchanges of confidence, among individuals, in support groups, on television, and through chat rooms, that faults and sins were commonplace, and therefore met the social standard of being normal. Increased reporting of the lives of public figures in the news and in history managed to bring it down to where the average person had little trouble meeting it.

Although these shifts have created moral messes in the criminal justice system and ugly words in the jury room, they might have improved things on the ideological front. The crash of certainties could have heralded a major etiquette victory, with everyone taking into consideration other people's experiences and feelings. With an appreciation of the complexity of human nature and attention to what goes into producing points of view, Good Guys v. Bad Guys could be played more thoughtfully.

Instead, the shoot-'em-up enactment of this plot line is more popular than ever. This tends not to happen in hysterical reaction to real threats; on the contrary, in times of natural or unnatural disaster, American behavior is generally exemplary. It happens during the lulls. When times are relatively peaceful and prosperous, our own political and cultural disputes are so incendiary that the smallest disputes burst into full flame, commonsense judgments are discounted, and draconian measures proposed. Idealists, even those expressly espousing peace and the protection of life, make their cases through intimidation. Acrimony in daily life produces its daily toll from previously obedient people whom trivial inconvenience has provoked beyond control. It turns out that none of those advances in compassion was considered applicable to people who failed to see how right one was. In theory, the chain of reaction models of bad behavior should exonerate everyone; in practice, it is impossible to live in a blameless mess, so we excuse only those whom we pity.

Rejecting the peacekeeper

Rather than ending domestic hostilities, the change made by the increase in sophistication was the rejection of the idea that these, unlike conflicts abroad, should be ruled by etiquette or its relative on the government payroll, diplomacy. This should not be surprising, because mundane conflicts, major and minor, are inevitable, and when they get rough, the rules of engagement are usually broken. What is different is the refusal to employ such rules routinely, to the point of denying the legitimacy of having rules, and then on to the next point of believing that morality rejects any such restraint.

Etiquette has always governed conflict. The very terms we use to identify the good and the bad—white hats and black hats (anachronistic as they are, now that black clothing is read as chic or of-the-streets or both, and white as Ku-Klux-Klan-lawless, or dead)—come from etiquette's jurisdiction over symbolism. Even conflicts to the death, such as wars and duels—the modern street gang type as well as the antique form—have strict rules regarding clothing, greetings, gestures, acknowledgment of hierarchies, and acceptable methods of execution. These hardly correspond to the etiquette of the society at large, and are rarely morally appetizing, but they nevertheless form a code known and recognized by participants and onlookers.

Etiquette's most direct peacekeeping function—inhibiting behavior likely to cause offense, deflecting reaction through apologies and reparations, and providing methods of settling conflicts without rancor—has been disputed on ideological grounds by people of presumably good will. Its rules, they feel, should be cast aside as unworthy of the righteous, whose passions were surely too strong to tolerate petty niceties. In institutions such as legislatures and classrooms, etiquette has been challenged on the indisputable ground that it interferes with the free and spontaneous expression of all thought and feeling. That is what it is intended to do. Positions cannot be aired when people are freely expressing their impassioned emotions, and so there is no hope of resolving conflict.

The results have not been pretty. Without benefit of etiquette, previously peaceful forms of conflict have turned vicious. Targeted fury over the tiny frustrations of everyday life is so close to the surface of even the most privileged segments of American society that apparently ordinary citizens turn out to constitute explosives that can be set off in an instant and lobbed at random victims.

The relatively civilized favor the adversarial model of conflict settlement. It is a technique modeled on our legal system, but it also applies to the other nonviolent method that is favored for settling differences, which is therapy. The premise there is that the unfortunate results of such previously recommended therapies as acting aggressively on self-interests regardless of the consequences of others can be mitigated by changing ideas, eradicating prejudices, and reversing emotions. Why it is thought that this is easier than telling people to cut out their nasty ways or no one will like them any more is not clear.

Love Conquers All

Remarkably, the American love story has remained essentially the same for centuries, triumphing over the reality of every era.

In it, two independent-minded people who are too busy attending to other matters (examples: piety, study, duty, career building, money making, fending off matrimony) to think about love, and don't believe in true love anyway, fail to recognize that they are destined for each other. After a quirk of fate manages to bring this to their attention, they will defy anything in the way of a marriage that will provide total fulfillment for each, and a lifetime of romantic excitement at a feverish pitch that no other couple has ever known.

Well, perhaps no couple has. Still, this was every couple's expectation in times when parents had to ratify courtships, coldly judging prospects in terms of their financial resources, social level, and general presentability; and it is every couple's expectation now that the young are freed from this narrow, typically parental tyranny to broker their own matches, judiciously evaluating prospects in terms of money, status, and looks. It was around for Puritanism, Victorianism, the sexual revolution, and two rounds of feminism. Other societies may believe in arranging marriages, keeping romance and marriage separate, or, more recently, eschewing marriage, but this is the American story.

The possibility—more than that, the likelihood—of its happening is believed by people who have never dated and by people who have often divorced. It used to affect the sheltered lady whose modesty made her react to a welcome proposal with a show of surprise and a touch of reluctance to admit her feelings; now it affects the experienced lady whose cynicism produces the same reaction. It affects the gentleman who declares that he has no intention of ever marrying but then does, as it has always affected the one who promises that he will marry and then doesn't. It lingers still, although many profess that marriage is no longer important, except those who are denied the possibility because they are too young or of the same sex or don't want to lose their pensions, who make the case that it is a basic right.

Another constant has been the assumption that the previous generation—any given previous generation—was too inhibited to misbehave and is taking out its resulting bitterness on the young. Elder generations assist in this because they have bad memories or want to set good examples. How the belief is maintained by generations whose childhoods were disrupted by parents' frankly pursuing their own satisfaction is a mystery, but the complaint of having been warped by Puritanical upbringing has not disappeared.

This belief produces a lot of mistaken people. In what are supposed to have been more innocent times, it was common for children to be mistaken about their parents' innocence and parents to be mistaken about their children's innocence. Now that the children all know about adultery among adults and the parents all know about sexual activity among children, the mistaken notions are more likely to be based on opposite assumptions.

That increasingly racier generations have steadily made the society ever more enlightened about sex—or ever more depraved, depending on one's morality or opportunities—is a childish illusion. Mores indeed change, but not in the straight projection that appears deceptively obvious to anyone keeping track of it for only the comparatively short time of one generation. As they observe, lewdness seems to increase, or prudery does, and it is easy to assume that whichever it is will keep on increasing forever.

Yet it doesn't. Somehow, we never do get to the point where people are all mating indiscriminately like dogs in an alley or, when sentiment happens to be going in the other direction, where people are no longer permitted to reproduce. Instead, a greater natural force takes over: the desire of children to distinguish themselves from their parents' behavior. The general rule is that prim parents produce wild children and wild parents produce prim children.

The society's behavior of choice, whichever it is at the time, is controlled by fear of violating the prevailing etiquette. This is most apparent when it operates on behalf of chastity, as it tends to produce impressive outbreaks of discretion on the part of people who are breaking the rules. However, it can equally serve to reinforce free love, frankly acknowledged, because it is morality, rather than manners, that determines the standard; etiquette is merely the method of translating morality's convictions into daily behavior. In either case, etiquette is a formidable force that soon operates under its own power. Social admiration is a huge come-on, and social disapproval is a killer.

Courting customs

That does not make etiquette a killjoy. On the contrary, it encourages romance by providing the forms of courtship by which it is conducted. After all, society has an interest in perpetuating itself, for which it realizes that erotic encounters are essential. One can hardly blame it for also wanting to keep enough order for children and property to receive the attention they need, so it also encourages less fleeting sociability. Besides, when its task is to set restraints, it may be largely responsible for adding untold (or rather frequently told) amounts of angst and excitement to the simple act of coupling.

American courting customs have tended to be more practical than Puritanical, especially among the Puritans. From the earliest settlements, there was the question of how simple laborers who worked long hours with little free time and lived great distances apart were ever going to prowl the winters to find themselves mates. The answer was to provide them with rest, privacy, and warmth all at once by popping courting couples into bed together with the understanding that they were to remember their religion and keep their clothes on.

This custom, known as bundling and variously said to be adapted from the Dutch, or from American Indians, did not seem ludicrously reckless to people unaccustomed to private beds, much less private bedrooms. Families who slept several to a room and travelers whom tavern keepers showed to already occupied beds probably fantasized as much about nocturnal solitude as other possibilities.

Still, nature was known to take its course, and there were pregnant brides and jokes about seven-month babies. It was not unlike the mid-twentieth-century dating system, where the privacy of the automobile (surely less comfortable than colonial straw mattresses, which at least lacked gear shifts) was not condemned just because it occasionally produced the same results.

This tolerance may have been influenced by the fact that bundling was as much of a benefit to parents as to their amorous offspring. Not only did it save the cost of candles and fuel that would have been needed to keep the parlor habitable, but it spared them having to stay up late themselves, listening to the inanities exchanged by the young and foolish. (Another early New England solution to that problem was the long, hollow "courting stick," which enabled the enamored to whisper to each other when neither they nor their elders cared to leave the hearth because that was their only source of heat.)

Additional American shrewdness was involved. More than one observer pointed out, with less grace than consumer smarts, the folly of buying a pig in a poke. The young John Adams, in his courting days, advised women that "tho Discretion must be used, and Caution, yet on the whole of the Arguments on each side, I cannot wholly disapprove of Bundling" as a way of getting acquainted before committing to a suitor.

The great Puritan preacher Jonathan Edwards and others of his ilk broadcast their suspicions about bundling, but the mothers and daughters of New England defended it with such rigorous outrage at the slur on their virtue that it survived into the early nineteenth century, when it succumbed to a combination of cheaper fuel and rhymed ridicule.

From bundling to parking, American courtship was characterized by its comparative freedom. However restrictive the laws and customs of the particular time, region, or social class, they were bound to shock foreigners, who noticed that these failed to prevent the young women in question from forcefully registering their preferences. Even when real money was involved, a circumstance that fires up family interest in sentimental arrangements, American daughters were famous for wheedling final control away from their fathers.

Fostering romance

Still, parents and other busybodies were necessary to manage the early stages. They ran the mechanisms, from church socials and barn raisings to debutante balls and philanthropies, by which eligible people were thrown together and which left enough freedom to seal the bargain. Various courtship forms came and went until they finally just went, shooed out by single people who found such assistance clumsy and offensive.

It was supposed to be so. Society was experienced at all this, and understood a thing or two about how romance worked. The answer is: only indirectly. It is a paradox that people who are eagerly in search of romantic partners are romantically unattractive even to other people who are eagerly in search of romantic partners. Why this peculiarly inefficient dynamic exists is another question. Something to do with shooting fish in a barrel. The immature assess themselves by attempting to capture the attention of a person who is too good for them, and the only definitive way of knowing that someone is too good for one is by that person's apparent lack of interest.

To break this impasse, civilizations devise methods that allow those of marriageable age to appear to be indifferent, even hostile, to the opportunities of which they are taking full advantage. The cover stories are that each activity is being pursued entirely for its own sake. Parental and community parties and dances had the deniability: "I hate these things, but my parents forced me to come." Singles bars and dating services, the replacement mechanism that the singles produced for themselves when they banished their elders, do not.

Methods of showing developing romantic interest were also conventionalized in such patterns as paying calls and going on dates. The stages were interpreted through frequency of visits, timing of calls, hints, teasing, compliments, and deep looks. It was all very artificial and complicated, but somehow every hobbledehoy could read the codes. When it was considered preferable for everyone to improvise, preliminaries were truncated, and the key to the codes was lost. Colleges were turning to legalistic codes requiring that all overtures be explicitly stated as the only sure way of finding out if one's interest were reciprocated.

Yet nature still takes its course, and the most crudely businesslike negotiations culminate, if they are successful, in the reenactment of the same old love story. There is, however, a new last-minute risk before the fade-out. Bridal couples used to have deniability about protecting their financial interests. The fathers or their representatives traditionally did the negotiating, tactfully leaving the couple free to rail against them and their materialism, when they themselves despised money and cared only for love. This position is harder to maintain now that they have to hire their own lawyers to draw up the prenuptial agreement.

Moving On

Not everybody is rich, but we know that the gold must be around here somewhere, so if it can't be found, then it must be time to widen the search. The perpetual frontier drama became a continuation of the immigrant belief that the response to failure should not be giving up but getting moving.

Nomads aside, it is not usual for a society to consider restlessness an attractive character trait. Strangers are generally regarded with suspicion, because they come without those compilations of background information that go into making a person's reputation. To those whose families have lived long in a particular place, it seems clear that the best people have stuck around, good riddance to the kind that doesn't, and it would be even better if those awful newcomers would go back where they came from. It wasn't long before Americans in various pockets of the country took to deriving pride from the length of time generations of their families had lived in the same place, and crediting themselves for the achievements of their ancestors.

These were the traditional methods of bragging before America changed the rules. They are in direct contradiction to our professed idea that it is only what the individual makes of himself that counts, and that this requires chasing opportunities wherever they may lead. Amazingly, the two forms of pride manage quite easily together. Deep emotional identification with a place one long ago left voluntarily, or at which one has just arrived, are confusing only to foreigners.

Time to go

To Americans, it seems natural to keep moving. Whether spurred by adventure or hunger, the hope of getting a start or the promise of getting a promotion, the desire to flee crime or the desire to flee punishment, mobility is the rule. It worked at least once in everyone's family history, or we wouldn't be here. We keep changing locations, dwellings, jobs, social circles, and religions.

Despite a high divorce rate, there is dissatisfaction with the cumbersomeness of changing family arrangements. Extralegal partnerships were supposed to facilitate moving on from bad choices, but appeals for legal protection in such arrangements are re-creating the conditions. Etiquette breakdowns seem to occur among parting couples who had pledged themselves to honor escape clauses as regularly as with divorcing couples. Even in the best of situations, the fortunate child chooses his college partly for its location away from home, and returns home—if the parents have not taken the opportunity to move—in the capacity of guest who lives elsewhere, or boarder who probably should. It is not only usual but deemed healthy for children to long to be free of their families, to the point that psychological doubts are cast on those who stay when they need not, and derision on those who keep closely in touch.

At the same time that we are charmed by people who live where they were born, we think them dullards to be satisfied to stagnate. The model combination of local and mobile is the athlete who is fiercely loyal to the town his team represents and just as loyal if switched to the rival team. Fans are ever ready to accept the fiction of the hometown boys on the newly arrived hometown team. It is a kaleidoscope society, where the patterns look orderly although the pieces are constantly shifting.

Treatment of strangers

To make all this roaming work, a special etiquette is required, one that has more in common with ancient Greek notions of how strangers should behave and be treated than with extant societies. Presuming that his object is neither to conquer nor to camp, the traveler in uncharted territory is dependent for food, shelter, and counsel on outposts of civilization along the way. Forceful codes about providing hospitality, which seem quaintly altruistic in a country dotted with motels and rest stops, were based on this necessity. What he is expected to give in return is news and entertainment, along with some verification of his identity. The habit of quizzing or confiding in strangers, now the amusement or bane of airplane passengers, is a remnant of that.

Odysseus is given clothing and food, and then must tell his story. Centuries later, this reinvented bargain constitutes the basis for what has evolved into the American character, with its generosity, curiosity, and quickly conferred but easily discarded intimacies, all available readymade in the welcome wagon.

Unfortunately, the glamour conferred on presentable loners is apparently not available at a group rate. The empathy underlying hospitality to individuals did not turn out to evoke in newly established populations a similar feeling about the plight of newly arrived populations. There is usually a noticeable failure to be charmed by the strangeness of their customs. Immigrants to nineteenth- and twentieth-century America were nervously or eagerly aware that they were expected to learn

American and even more specifically local "ways" in addition to the English language, and to concede that these, being "modern" (a term of approbation at the time), would be an improvement on their own, not least because they would presumably not (although they often did) countenance the newcomers' being kicked around by bullies, as may have been the custom at home. In theory, all immigrants would keep moving only as long as necessary to find the right place in which to settle down and turn into one of those old families looking askance at new arrivals. "Right" being a subjective term, which individuals and generations keep redefining, that and changing economic conditions have been enough to keep most people on the go.

Escaping etiquette

Beyond that, moving on, like work, has become more of a goal in America than a means to reach one. It has an appeal subtler than that of abandoning bad conditions for the opportunity to fashion better ones. This is the seductive, although dangerously misleading, notion that in fresh territory, there are no rules, and therefore one can achieve the ultimate liberty, freedom from etiquette.

Only hermits can manage to live like that. What has been mistaken for etiquette freedom is the headiness travelers feel when they leave the jurisdiction of those who matter to them (and thus have the power to shame them), and are sufficiently provisioned and protected to ignore the rules and opinions of those they pass among. That has been one of the great lures of travel, from the Crusades to the Grand Tour to the Interstate Commute. It fails to allow for the fact that community life has always been impossible without behavioral restrictions. People who venture into new communal arrangements with like-minded people can sustain the illusion of getting along without etiquette only until a holiday-like amiability wears off and the first conflict arises between one person's wishes, habits, or desires and another's.

Nevertheless, the illusion is powerful enough still to keep people roaming. After pushing the frontier along until it came to a geographical stop, this focused on whatever unpopulated pockets could be found. Nature was the natural place to practice natural behavior. Or so it seemed until the bitter struggles between those who had different views of the ways to use natural resources demonstrated once again that human nature is no more peaceful than Nature herself.

Then a whole new world was discovered, and stirring declarations were made that its limitless space should be kept free. Cyberspace is, indeed, proving elusive to regulation, and attempts to impose legal restrictions are still met with cries of outrage. Etiquette, in contrast, is accorded astonishing respect, surely more than it receives when out in the society at large. Any freedom cries that might have been raised against its presence in cyberspace for stifling free expression were drowned out by the outpourings of obscenities, viciousness, and junk mailing that flooded the various venues and made them unworkable.

Once again, it was demonstrated that no activity functions without etiquette, not even ones expressly intended to support free expression. Court cases cannot proceed fairly and educational classes cannot pursue knowledge unless participants are required to speak respectfully and in due turn. People trying to handle their e-mail or use chat groups to chat were being driven mad by rude spoilers, to the point where they were driven to reinvent etiquette and demand (sometimes rudely demand) compliance. Etiquette rules, labeled as such, are posted all over the new world and last frontier.

Ever After

Here is where the story line falters. After implying that things will go on happily ever after (or—now that we are more sophisticated than we believe people used to be—sadly but more wisely ever after), the action stops. There can be retakes featuring another adventure, another romance, another generation pursuing one of these goals, but no sequel. The midlife crisis movie, in which someone with position, family, and money complains that that is all there is, only ends in the whiner's going through a new episode that ends in some form of love.

This problem is inherent in drama, where action should conclude in something as satisfying as marriage, victory, the dawn of a new age, or the destruction of the universe. Life goes on, past the idea that getting oneself well placed is the goal and that everything bad is fixable, attitudes that are harmless enough in the movies but have seeped dangerously into our ideas about philosophy, religion, psychology, and health. This is a decided disadvantage of using entertainment as a guide to life.

Chapter 5

The Stars
Be Anything, but Be Yourself

"YOU CAN BE anything you want to be."

"Just be yourself."

If American children listened to these instructions, which are dispensed to them as the fundamental guide to modern life, someday a child might think to ask what they meant. There would be a devastating disruption in our wisdom-passing system if this led to the real question:

"Oh, is *that* how you become a star?"

Although commonly twinned, these statements are contradictory. Are you supposed to get busy changing yourself to become like those who have succeeded at becoming whatever it is that you want to be? Or should you direct your efforts at resisting outside influences, in order to prevent others from changing you, instead honing your ability to respond only to your own feelings?

The correct answer would be yes. Self-improvement and self-satisfaction are thought to be compatible.

It was not always so. Of the two, self-improvement is the older American goal, in the sense not only of improving one's circumstances by retreating from the old country and advancing in the new one but of improving one's naturally sinful self by developing and practicing the virtues. Modesty being one of the old virtues, self-satisfaction would have been a sure sign of failure. One era's healthy confidence is another era's impious arrogance.

That is not to say that the practice did not thrive under an appropriate supporting theory. We have the example of the rich who refrained from congratulating themselves on their cleverness, which would have been sinful pride: Instead, they congratulated God on His cleverness in finally having lost patience with the meek and realized that those who had already helped themselves were a better investment.

This was an early sign that the manners-and-morals agenda controlled by religious authorities would be giving way to more immediately rewarding definitions of virtue. The cycle was completed in our time, when religious institutions came to seek moral validation in popular approval. It had always been necessary for them to maintain a self-sustaining quest for attendance and donations, but tailoring theological demands to avoid offending those who could not meet their strictures, or who declined to do so, was a twist on the previous expectation that congregants, not their ministers, be the ones to shape up. Whereas people had been urged to be upright, they are now enjoined to make sure that they are comfortable.

Consigning extralegal morality to the conscience is in keep-

ing with our faith in individual judgment. This still leaves plenty
of room for socially mandated self-improvement in such areas as
beauty, health, consumer judgment, and income.

*Seeking
identity*

But first it is the task of the individual citizen to figure out who he is and what he
wants to become, choosing not just an occupation but a persona. If the promise of success and the suggestion of passivity make this
sound easy, that is misleading. The mandate to be oneself is used
to suggest not simple acceptance of inclinations and limitations
but a laborious peeling away of learned behavior. The mandate
to improve oneself requires equally laborious training. When a
ceaselessly energetic program of self-improvement and a deep
and constant sense of self-satisfaction are expected, a casual or
occasional approach is indicative of yet another aspect of the self
that needs improvement. A lifelong struggle is required to con-
ceive, develop, and defend an original version of that elusive
concept we now call "personality."

This only seems like a fad of the analytic age, to be practiced
by people with too much time on their hands, and proof that
our hardy stock has deteriorated into foolishness. It can be
traced to the American experience of self-reinvention, and to
the lesson learned from it: That as society uses surface indicators
to peg people in positions they may not care to occupy, the
individual ought to be able to take control over those indicators
and refashion them to achieve the result he or she would prefer.

And so we go to work on ourselves, a nation of hard workers
working at being ourselves. During the teenage period, anxiety
is expected to focus on fashioning oneself to meet the standards

of one's peers and/or those of desirable future peers in a world of infinite possibility. A second period in middle age is therefore devoted to disappointment that one did not get one's expected share of those infinite possibilities, and to efforts to refashion oneself to get compensation. The pattern is to be overcome with anxiety about who you are, make yourself over to achieve your aim, be overcome with anxiety about who you are, aim at whatever was skimpy or missing (typically either spirituality or sexuality), and make yourself over to achieve it.

The relationship this renovation project bears to the preoccupation with finding one's "identity" is staggering to contemplate. Is there a "truer" identity independent of the actual circumstances, attributes, and history with which one finds oneself? Is the identity to be found in exercise of the creator's imagination rather than the person the creator is working upon, even though the two are one and the same? Has the habit of fooling with one's given identity created the compensating desire to pursue the very identity that one has altered? Peculiarly enough, people who believe so strongly in the beauty of the natural self that they are on guard to prevent civilizing influences from interfering with it describe the happy state of "being myself" as boorishness.

Thus the modern American search for individual identity may appear to be rather more philosophical than it is. There is much anguish along the lines of "Who am I?" and "Am I in touch with my feelings?" and "Is this the real me?" and "Am I being true to myself?" but this is not what more introspective societies might consider soul searching. Given an interest in the wider questions about the essential nature of mankind, others might dismiss the who-am-I fretting by asking who else anyone could possibly expect to be.

*Creating
a
character*

That is because they fail to share our faith in our ability to shed inherent and inherited conditions. Our terminology, which suggests a quest to find what is already there, is misleading. We mean something more creative than merely delving into the labyrinths of human nature.

Reinventing the self, as opposed to merely changing one's ways or enhancing one's attractions, is not a peculiarly American concept. Rogues have always attempted it for nefarious purposes and dandies for aesthetic affect. Before cyberspace made it temptingly easy for anyone to create a temporary identity as a casual amusement, it was not an unusual holiday hobby to spin fictional biographies for people one would be unlikely to encounter again.

What is different about the American approach is how widespread and accepted is the practice of significantly altering the superficial but key aspects of one's identity. It is also legally possible, as there are minimal requirements to report in when we make changes—of name, of address—that people of other countries would have to explain and register if they were allowed permission at all.

The importance of controlling one's identity, as distinct from one's destiny, is thoroughly supported by the society. An education system that has faltered over defining, much less teaching, morality is geared to extract any feeling or opinion that might be a sign of self-expression on the part of an emerging self. Before developing character, we each have to work up a character.

Shooting
for
stardom

The synthesis of being oneself and becoming what one wants to be is "making something of yourself." But—what is one to make? Our national product is the star.

Perhaps there is another explanation for the phenomenon of individuals acting as if they were each the boss of an old-time Hollywood film studio, or an enterprising agent creating stars out of the raw material that is ourselves. When we divert our gaze from mind and soul to do a cool appraisal of our outward attributes in terms of what we present to the audience around us, it is only an exaggeration of the common human impulse to make personal adjustments that might win approval from others.

But what an exaggeration it is. This quixotic project speaks to the country's deepest article of faith: that if conditions are fair, all enterprising individuals will rise to the top (resting on an unstable bottom of the feckless, one would assume). Whatever this assumption may be responsible for in the way of political bitterness, personal depression, and litigiousness, it has spurred the home-based theatrical imagination amazingly.

A slew of characteristics over which people from other societies might assume they had no control is examined for possible improvement. Having changed—or benefiting from our ancestors having changed—our nationality and domicile was only the beginning.

The possibility of escaping class designations, ethnic and family affiliations, and personal reputations was immediately obvious. The ability to change and choose our own names became an American right. The ability to choose our work, free of inherited or inescapably contracted conditions, became a matter of free choice after the abolishment of indentured service and slavery. Eventually, we got ambitious and started messing seriously with appearance and gender, doing away not only with social barriers but with natural ones. Taking advantage of all these possibilities would create an entirely new person. From a successful mix, we get our A Star Is Born metaphor, which is understood to mean, rather, that the star is created.

Changing names

Stars need glamorous, important, and memorable names, but that is begging the question. A name that is considered glamorous, important, and memorable is often one associated with a star of one sort or another, which accounts for the number of American babies who were named Shirley and Elvis, Jefferson and Che, or Dylan and Vanessa, and pinpoints the decades in which they were born. We can make up whatever given names we wish for our children, rather than having to chose from an authorized list, as some countries still require, and when bestowing and changing names are a matter of free choice, fashion rules.

Many nineteenth- and early-twentieth-century immigrants changed their family names, sometimes involuntarily at the insistence of impatient immigration officials or already assimilated relatives, to make them sound American, which is to say English. Shedding foreign or ethnic associations in the hope of disappearing into a fully American identity was one motive, and providing a sound that other Americans could easily pronounce was another. In the late twentieth century, those who received such names, as descendants, admirers, or slaves, made similar changes, but in the opposite direction, motivated by the hope of reclaiming a pre-American identity or producing a distinctive sound.

Given names are even easier to date, since they must be conferred on every newcomer arriving by birth. One year may be materialistic, and babies will be named like corporations and banks (Madison, Tiffany), and the next traditional, with names from the Bible (Adam, Noah), like those of the earliest American babies. Or there will be a fad for a particular letter, such as J (Jennifer, Jason, Justin, Jessica) or Z (Zoe, Zachary).

More telling is what the bearers of these names do with them. As outright legal changes are relatively easy in America, much can still be done to catch up with popular trends. Middle names, rare in colonial America, became increasingly common, partly as a convenient slot for parents to stash family obligations and compromises, but also to provide leeway for the bearer of the name. The persistence of nicknames in adult life, once a sign of intimacy or a source of embarrassment or both, were retained by adults when they took up other forms of youthful manners.

There is a political angle to this as well. When the populist style is in the ascendancy, no occasion, not even one's wedding or ascendancy to highest office, is considered formal enough to support the use of one's formal name. Private citizens now often use nicknames and eschew honorifics while otherwise attempting to retain some formality, as a result of which the formal, third-person invitation or announcement has become a hybrid of styles ("Bill and Christy Hardstone request the honour of your presence at the marriage of their daughter, Dr. Isabelle . . .").

Compounding this is the issue of whether married women should adopt their husband's names or retain their father's names—or revive their grandfathers' names, which is what they do when they take their mothers' maiden names. There are strong feelings on all sides of the question and no possible solution that would fairly recognize a woman's affiliations with her maternal and paternal ancestry, her husband, and their children, never mind her children by a previous marriage or a husband acquired after she made a professional name for herself. This has produced a variety of ad hoc solutions, such as hyphenations and invented names, along with a rate of change and state of confusion that injects acrimony into the mere act of addressing people with every intention of showing respect.

Combined with the emotionally charged issue of which honorifics should be used for women and for doctors of philosophy, this is potentially so explosive that surnames and titles, the great signs of hard-won dignity, have all but disappeared in common usage. We seem to be returning to the pre-surname era of given names followed by descriptions ("Edward the blacksmith, who is the son of John," "Chris the therapist, whose mother, Tammy, works at the bank"). That etiquette should impose standard forms of whatever kind is considered outrageous authoritarianism in a matter that individuals ought to be able to decide for themselves. Thus, a practical and graceful reform, that of using a standard title ("Ms.") for all women with their own given names rather than their husbands' and their own preferences in regard to their surnames, is resulting in the rejection of all courtesy titles.

The chaotic approach draws on the American experience of triumphing over adverse natural and social conditions, producing medical and technological wonders, and achieving moral, artistic, and personal success by breaking social rules. It retains an enormous influence on the ordinary behavior of the ordinary citizen—a strong focus on self, as opposed to community; personal expectations so high that disappointment or disillusionment are commonplace; and an overwhelming sense of grievance, if not despair, when life has its downs as well as ups.

Assimilation

The affiliations that surnames represent in the way of origins and family ties have also been regarded as fungible, beyond the shedding of unwanted or handicapping ties upon arrival in America and the acquisition of American ones. That opened the possibility of adjusting one's background at will that was to have a profound and lasting influence on immigrants' American-born descendants.

Until the last few decades, the assumption was that immigrants would naturally want and need to adopt the language, dress, customs, and loyalties of the new country. Whether the old ways were a source of solace, sentiment, or shame, they were to be sidelined by the effort to assimilate to the American way, whatever that was. Yet the more cultures that contributed to American life, the blander the exemplary American culture became.

The reversal was led by blacks after a century of espousing that standard without notable success. Even now, the best American customs and manners once claimed as the special skill of our finest citizens—the meticulous dress codes, the careful forms of mutual respect, the beautifully set tables, the formal balls, the ritualized extended family holidays—survive chiefly among the older black families, who practiced them for their own sake; doing so was not helping them into the mainstream, despite white claims that the barrier was cultural rather than racial. The mid-twentieth-century reaction of African-oriented black pride was an eye-opener to other segments of the society who had made greater progress, but only if they passed as homogeneous Americans. Instead, they could turn back to the old country, whichever it was, and feel authentic. They could reclaim the emotional allegiances their families had regretfully or thankfully renounced.

Among them, they made those longtime barriers, race and ethnicity, seem vibrant and exciting. Children of haughty New England and southern lineage were begging to be let in.

All of this was terribly American. There was no profound social upheaval, no major commitment to learn foreign languages, and prejudice was not ousted by enlightenment, but there was a significant change just the same: new cultural boutiques had been opened for American shoppers.

Designing cultures

Cultural consumerism had been going on for a long time, mostly in connection with changing domiciles. People would move to Texas and acquire the habit of wearing boots to their office jobs, or to Charleston and acquire the antique furnishings and portraits to match. Aside from food enthusiasms, however, adopted ethnic affiliations had previously consisted of everyone's pretending to be Irish on St. Patrick's Day. Now everyone could have an ethnic origin. For some it offered the enticement of betraying the traditions of their parents by taking up those of their grandparents.

The newly discovered cultures-of-origin were, of course, mostly fiction, but then so were the foreign fixations of Americans who were pleased to consider themselves an old aristocracy. Africans didn't recognize the continent that had such meaning for African-Americans any more than the English mistook Boston for London. It was just satisfying to pick a culture to root for and adopt or make up manners to go with it. Being good at this is a recognizably American trait.

To dismiss this as fake, or superficial, is to endorse another fiction, that of the "authentic" culture. Apparently static societies, where everybody remembers things being done the same way forever, may unwittingly be bigger frauds. Slow alterations in rituals and manners may be imperceptible. Memories being short, scholarly examination can often show that ancient tradition is the term used for one that was invented a generation ago. By the time something is recognizable as a national costume or characteristic, it is probably surviving only as a souvenir. An American who refers to a custom or an artifact as being old at, say, two hundred years may arouse amusement from a European whose standard for age is three or five times that; but, in fact, they may well be citing examples from the same period. Historians of tradition point out that British, French, and German court ceremonies are largely constructs of the late nineteenth and early twentieth centuries, spurred by the twin needs to develop nationalism and tourism

Shedding affiliations

Sure it is fickle to change habits, sentiments, and loyalties, keeping and choosing what one likes, neither sticking to one's inheritance nor committing to what one has chosen. But it is also flexible. Consciousness of change, and of the possibility of more change, can encourage conformity with high principles.

Or low. The lowest may be when it moves from the abstract concept of country to be applied to individual human beings. Americans have no corner on divorce or brevity of other arrangements for coupling, but it is unusual to find foreign societies who regard their families of origin as optional appendages. Hating one's family and cutting off relations is not the same thing as failing to see why it should have claims above those based on mutual amiability. Parents who present themselves as their children's friends should be careful about launching such a dangerous idea. Theirs must be the children who, once grown, complain that they don't understand why they are made to feel obligated to pay annual holiday visits to their parents, whom they point out they "didn't choose," rather than their friends, whom they did.

Another unfortunate side effect was to undermine the legitimacy of a national etiquette that can be used and understood by the entire population. Enthusiasm for customs associated with one's heritage, sometimes even accurately, led to claims that misbehavior by previous standards was condoned by the culture of the miscreant, and therefore ought to be excused and respected.

This opened a whole new area of excuses, culminating, perhaps, in the legal defense made by a Harvard student who was caught committing robbery during vacation that it was done to demonstrate that he still observed the traditions of his barrio. This ploy, with its staggering insult to his own people, was unsuccessful in court.

Even genuine foreign customs can create havoc when they go against American ones, as when immigrants attempt to force arranged marriages on their daughters. At best, benign ones create confusion that interferes with the predictability and intelligibility that an overriding standard of etiquette brings to a large society. The problem is not unlike those inherent in the argument that immigrants should not have to learn English. Foreign etiquette has helped create what we recognize as American etiquette and continues to influence it, but cannot be allowed to trump it.

Moving up in a classless society

Debate about the American class system is endless, fierce, and unperturbed by the fact that we do not have one. We do not have a class system in theory, as everyone will grant, but we do not have a class system in fact, either. Challenged to define it, everyone who claims it exists describes another method of categorizing people—by their money, the age of their money, their choice of possessions, the age of their possessions, their date of family immigration, their education, their occupation, their statistical chances of success, or their knowledge of etiquette and how they put this knowledge to use (whether by obeying the rules or by using them to humiliate others).

All of this is very interesting to those who are proud or aggrieved about how they are rated, but it still does not define an operating class system, meaning a static stratification for assigning privileges and duties, which can only be entered through birth or marriage.

What it does approach is describing the basis for establishing a class system. Aristocracies are not founded by recruiting those who have the innate taste to realize that the model of a duck in the library is superior to the model of a flamingo on the lawn (unless it is a fluffy duck and an ironic flamingo, in which case the judgment is reversed). They are established by the powerful to perpetuate their power, to placate those they find threatening, and to secure those they find useful. Raw amounts of money, property, and military power, plus the luck to be on the scene at an early stage when the civilization has not quite jelled, are the traditional qualifications for ennoblement.

What we really mean when we use that term is an end product of inherited nobility, which is relief from the necessity of doing all that vulgar grabbing that secured the position in the first place. This is supposed to produce the leisure and security to reach a level of refinement unobtainable to those who must strive to achieve position.

Except that it does not work that way. The term "well-bred" is a misnomer. Even those who are born gloriously unequal are not born refined, and must learn from the same starting point of ignorance as everyone else. Presumably, the opportunity to learn, through observation, is greater, although this may be balanced by a lack of motivation when one starts at the social pinnacle. Being born with a silver spoon in your mouth does not suggest how interesting it would be to examine the hallmark, while being brought up in a barn could keep one alert to find a way out of there to the manor house.

Clashing classlessness

No sooner had we declared ourselves a classless society than we all started arguing about who is in which class. That should be a tip-off. In a genuine class society, there is usually a book where you can settle this point by looking up names.

The traditional criteria of money, power, and getting there early works for the achievers, but less well for their descendants. To be sure, these may provide them with fortunes, renowned names, and useful introductions. Without the official recognition that comes with a handle to the name, however, holding onto these advantages requires them to vie with energetic upstarts. In a vibrant society of people out to establish themselves, they can be left with little more distinction than membership in organizations limited to people of similar backgrounds.

Meanwhile, hordes of other people will be on the move up through the economic class system, which is very much a reality. That is a system with no security at all, changing its membership the minute one makes or loses enough money, so when economic enterprise took off in the nineteenth century, even those who had been only moderately well off were looking for ways to consolidate their advantages.

It was attempted through citing that caveat about refinement. The nouveaux riches had only money, charged the vielle riches, and none of the graces that should go with it. Class warfare to be fought using taste, not money, was declared: You would be ranked not by how rich you were but on how you behaved and what you enjoyed or pretended to enjoy. You could build a palace, fill it with Old Masters and a bejeweled mistress of the house, feed and entertain everyone in town, and still lose on the grounds of being vulgar.

Thus a powerful national ranking system developed in which people were judged by, of all things, their manners. Knowing how to behave politely was something that financial reverses could not diminish and riches could not buy, so it would stave off the social upheavals that threatened to accompany the financial ones. Once they changed the contest, declining old families were able to terrorize captains of industry, as William Dean Howells wittily depicts Silas Lapham being nearly destroyed over the glove issue in his novel about that gentleman's rise.

Using different artifacts, the technique worked equally well when used by shopkeepers against laborers.

Not for long, however. Manners could not be bought, but they could be learned. A national frenzy of interest in etiquette accompanied the dramatic financial doings of the time. Everyone at every level had hopes of moving upward or pushing others back down, so they were all studying etiquette. Even those who had set the terms had to keep at it, because the only way to prolong the match was to keep changing the rules.

The idea that using the wrong fork puts you out of the game remains in the national memory still, but that was a hurdle devised by the earlier usurpers to trip the later ones. Old Dutch New York society considered the proliferation of forks to constitute a transgression; refined people had just big forks and little forks, and would not indulge in the vulgar display of newfangled silver on the table. Thus their eating habits were more similar to those of the poor than to those on the move.

Bewildered aristocrats

With such ever-increasing subtleties, and the quick turnovers as tycoons either caught on and hung on or fell by the wayside, only to act as guardians against newer aspirants, it was difficult to keep track of who was in society and who was out. How was it possible that people who were scorned in their hometowns and ignored in major American social centers were hobnobbing with, of all people, European aristocrats?

It was to them that ascending American society looked for confirmation. A yearning for the definitive pronouncements of those certified creatures, compounded, no doubt, by plain old snobbery, occasioned backsliding of monumental proportions.

Forgetting their ancestral pride in rebelling against decadent foppery, the squabbling rich of all pedigrees scurried to them, eager to explain all their nuances and receive their support.

The Europeans let them down. With their bankable titles, they were brokering marital deals with American heiresses and were flummoxed by these petty distinctions. Surely all the Americans were more or less equally arriviste compared to their august selves, so the richest, with the prettiest daughters, should have the honor of refilling their coffers.

In the end, those distinctions were paved over in America, by the progress of time and the power of success. John Adams, who had been the bourgeois among the landed Founding Fathers, was the founder of what came to be considered the most aristocratic family in America—although not before a Lafayette Square neighbor of Henry Adams, of the Blair family, famously remarked that "we of older blood do not think him such a great aristocrat." The Vanderbilts, who, in a later era, had epitomized the intrusion of vulgar money into genteel old society, became symbols of the upper-crust establishment.

The national etiquette competition, which, for all its vicious prejudice, at least aimed at judging people by their good behavior instead of their more tangible assets, deteriorated into competition for "good" restaurant tables as judged by how ingratiating competing patrons were to the presiding employee. In its way, this was a triumph for democracy: the proletariat ranking the swells.

Ranking by job

Nowadays, the companion ranking system to money is how it is earned. The job description has become the primary means of pinpointing social identification and worth. The chief definition of what one would aspire to be had moved from character to occupation, and American children who were once told that what they wanted to be was good were then instructed that what they wanted to be, instead, was president.

At different times, various other occupations have appeared to be worthier of the aspirations of the young: lawyer, movie star, astronaut, stockbroker, rock star, business consultant, basketball player, and—at least in the aftermath of the World Trade Center disaster—firefighter. Some that seemed likely to be permanently valued, such as soldier or police officer, might be idolized at one time and vilified at another. Others that seem forever condemned to be ridiculed, such as computer nerd or clothing mannequin, might become suddenly glamorous.

The change that lasted was personal identification by job. Kindly parents offered as career guidance, "whatever it is that makes you happy is fine with me," but that is not to be taken literally.

Neither is the devotion to the job of choice. That is only the first step. The tremendous variety in types of work to be done by those willing to take the training and pursue the opportunities barely disguises the consensus that every job can open the way to pursuing the prime American career of being a celebrity. Whether one is a zoologist or a brothel keeper, an evangelist or a cook, a fashion designer or a cabinet officer, a lawyer or a criminal, the object is to become famous enough to earn a handsome living dispensing opinions, endorsements, and memoirs.

Few will achieve this stardom, but everyone is supposed to be uplifted by the possibility, and better off for undergoing the preparations. What training is necessary, we do not know, as

172 Judith Martin

chance and determination seem to be the deciding factors, perhaps accompanied by talent, perhaps not—but we are certain, at
least, that looks are involved. And looks, like so many other
aspects of the self that might appear to be beyond choice, are
coming more and more under the bearer's control. Once the
onus was dropped against using in everyday life such basic tools
of the theater as makeup, hair color, and body padding, resentment grew that heredity and aging should control something as
significant and influential as one's appearance. Exercise and
elective plastic surgery were added to the toolbox enabling the
artist inside to realize her, and sometimes his, vision.

Superimposing one's own design on the natural version is
interpreted as a triumph against an unfair enemy. That this goes
strongly against the contemporary American attitude toward
Nature only shows how important the matter is. Stars need to
be fit to be seen and admired.

They must therefore present themselves not only attractively
but in types suggestive of popular roles. Whether these are taken
from life or life from them is a moot point, because they draw
from each other. Each, however, has its own look, its own manner, and its own etiquette. The variety makes present-day America appear to be the back lot of a studio, where unrelated types
from different periods and genres coexist in a chaotic society:
the old-fashioned patriot and the feisty protester, the queenly
society leader and the spunky bar girl, the selfless caregiver and
the self-centered artist, the naturalist and the boulevardier, the
city tough and the wily yokel, the roaming do-gooder and the
iron homesteader, the small businessman and the international
CEO, and so on.

They have their foreign counterparts, although there are also strictly American types:

The American Girl, who has the confidence and strength of pioneer women with the unstoppable enterprise and flair of self-made merchants, and saucily flaunts her freedom in the face of Old World criticism.

The Ugly American, who is driven to improve the world for foreigners he will never fully understand. (The term is mistakenly used to describe his opposite, the callous and ignorant American Tourist, but that character has been taken over by the German Tourist, the French Tourist, the Swedish Tourist, the Japanese Tourist, and others.)

The Relentless Reformer, who draws ridicule and hardship in dogged pursuit of a cause that may ultimately turn out to be as heroic as ending racial segregation or as futile as banning liquor.

The Charismatic Rebel, whose alienation is discovered to arise from suffering parental or social injustice, provided he is won back by love before doing major damage.

The surprise here is not that there are so many types, but that the same people appear as so many of them over the course of their lives, and that they embody them so well. The American Girl was so captivating that the foreign, homegrown product, refined into placidity, was no match for her. The heiresses who provided European nobility with its American great-grandmothers were as prized for their charm as for their money, and an American actress taking up the role of European princess consort demonstrated royal bearing to those who only inherited their thrones.

Such facility and adaptability is cited as evidence of superficiality. So it is, in the sense of using outward signs to convey more basic values, which is what etiquette does for national and individual character. And so it sometimes is in the sense of disguising emptiness with playacting.

The fresh start

There is something of a metaphysical morass underpinning these endeavors, all the same:

There is a sense of self as sacrosanct and yet infinitely malleable, the latter derived from a strong belief in cause and effect as applied to human development. We believe so thoroughly in the goodness and power of humanity that we define badness and sadness as physical or social illnesses, and pinpoint individual or social failure for them—poverty and crime as social failure, and illness and death as the fault of doctors or of the sufferers themselves for their bad habits or pessimistic attitudes. Yet the same optimism is what presses us to persevere at offering comfort and seeking cures.

There is suspicion of authority, along with the conviction that society is obligated not just to tolerate the individual who defies its conventions but to indulge and admire that person— whether it is the sidewalk crusader who expects passersby whom he humiliates to recognize his moral superiority, or the artist who expects public financial assistance for his ridicule of whatever the public holds dear and sacred. Children are urged not to care what people think of them in their quest to become popular and celebrated. At the same time that this encourages freelance nuisances, it keeps a check on the empowered, who might otherwise make more serious nuisances of themselves.

There is a suspicion that character development may be more trouble than moving on and creating a new character. This speaks deeply to the question of self-invention: You are what you are now, wiping out mistakes and putting out of decent bounds any attempt to hold people responsible for their own pasts, even their immediate pasts—although people have a tendency to insist on retaining credit for any good points they may have in their pasts, and credit companies have a way of keeping records of bad debts. While the perpetually fresh start hampers the power of public disapproval as a system of control, it fosters the generous notion of redeemability to all, possibly occasionally inspiring reform from within to compensate for the weakening of outside pressure.

There is the constant claim of the right to decide moral matters for oneself, to the point where the justice system began to harbor jurors who would admit, in retrospect, to acquitting defendants whom they believed to be legally guilty, using their own ideas of justifiable motivation and extenuating circumstances in place of those employed—and legally required—by the system. As if it weren't difficult enough to run a society under these circumstances, the example of self-designed morals culminated in emboldening individual citizens to mess with etiquette. Having the usual gradual influence that members of any society do on changing etiquette was no longer enough. Manners were being considered fit modes of self-expression rather than social codes. People wanted to invent their own, almost inevitably from their own point of view, which only aggravated conflicts and confusion. Yet there were etiquette reformers who approached it as the Founders had—which is to say that they sought reasonable change, set modest goals, and appealed to an American sense of fairness (it is difficult now to believe the tremendous defiance and ridicule that greeted the campaign to stop people from strewing trash around public places or the one to take the gender designation out of occupations, changing "fireman" to "firefighter" and "stewardess" to "flight attendant")—who succeeded in etiquette's true goal of making human relations easier.

The natural look

Finally, there is an unaccountable general disdain for the artificial, coexisting with our admiration for the theatrical. Training sessions for expressing the natural self are as popular as cosmetics for achieving a natural look. The idealization of sincerity, to the point of vaunting blunt and rude frankness, reflects the desire for a closer connection between manners and morals, on the part of idealists who are deeply troubled that there is a gap between soul and surface. The remedy was supposed to be renouncing all outward manifestations that were learned, rather than spontaneous, which would, and sometimes did, stifle the practice of etiquette. Even if that were possible, it would have required sacrificing our talent for dramatization and reform, which, to Americans, would be—well, unnatural.

All of this has been analyzed in psychological, political, sociological, and economic terms, but not theatrical ones, much less those of manners. After a period of denial, we are again obsessed with etiquette and, like the Victorians whom we so freely ridiculed for the same focus, beginning to admit it. Controlling and altering personal attributes and behavior to create the effects that convey our values and whatever else we consider to represent our identities, with the dual object of reforming the world and turning ourselves into stars, is too basic to our national character to renounce.

Chapter 6

The Supporting Cast

All Those without Whom

I F EVERYONE IS an aspiring star, then who are all those other people? Rivals, critics, and hangers-on? The powerful who thwart one, and the masses who fail to appreciate one? A whole nation of such types, with their annoying claims and outrageous presumptions?

Openness becomes snippiness

One might suppose so, from the way that America-the-friendly turned irritable. Foreigners who had sniffed at the open young country for ignoring the protective conventions with which they kept their own crowded conditions from crushing them might now concede that America is approaching their standard of buzz-off propriety. All that seems to be left of that easy public sociability is the dregs, the nosiness and bossiness directed at strangers ("How much did you pay for your house?" "Is that a dye job?" "Why don't you go ahead and buy the kid what he wants?"). The rest is shoving and suspicion.

American kindheartedness can still be found in the largesse of its charitable impulses, and the way the citizens rally heroically during emergencies. What is missing is the casual cheerfulness that was noticed, sometimes sourly, by two centuries of visitors. This was the spirit that went under such names as neighborliness and informality and helpfulness, although it went beyond the neighborhood, characterized formal observances such as religious services, and may have hindered as often as it helped. It is severely missed by Americans, which explains why so many spend their leisure yearning for defunct wars, fixing on the American Revolution, the Civil War, or World War II as periods when they believe human relationships were nobler.

Emergency etiquette

Even allowing for gloss on the historical record, we have all witnessed this goodness in the form of sudden surges of courtesy. During every earthquake, hurricane, flood, fire, or hostile attack, the people of California, Florida, Missouri, Oklahoma, or wherever disaster occurs, and strangers who rush in from elsewhere, can be seen helping one another in large ways and small, at least until the second shift of scammers and looters arrives. It is not just the daring rescue or the courageous sacrifice that is demonstrated, but those minor forms of courteous consideration that no longer characterize everyday life—putting aside one's own needs to share and commiserate with others.

The 2001 World Trade Center attack was such a striking example of this uplift in general demeanor that there were predictions it would change American behavior forever, continuing to inspire routine observances of etiquette when the dramatic sacrifices were no longer needed. All over the country, people who had been in the habit of making scenes when they felt thwarted started waiting patiently in line to the extent of sometimes inviting others to go head of them, driving according to the rules and courtesies of the road, showing concern for their families, getting in touch with friends, and offering signs of gratitude and respect to public officials. In turn, public officials were softening their differences with opponents to work cooperatively.

It was as if whiny children had been shocked into behaving themselves with the classic parental threat, "If you don't cut that out this minute, I'll give you something to whine about." When there was something to whine about, we abruptly quit whining.

However, the cry that followed, to "get back to normal," was soon heeded. We have yet to know whether this brief sample of life in a polite society will have any lingering influence. What it would take to sustain such politeness when no great threat is looming is a shift in emphasis in the constant tradeoffs we must make between the freedom of the individual and the well-being of the community, ever one of the most difficult problems in a society that treasures both.

We have now sacrificed such previously treasured freedoms as full self-expression by aggrieved people in airports. It is by no means clear that Americans are willing to give up the right to be obstreperous in situations where their behavior would destroy the activity at hand for other participants. Cases in point (admittedly, less lethal than what is feared in airports) included a legislator cursing his distinguished colleagues during a session so that the debate could not continue, many an athlete defying the umpire who then had to stop the game, and students curtailing classes or lectures with shouted opposition. The right to free expression in a movie theater while others are trying to follow the dialogue has not been tested in court, but as a practical matter, people debating whether to go to a theater or a video store should remember that free expression has been winning these contests.

Etiquette has generally found itself on the side of the community, which is doubtless a factor in its unpopularity when public sympathies are impatient with rules that restrain the individual. This has obscured the fact that many such rules are designed expressly to allow individuals to get their share of free expression—the turn to speak in the legislative session or class—when the absence of rules would deny this, either by turning it over to the most forceful disrupter or by forcing the activity to disband.

The sacredness of our principle of free expression is not in question here, but rather whether it trumps all our other principles, as some believe. Similarly, the embracing of honesty as a trump virtue, overriding the virtue of kindness, has menaced etiquette by allowing people to believe they are virtuous when they inform others that they are fat, boring, or stupid, merely because their insults honestly express their beliefs.

The change that would be needed to make the public sustain the behavior it so much admired during the 2001 crisis is not a sustained crisis that would stimulate or scare people into a state of politeness, however nostalgic we may eventually become about the good old days when buildings were being destroyed, masses of people killed, and our faith in humanity was being renewed. We need to achieve—rather than restore, because we have never managed to get it right—a more even balance between duties owed to oneself and duties owed to others, which ultimately serve the individual by making the human environment more pleasant.

As usual, the results of one reform created the need for another. The twentieth-century vaunting of self was, itself, a reaction to an imbalance in favor of powerful elements of the community demanding self-sacrifice from others. That had been bolstered by a bogus etiquette rule that it would be rude of them to complain, paired with a moral injunction that it would be wrong to attempt making things more equitable. The former was disobeyed immediately, and the latter eventually exposed.

Blaming politeness

Once again, however, revolutionaries had defined etiquette as the enemy, failing to distinguish between particular rules and attitudes that were offensive and the principles of manners on which the rules were supposed to be based. They would have found a stunning contradiction between the two, just as we identify laws that we declare unconstitutional. The very idea of women, children, and servants forming a supportive class (used here to reflect the historical attitude), along with all the customs and slights used to reinforce it, violated the American manners system, which is based on equality.

Etiquette was not the enemy, and a reign of rudeness is not the solution. By condemning the system, reformers distracted themselves and their targets from the real solution, which was to change the rules in order to make them conform with the principles. When an oppressed group starts saying, "Stop being polite to us," it is unfortunately taken at its word, especially if this is reinforced with its own demonstrations of rudeness. It has taken decades of such reform-motivated rudeness to produce the discovery that what is needed is an equitable distribution of dignity and consideration rather than an equitable absence of it.

For all the legally sanctioned and socially tolerated injustices that have flourished in America, foreigners have always been struck by the liberty accorded to women, children, and free servants. We may look back in amazement and shame to times when these and other elements of the society were exploited and patronized, but that is not what was being said about us at the time. Then, as now, the word was that American women were shameless, American children out of control, and American servants uppity. That is what comes of spreading ideas about equality, they would say. Spoiled, spoiled, spoiled.

Americans, meanwhile, had their own complaints about equality. Those who felt that, notwithstanding claims-at-creation, one must earn it by attaining adulthood, acquiring property, and braving the rough world in manly fashion, complained of the responsibilities involved in looking after—which is to say supporting and engaging in the thankless task of shaping up—those who patently failed to meet their criteria. The latter were making the same complaint about one another: women about servants, servants about children, and children about women, as well as women about other women, servants about other servants, and children about other children.

The absence of a hierarchical structure compounded traditional prejudices and ordinary rivalries. There was not a clear distinction between the lives of the youngest and oldest, the richest and poorest, men and women; they faced the same dangers and did as much hard work.

We know what happens when people truly appear to be roughly equal: They have all the more jealous incentive to delineate what differences there are, in the perpetual human quest to have comfortable numbers of people on whom to look down. The wonder is not that everyone failed to be accorded full respect but that the women, children, and servants escaped at least some of the forms of disrespect that prevailed elsewhere.

This may have had less to do with idealism than with a distribution of power and powerful ideas that were different from those of less flexible communities. Among the settlers, and as the population spread out, there was often a scarcity of women that encouraged men to vie for their continued favor when alternative suitors were so obviously available. As we know from courtship, this tends to have a favorable effect on manners. Even in the roughest pioneering communities, there was considerable doffing of hats, declarations of "yes, ma'am," and voluntary protection of ladies from those other uncouth men. Chivalric trifles these may be, but, like chivalry itself, this was an improvement on a standard that condoned a lot worse.

Children, not being scarce, had no such advantage, nor did servants, despite their ability to make themselves scarce. However, the histories of their putative betters were not well concealed, and this made them prone to harboring ideas about themselves. Children had heard, and servants overheard, family histories that illustrated an effective way to deal with unsatisfactory conditions—clearing out as soon as feasible. The superiority of adulthood only works on children for so long, and it was difficult to convince servants to regard their employers as their natural superiors, when the latter used grandeur and haughty ways but had backgrounds as humble as their own. It seemed that, whatever harsh treatment was applied to administer the idea that certain Americans were to be content with supportive roles, the women were incorrigible, the children undutiful, and the servants insubordinate.

Women

Applying the convention of female weakness to pioneer and frontier women was a stretch, and they left their more fastidious descendants the legacy of moving freely in public without expectation of masculine annoyance. To the modern way of thinking, these women's proven strength and independence should have prompted refusals to accept any sort of secondary status. Instead, it fostered something like a reaction not uncommon in contemporary professional women with families—that a ladylike life of being looked after and pampered did not sound so bad.

Illustrations of this fantasy came from abroad, where sole responsibility for providing the prototype for the ladylike life was borne by the rich. They also had the burden of providing the prototype of the gentlemanly life. Nobody else could afford to do so.

The two versions were not all that different in Europe. Unless an opportunity for glory or adventure presented itself, what rich men, as well as rich women, earned was mostly the title of idle rich. This was in contrast to the class taxed with working ceaselessly, to whom they gave the title of shiftless poor. When people now assume that women didn't work for a living until the twentieth century, they of course fail to count the majority of women who were peasants, servants, and worse. Before the rise of the middle class, it was money, not gender, that divided the working world from the gentry, although there were such gender distinctions within those categories as rich women's being charged with supervising the indoor staff while rich men were charged with supervising the outdoor staff.

In early America, where idle rich was neither a sanctioned nor a viable concept, much hilarity was garnered by women who lay claim to the ladylike life because their husbands were colonial officials or prosperous land owners or merchants. By the time the Industrial Revolution came up with the division between the working realm for men and the domestic realm for women, however, America was highly receptive. Confined to the new middle classes of Europe, the pattern of gender division was adopted in America by those who could afford it, including men who could have afforded not to work.

There were two different tasks to be accomplished to achieve and sustain success, and as these were mutually exclusive, they fell to the two marriage partners. To get ahead in the world required money, as always, but money was not enough. As conditions became less primitive, gentility began to seem not so comic after all. The aggression needed to amass a fortune was antithetical to the grace needed to preside over it decorously, so the husband was supposed to accomplish the former on behalf of the family, while the wife accomplished the later.

A new figure of fun emerged: the awkward husband bumbling unhappily about in the social and cultural world to which his wife had risen. He survives to this day, in cartoons about husbands falling asleep at the opera, to which they have been dragged by their pearl-bedecked wives who are no more musical but recognize the opera house as a major venue for those twin markers of social advancement, culture and couture. The fact that formality has become scarce in opera houses, with the jeans now outnumbering the jewels, has not dislodged the joke.

188 Judith Martin

In the end, this was held against the opera more than against those upwardly mobile husbands, who were accorded sympathy that was not directed at, for example, English industrialists parlaying their fortunes into country houses and retiring their working skills to take up the seasonable sports. Because work was not a barrier in America, the jobs of earning and rising did not have to be done sequentially, so the husband pursuing a family fortune could fully delegate to his wife the task of pursuing family prestige, and thus leave her to be scapegoated for undertaking it. The wives may have taken to social advancement with unabashed enthusiasm, as the chief outlet for their ambitions, but success would also bolster the business, whereas in England, until recent times, renouncing business was a prerequisite for infiltrating the upper class. Thus European men were free to participate in society, and not free of suspicion of the machinations to cut a figure in it.

Turning money into prestige

The dynamic of turning money into social prestige is always the same, whether it requires years or decades (setting it at centuries is a European exaggeration not borne out by their own history). It is done through consumerism, marriage, and myth, in that order, and in America these were female specialties. For that matter, the resistance was also manned, as it were, by women— so effectively, that newly rich Americans found it easier to marry their daughters into the European aristocracy than into the families of immigrants who had preceded them.

The mythology of money being hallowed by age obscured from American women and Europeans of both sexes what American men knew all along: that their bailiwick was more exciting than society. Ideally, one wants both, but few Americans have taken happily to the work-free life, surely a reason, in addition to good-heartedness, that unemployed American women ran community organizations in such a high-powered, businesslike manner. We remained impressed with the English ideal of country life but bored with the reality. Those who are most enamored of its tweedy clothing and dog hair–covered decorating styles (available to us, and now to them, through the enterprise of American designers)—New Englanders and the products of their business schools—would be the first to go stir-crazy in the challenge-free life they represent.

Built into the premise of America and accentuated by the dramatic economics of the nineteenth century, social competition was everywhere that the possibility existed, however remotely, of being able to rise—as was the companion desire of preventing newcomers from rising to one's present level. Farms, factories, and frontiers were not free of such vying. A huge number of citizens were studying etiquette books, which were being produced rapidly (thanks to the inattention given to their lifting portions from one another, which made for remarkable agreement on rules, as well as of the language for expressing them) and sold in great numbers. This activity was not a contradiction of American cooperation, solidarity, and neighborliness or a special penchant for snobbery beyond the normal human allotment. It was the social equivalent of staking out fresh territory, putting up barriers, and defending them while challenging those of others.

Since etiquette was the weapon used in this contest, women who were hoping to advance themselves became serious students of etiquette. If they were hoping to bring their families along with them—the rich also had the popular option of bringing along the daughters and leaving the husbands and sons behind as invisible sponsors—they also became its teachers.

Thus etiquette came to be thought of as women's work. Elsewhere, it was run by kings and studied by courtiers; in eighteenth-century America, the preachers and the Founding Fathers found it fit matter for their deliberations. Once it came under the jurisdiction of women, the fact that distinguished men had been theorists of etiquette was forgotten, and the subject came to be considered a perhaps necessary, but nonetheless trivial and exasperating, field.

Women's work

For that reason, etiquette came to play an enormously important and yet complex and contradictory part in the feminist movements of the twentieth century. At issue was whether etiquette—by which was meant the more or less chivalric style in place at the time—should be utilized, altered, or abandoned.

As women had been handling the teaching and supervision of etiquette, they had an appreciation for its symbolism that put it high on the movement's agenda. The more legal points that were gained, the more etiquette issues seemed to arise, and however ponderous the courts appeared to be in settling its caseloads, the public was even less able to achieve consensus on the issues that fell under its jurisdiction, such as precedence, dress codes, and nomenclature.

The campaign for suffrage was a legal issue, and although it coincided with dress reform, the latter was argued on the grounds of health and freedom of activity rather than symbolism. Corsets were condemned as squashing the internal organs, not as reshaping women's bodies for male enjoyment, as brassieres were to symbolize for a subsequent wave of feminism; bloomers were advocated to facilitate bicycling and walking, more than to symbolize the assumption of male freedoms, as trousers had done for the occasional eccentric woman before and since, until they became standard female attire.

The clearest symbolic gesture was, then as now, keeping the maiden name after marriage. However, for its opponents, all aspects of the movement added up symbolically to indicate that feminists were in a genderless state in which men's rights could legitimately be denied while the courtesies that had been acknowledged as due to women could be simultaneously withdrawn.

Resisting change

Fear of that, in addition to simple attachment to tradition, may have contributed to the vehemence with which many women who support the legal changes wrought by feminists have resisted the etiquette changes. Presumably, that is what is meant by women who declared, "I am not a feminist," and then continue by declaring support for the list of legal rights attained through the feminist movement.

That round of drastically needed etiquette reform, which began with reviving the use of the maiden name after marriage and relaunching the useful and practical honorific "Ms.," turned out to be etiquette obliteration instead. Hardly a gesture was left unanalyzed for suspicion of symbolizing female weakness. Gender-specific courtesies were effectively discouraged through the widespread use of humiliating public rejection of obviously well-intentioned gestures. The resulting ill-will had the wanted effect of demolishing forms of politeness still in use, but it also left people on all sides of the question too angry to work out which rules might be kept for their charm or sentiment and which should be discarded as degrading, and incapable of agreeing upon what alternative of precedence, nomenclature, and clothing symbolism could be developed to replace forms being dropped.

This has not only shorn life of some harmless graces but, more seriously, hindered people from understanding when gender differences can properly be expressed through etiquette rules and when to do so would be insulting. For example, should a gentleman carry something heavy for a lady? We would find it appalling, in terms of traditional courtesy, to see a wife carrying her husband's luggage if he is able-bodied and unburdened. An equally wrong note would be struck if a businessman offered to carry a colleague's briefcase for her, because it would emphasize her social identity at the expense of her professional identity as a businesswoman. They should carry their own. Now suppose that the man has hired a car service and the driver who picks him up at the airport is a woman; if he does not allow her to carry his bag while he goes unburdened, he is undermining her ability to do her job.

Complicated though these questions are (and in life they would be additionally complicated by such factors as age, state of health, and employee status), they can be understood and codified to eliminate what is inconsistent with our principles without destroying what is pleasant. Yet a combination of acrimony and ignorance has left us in a state of etiquette chaos in which we are still flailing. The absence of a universally accepted standard, along with the habit of suspiciously analyzing whatever forms are proposed, means that no one is safe. The likelihood of guessing wrong is not considered when people flare up at what they consider to be wrong choices. Many people have found it easier to drop using honorifics, dressing up, and deferring to others rather than hazard a guess when the consequences are so severe.

Children

That children are born without manners had been considered by Puritans to be an enormous failing on their part. Eventually, the young were successful in overturning this view to the extent of convincing adults that it was the adult manners that were out of line with society and an embarrassment to youth.

This triumphant progress was due not to the machinations of the young but to the yearnings of their elders. The adulation of family life in the nineteenth century and of youth itself in the twentieth century carried children from the bottom of the social heap to the center of the domestic circle to the pinnacle of consumer society.

At every time, there will be individual children who are indulged and ones who are abused; there will be adults who idealize children in general, in addition to their own in particular, and ones who revile them all. In the current era, we are forever invoking the sacredness of children as representing the future of humanity while, in the meantime, regulating them out of the grownups' way with restrictions similar to "no pets" rules.

Child-rearing theories

Attitudes may also be conditioned by the particular circumstances of the period— whether the children appeared because the parents were unable to circumvent the process or appeared via fertility clinics through great personal cost; whether they were contributors to the family income or drains upon it; whether they tended to die in babyhood or turn surly in the teenaged years; whether the custom was for even prosperous parents to send them out as servants as early as the age of eight to learn manners, or to sponsor them at the college of their choice to pick up the manners of their peers.

However, there seems always to have been something distinctive about the behavior of American children. Through circumstances and the national ideology, a certain self-awareness and independence was observed to characterize them, although less flattering terms were used as, even in America, these traits are more admired in theory than in the young flesh.

The Puritans certainly tried their best to get it out of them. They threatened death for parental disobedience, perhaps more convincingly than the modern parent who says, "If you don't cut that out, I'm going to kill you," but apparently no more literally. Respect for elders was one of the major items on their etiquette agenda. The child was supposed to bow, beg permission to be allowed to eat at table, and keep his thoughts to himself. Punishments included beating, restraints, and public humiliation by means that we would consider devilish or fiendish. Cotton Mather even resorted to using psychology, opining that it was worse than a beating for his child to know that he had disappointed his august self.

Still, the complaints continued that the children were not sufficiently intimidated. Gentler ideas were already circulating. Dutch settlers had brought their freer child-rearing methods, and New York was beginning to recognize what would inspire it to great and profitable industry—that youth should not only be trained but amused. Well-to-do southerners were stressing graceful estate manners rather than manners supposed to bring children to a state of religious grace. Revolutionary thought added notions about the sovereignty of the individual, adding yet another task—but one promising an eventual end—to the job of child rearing, that of teaching self-reliance.

When the Victorians launched their ideal of the household fueled by love, with its angelic mother, benignly authoritative father, and happily blooming children, America was again receptive. The holiday rituals were adopted, the books were read, versions of the costumes were sewn, and attempts were made to stuff luckless American children into them.

It still didn't look the same. Try as they might—and many American parents no longer believed in trying—they were not producing the dutiful, obedient, docile children the English were conjuring up. Little Lord Fauntleroy had an American mother but he was no American child, and the sooner he worked his way back into the English side of his family the better chance he had of hanging onto his own curls.

Observations from Mrs. Trollope's boy, Anthony

In his travel book *North America*, the novelist Anthony Trollope described the commanding demeanor of American children he observed in his hotel dining room:

. . . the children—babies, I should say if I were speaking of English bairns of their age; but, seeing that they are Americans, I hardly dare to call them children. The actual age of these perfectly civilised and highly educated beings may be from three to four. One will often see five or six such seated at the long dinner-table of the hotel, breakfasting and dining with their elders, and going through the ceremony with all the gravity, and more than all the decorum of their grandfathers.

When I was three years old I had not yet, as I imagine, been promoted beyond a silver spoon of my own wherewith to eat my bread and milk in the nursery, and I feel assured that I was under the immediate care of a nursemaid, as I gobbled up my minced mutton mixed with potatoes and gravy. But at hotel life in the States the adult infant lisps to the waiter for everything at table, handles his fish with epicurean delicacy, is choice in his selection of pickles, very particular that his beefsteak at breakfast shall be hot, and is instant in his demand for fresh ice in his water.

But perhaps his, or in this case her, retreat from the room when the meal is over is the chef-d'oeuvre of the whole performance. The little precocious, full-blown beauty of four signifies that she has completed her meal—or is "through" her dinner, as she would express it—by carefully extricating herself from the napkin which has been tucked around her. Then the waiter, ever attentive to her movements, draws back the chair on which she is seated, and the young lady glides to the floor.

A little girl in Old England would scramble down, but little girls in New England never scramble. Her father and mother, who are no more than her chief ministers, walk before her out of the saloon, and then she swims after them.

On another occasion, he remarks on "tyrant children," while watching such a one order dinner on a steamship: "'Beef-steak,' the embryo four-year-old senator would lisp, 'and stewed potato, and buttered toast, and corn cake, and coffee,—and—and—; mother, mind you get me the pickles.'"

This gentleman who tarried about in his nursery long after the age that Americans were commandeering restaurateurs is the very one whose mother reported that Americans had a "total want of all the usual courtesies of the table." While the son's description is sardonic (and Anthony and Fanny Trollope were, of course, watching different individuals of different circumstances at different periods), he understands that these were not primitives who would grow up eager to trade their liberty for European refinement, which she saw as the best hope for America.

Child rearing reversed

Concepts of equality and independence that had filtered down to the young, and at the same time restrained their parents from exercising dictatorial power over them, were already producing strong-willed American children when another factor arose. Immigrants were no longer arriving for the purpose of reestablishing their own cultures on fresh American territory, except with a better deal for themselves; they were coming to partake in the American way, knowing that it would require much study and practice to earn a place in it. Learning the language, the look, and the manners was a prerequisite, and if one was to advance significantly, it was necessary to move from immigrant enclaves to mainstream business and society, where these skills were judged with an inhospitable eye.

Realistically, this could rarely be done in a single generation. At best, it would be their American-schooled, if not also American-born, children who would justify their travails. Thus began the overturning of generational power, of which anyone born before the computer-literate age has had a fresh taste. American manners and attitudes were being taught to immigrant children

in the public school system, and immigrant parents were await-
ing their secondhand after-school instruction the way a recent
generation awaited their youngsters coming home to retrieve
their lost word-processing documents or program their VCRs.

With the superior knowledge naturally came a sense of superiority. These were children, and they had access to a body of
vital information on which their parents had only a tenuous
grasp. Having the final word on what is done and what is not
done, especially in areas of such interest to young people as
fashions and courting customs, bestowed great power, even
though it was often hotly contested. Parents may have resisted
having their children turn away from their own culture, and
they may have suffered to see their children regard their own
looks and ways with shame, but they also ached to have the
family succeed in America.

To have one's children do better in life than oneself would
combine American faith in progress in general with the penchant for improving the self indefinitely. Galling as it was, parents, especially immigrant parents, were at their children's mercy
to decide how that should be done. If fitting in was a requirement for success, children were the authority on that. If it
meant fitting in with the ways of the children's contemporaries—achieving popularity—even parents who were masters
of the mainstream culture had to rely on the information of
their children.

"But everyone else is allowed to do it," became an effective
argument to parents, who were expected to accept the truth of
it on faith. Not surprisingly, the standards that were most eagerly
reported allowed great license for the young. The American child
who preempted adult ways and authority was learning to dis-

dain them and create ones more to his taste. Someone has to set the standards of daily behavior, and as there is a tendency to respect those who seem sure of themselves, and as that sense of fallibility tends not to kick in for the first quarter of life, this task has been undertaken by the young. That which used to be disparaged as youthful peer pressure could, under conditions of equality of age, be considered the Voice of the People. What this amounts to is respect based on age after all, only in reverse.

Original innocence

Although there are those who deplore it and voice regret for the days when parents would not be so easily fooled into surrendering their power, modernism is not entirely at fault. This can be traced to our Enlightenment heritage. A belief in what may be called Original Innocence surfaces periodically as a philosophical influence, holding that people are born good and later corrupted by the ways of the civilized world. Therefore, the nearer one is to birth, and the farther from experience, the wiser and more virtuous one is.

Appealing as this notion is, with its adult humility and sweet confusion of soft rosy cheeks with soft rosy impulses, it has a lot to answer for. Peculiar educational theories, intergenerational hostility, and do-it-yourself child rearing all sprang from a belief in the moral superiority of the immature, a theory not obvious to observers, however fond, of little ones at play. It strikes at the heart of manners, as it condemns controlling one's feelings, however ugly, or censoring one's thoughts, however insulting. Indeed, vast amounts of money and energy are put into training that is directed at reversing any inhibitions among grownups against thus provoking others.

As the inevitable happened, there has been an attempt to add

yet another form of retraining, known as "anger management."
That etiquette's mandate has always been to teach patterns of
behavior that minimize provocation and provide methods of dif-
fusing conflicts has not earned it a place in this cycle of encouraging children to be free of constraints, schooling adults to be
childlike, and then classifying the results as individual psychological problems. Antisocial behavior on the part of people who
have not been socialized remains a surprise, however widespread it becomes. Mannerless children are treated as "dis-
turbed," no matter how common they become.

The belief that childhood is naturally virtuous persists, along
with its corollary that the first parental duty is to refrain from
spoiling this by imposing the rules of etiquette. Well-to-do children may be sent out for a professional etiquette lesson or two,
typically concentrating on restaurant skills, but etiquette at
home is still considered to be incompatible with love. Even the
public outburst of frank child loathing, taking unpleasant forms
from banning the presence of children to characterizing the
instinct for parenthood as inherently egotistical, has not suggested that politeness enhances, rather than ruins, the young and
that it does not come naturally or easily.

If the rude child is considered a public nuisance, the polite
child is even more so. Many consider it their public duty to sab-
otage any efforts they may observe by parents to teach their
children manners. Etiquette that implies respect for adults is
especially incendiary, as parents who teach their children to say
"sir" or "ma'am" can attest, but it doesn't have to undermine
the critics' own status as ersatz children to attract derision. Even
prompting a child to say "please" or "thank you" may inspire an
adult rebuttal: "Oh, let him alone," "She's only a child," "He

doesn't have to thank me." If the child exhibits manners without prompting, there are dark suggestions of his or her being deprived of childhood, or of humanity itself. If we believe that a "real" child acts only as he pleases, free of civilizing limits based on consideration for others, a polite child must be a robot.

The parent as advocate

The model parent, in contrast, is loaded with proscriptions. Commitment to an absolute notion of equality suggests giving the opinions and wishes of the young equal consideration with the parents' own. Original innocence, youth culture, and humble awareness of their own fallibility further suggest that it may be as unwise as it is undemocratic. Many devoted parents have come to see their job as zealously battling outside authorities on the child's behalf, defeating the child's rivals, and attacking the entertainment industry for not providing better child-rearing instructions and examples. Occasionally, as when children's athletics are supervised by parents not noticeably interested in using them to teach sportsmanship, this turns vicious.

These attitudes have taken hold most strongly among educated and well-to-do parents but have had a strangely equalizing effect. Unintentionally, the outcome may have restored an ideal of equality at birth that their advantages had been skewering. The rich, as well as—and sometimes more than—the poor, were coming from etiquette-deprived homes.

When Americans devoured the complex etiquette books of the Industrial Revolution, it was not entirely in a spirit of social competition. There was also a moral commitment to the belief that the absence of a hereditary class system would foster a hierarchy based entirely on how one conducted oneself. It would not be equality in the sense of everyone's being at the same social level, but equal opportunity to rise. Learning and practicing good manners were available free to anyone willing to put in the study and exercise the discipline, so America's ladies and gentlemen would be those who had the highest personal qualifications, for which neither money nor position could substitute.

Belief in this ideal has made many a rural or ghetto or slum kitchen into a strict classroom of etiquette, where reluctant pupils acquired the basic manners of ladies and gentlemen. They were therefore prepared should the other advantages follow—but they rarely did. Furthermore, the privileged could still win by using esoteric etiquette from their wider experience—hence the continued citing of the what-fork-to-use test—and by mixing in knowledge of trends and fashions from the greater commercial world.

Disillusionment set in. Probably the last public examples of faultless behavior as evidence of quality deserving of the highest consideration occurred when Dr. Martin Luther King Jr. insisted that politeness be observed in civil rights protests of the 1960s. Although it was ultimately an effective tactic, it was dropped after his time, in favor of harsher methods.

By then, oddly enough, a sort of equality of behavior was actually achieved. Prosperous parents were withdrawing from endorsing, much less teaching, etiquette, even in such simple matters as eating or thanking. The idea that bad manners showed that one was "brought up in a barn" was meaningless, first because poor people had learned manners, and then because the rich no longer did. Competition based on fashion raged ever stronger, but the manners of the drop-out child of an unwed crack-addicted teenager were not likely to be noticeably different from those of the child of two lawyers attending an expensive school.

Servants, a k a Help

"I hope America will come to have its pride in being a nation of servants, and not of the served," wrote Ralph Waldo Emerson. It did not.

Good Americans have always had trouble with the idea of having servants, and all Americans have had trouble with the idea of being servants. Despite the country's history of slave owning and ongoing forms of exploitation, it strikes those served, as well as those in service, as an unnatural relationship for which there is no satisfactory etiquette in either direction. Only the callous and the obsequious seem to manage without making the situation strikingly awkward.

The question of dignity in the job ought to be covered by our respect for honest work. Criteria commonly used to justify the low esteem in which the job is held (other than its low pay, which is a reflection of the low status) can be found in jobs of currently high status. A corporation executive is on constant call, an artist works with his hands, an athletic director comes into contact with sweaty bodies, and a doctor does all of these. Wives and mothers acquire an odd combination of high praise and low esteem for doing the same work in their own households.

The psychological impermanence of the situation also ought to mitigate attitudes toward it. Americans do not "go into service": They take domestic jobs when none others are open to them, cherishing the hope, however forlorn, that it is a temporary measure until things get better. They may not often marry the sons of the house, but there are enough instances of their own sons rising to prominence to illustrate its being a stopgap job rather than a career.

None of this has lifted the position in the slightest. The very name of servant riles household workers and embarrasses all but the most retrograde employers, and nobody has been able to come up with an adequate substitute. The term "public servant" is used with pride by our highest officials, but the private servant and her employer have always been skittish about the word and employ euphemisms.

"Help" is the most venerable term, still in use. As no self-respecting American would want to be served by another person, much less serve another, we all look after our own and our families' personal wants—or so this suggests. However, we are also generous and cooperative, so we help out one another.

The Beecher sisters' assessment

Harriet Beecher Stowe and her sister, Catherine E. Beecher, mindful that "Great merriment has been excited in the old country because, years ago, the first English travelers found that the class of persons by them denominated servants were in America denominated help, or helpers," explained the origin of this usage in their household polemic *American Woman's Home*.

"The term was the very best exponent of the state of society," they wrote. "There were few servants, in the European sense of the word; there was a society of educated workers, where all were practically equal, and where, if there was a deficiency in one family and an excess in another, a helper, not a servant in the European sense, was hired."

This refers to the program of sending children out to work in the houses of their parents' peers, like today's neighborhood teenaged babysitters, with the social standing of equals who were pitching in to help the family with the tasks it also performed. Europeans who found that hilarious would only have been showing their ignorance of their own customs. In feudal European society, the upper-class young were sent out to be servants in other castles as training for the waited-upon lives they were to lead. Full-grown aristocrats acted as body servants for royalty, vying jealously for the privilege of dressing the king or, even now, carrying packages for the queen.

The custom of employer and employee taking their meals together, which was observed in early America, sometimes even with slaves, and continued in rural America among farmers and their farm hands, was also considered comical. It, too, had its upper-class European counterpart in feudal times, when the lord and lady were served in their Great Hall, along with all their household, with the imperious salt cellar marking who belonged above and who below.

Operating in a time when the American household situation had turned bad, the Beecher sisters were rapturous about the days when "mistress and maid" lived and worked together with equal dignity, whichever one being less skilled at the job helping the other. Not only did the job get done, they claimed, but it was only one part of a sort of college curriculum, complete with intellectual and artistic seminars:

Then there were to be seen families of daughters, handsome, strong women, rising each day to their in-door work with cheerful alertness—one to sweep the room, another to make the fire, while a third prepared the breakfast for the father and brothers who were going out to manly labor: and they chatted meanwhile of books, studies, embroidery; discussed the last new poem, or some historical topic started by graver reading, or perhaps a rural ball that was to come off next week. They spun with the book tied to the distaff; they wove; they did all manner of fine needlework; they made lace, painted flowers, and, in short, in the boundless consciousness of activity, invention, and perfect health, set themselves to any work they had ever read or thought of.

The term "help" stuck, but the harmonious relationship and uplifting program were not in evidence when Mrs. Stowe and Miss Beecher issued what amounts to a domestic manifesto. Although it includes advice on candle making, "deodorization and preservation of excrementitious matter," and not wasting money on artificial light and warmth at night, their book can hardly qualify as "household hints," as there is no waffling about their opinion of the mistress of a household who is ignorant or contemptuous of how it is run. Things had so deteriorated, they reported, that women had to keep fit by working out in health clubs instead. "Our land is now full of motorpathic institutions to which women are sent at great expense to have hired operators stretch and exercise their inactive muscles. . . . Does it not seem poor economy to pay servants for letting our muscles grow feeble, and then to pay operators to exercise them for us? I will venture to say that our grandmothers in a week went over every movement that any gymnast has invented, and went over them to some productive purpose, too."

The authors identified a number of historical causes for what seemed to have become a competition in snippiness and surliness between mistress and maid, now equally incompetent at housework.

There were Pilgrims who started behaving as they had observed privileged classes to do toward inferiors (such as themselves) as soon as they acquired some clout in the new world. The more they did to emphasize their own superiority, the more their designated inferiors conceived a similar notion about themselves.

There were miserable working conditions, exacerbated by the notion that the long hours and scant wages bought the employer the privilege of supervising the servant's religious, moral, and social life. Even the exceptional employers who provided decent working conditions showed contempt by being inordinately proud of doing so, the authors observed.

There was "all English literature of the world," describing the master-servant relationship in feudal terms, with "the master as belonging to a privileged class and the servant to an inferior one. There is not a play, not a poem, not a novel, not a history that does not present this view."

There was the pernicious "near presence of slavery in neighboring States." For all the talk of equality, the ultimate example of inequality operated right along side of it.

There was, at Women's Rights Conventions, "a great deal of crude, disagreeable talk" downgrading the value of domestic labor. The Beecher sisters endorsed the position that "every woman has rights as a human being which belong to no sex and ought to be as freely conceded to her as if she were a man,—and first and foremost, the great right of doing any thing which God and nature evidently have fitted her to excel in," but objected to the "dissatisfaction expressed at those who would confine her ideas to the kitchen and nursery."

All these influences contributed to the key problem that was destroying the system along with household peace. That was a giant manners problem: Disrespect for the job and anyone who performed it, including the mistress of the house (who, as the person who needed help, couldn't also be "help," and would come to invent her own euphemisms, such as "domestic engineer" or "estate manager"). Employers behaved as badly as if a firm class system protected them against the possibility of their and the servants' fortunes being reversed, which alone should have inspired cautionary politeness. And that was before servants began writing books about their employers' habits and manners.

The uppitiness of which employers and foreign observers complained was matched by the servants' complaint of being put down:

"I'm nobody's servant" was the servant's mantra from early times.

"Managing republican servants is a task quite enough to make a Quaker kick his grandmother," Fanny Kemble reported.

Mrs. Stowe's abolitionist novel, *Uncle Tom's Cabin*, may have started the Civil War (as President Lincoln is supposed to have acknowledged upon meeting "the little lady who made this big war"), but the campaign to free domestics was ineffective. Their injunctions to employers, including paying good wages without resentment, providing quarters comparable to their own standard of living, understanding the work themselves so as not to make unreasonable requests, refraining from adding tasks for which they have not contracted, acknowledging that the employee's private life was none of their business, and giving them sufficient time off to have a private life in the first place, went unheeded for more than a century.

When they demanded respect for household employees, they also thought to caution well-meaning employers who attempt to "make pets" of them instead of letting them do their jobs that this, too, is a form of disrespect. From Ralph Waldo Emerson's embarrassing his manservant by trying to make him sit at table with him long after that custom had disappeared, to the twentieth-century employers who summoned their cleaning ladies to talk over race relations with them, the pretense at friendly "help" had become an imposition.

No dignified professional manners between employer and domestic employee have changed the situation. Employers continue to exhibit callousness or to force chumminess, and the employees' behavior veers between the same sort of anger and intrusiveness that Mrs. Kemble bluntly called servility and insolence.

Distancing and upgrading

Small wonder, then, that when women have resigned and children have rebelled from the status of supporting players, servants are also managing to find a way out, although by a different route. The change in one direction is to professionalize the ad hoc arrangements between householders and their "help," preferably so they hardly have to deal with one another at all, and, in another direction, to escalate the "help" fiction to the point where the workers actually are treated as if they were friends, complete with exchanges of confidence, loyalty, and birthday presents.

A prime example of the former is the cleaning service.

Although the cleaners are still drawn from the ranks of new immigrants hoping to work their way up and out into more respected jobs, they and the people whose houses they clean are released from any semblance of a relationship. The cleaning service may offer reliability, supervision, and bonding, thus freeing the employer, who most likely has her own job to do outside the house, from filling in at absences, spot checking, snooping, moral responsibility for the working conditions, and psychological responsibility for the worker's feelings. Its biggest attraction, however, has to be that it circumvents the need for an etiquette between "mistress and maid," when neither continuing the fiction of "help" in a business arrangement nor maintaining professional distance in a domestic setting seems quite right.

An example of the latter would be the hairdresser.

As more and more formerly domestic services are being jobbed out without the advantage of separating "mistress and maid," they are being sorted as to which commands professional respect, which should carry the disguise of friendly help, and which are left, like the domestic who works without an intermediary, to the same old confusion of etiquette and temptations to rudeness.

Generally, the etiquette of friendship is applied to services that are most intimately connected with appearance—not only hairdresser but dress designer, interior decorator, party planner, personal shopper, and personal trainer.. Although, or possibly because, those connected with physical or psychological health would seem to be more intimate, such support staff as therapists, grief counselors, nutritionists, chefs, and caterers are treated as professionals.

That leaves a lot of people still trying to upgrade into one category or another. If they deal with the children or old people in the family, such as nannies and nurses, or work around the house without intermediary employers—gardeners, as opposed to gardening services; drivers, as opposed to car services—they have a difficult time doing so. For them, the etiquette skirmishes with employers are still going on, and the question of which one of them is in more desperate need of the other is not as decisive a factor as which can best carry off a haughty demeanor.

"WE ARE REGISTERED AT . . ."

Chapter 7

The Show Stoppers
Emceeing Ceremonies and Celebrations

"YOUR WEDDING IS all about you, so you want to make sure everything is perfect."

"How many Valentines did you get?"

"Our baby's birth was the most beautiful experience of our lives."

"Christmas is for the children, and we don't want to disappoint them. Here are their lists of what they want."

"Well, it's my birthday, so I get to choose."

"Sure, New Year's Eve is fine for you—you're in a relationship—but how do you think it makes me feel?"

Ingredients of celebrations

We seem to have a theme uniting American holidays and ceremonies. The idea appears to be to provide opportunities for individuals to star in a variety of extravaganzas, which they should first redesign to suit themselves. Into every life, no matter how drab, will come the occasional chance to put on a smashingly big number. The downside is that this requires coercing others to act as audience and sponsors, and people sometimes have ideas of their own and are difficult to control. A lot of anxiety goes into these productions, because they can as easily be flops as hits.

To note that this was not always the American approach to special occasions is not to suggest, although people often do, that attitudes used to be finer and important occasions more uplifting. It is often lamented that changes over the years took us from the meaningful to the crass, as people were more spiritual in the seventeenth and eighteenth centuries, and more mindful of tradition in the nineteenth, but this does not happen to be the case.

One might think that the Puritans and other settlers in colonial and early America could be counted upon to conduct their holidays in a pious and sober fashion. One would be seriously disappointed. That would have been against their religion, as well as contrary to their inclinations. Exceeding even their own impressive reputation for being no fun, religious leaders of the time condemned religious festivities as an oxymoron, religion being a solemn, not a festive, matter. Christmas was denounced as pagan, Popish, and, in some communities, illegal. Being married in church was considered not a blessing but a cheeky attempt to draw God down into the mundane arrangements people make for their own convenience.

Undermining that stern reputation (at least to those who have been forced to square the facts with our picture of our strait-laced forebears) is the purpose and spirit that characterized any breaks from the routine of their harsh lives that they were able to seize. Their idea of a boisterous good time featured widespread drunkenness and debauchery, mischief and begging, customs that survive in the carnivals that still serve as a prelude to Lent. Such goings-on may have galled the sober, but they were certainly traditional.

Wills, bills, and lawsuits from the seventeenth century testify to the burden of the bereaved in having to supply the community with alcohol. A routine hazard at burials was adults, children, and sometimes infants falling drunkenly into the open graves.

Domesticating holidays

General agreement that order and propriety might be observed during time off was an innovation of the nineteenth century, which also undertook to supply emotional content and decorating ideas for such occasions. The major holidays and ceremonial patterns that we now celebrate, along with the spirit and the rules we expect them to have (and complain that they have lost), were dreamed up by Victorians. It was a regular industry. They took old cultural patches they found around at the time and joined them, using not the thread of history but the glue of sentimentality to hold them together. Our rituals for Thanksgiving, Christmas, and weddings are among their imaginative pastiches. To Victorians, the official solace of choice for the stress of the working world was lawful love rather than liquor.

As the twentieth century progressed, those charmingly warm family holidays beside the hearth were making people perspire. There was a lot of work involved, both in getting ready and in maintaining the fiction that family togetherness was balm to the soul. The suspicion arose that not a few family members had reversed the instructions and started using the workplace as a solace from the stress of home life.

Maintaining the tradition that occasions should take their meaning from the spirit of the society, rather than interrupting them to interject uncomforting and discomforting ideas, people began using holidays to showcase personal and group identity.

The holidays that have increased in popularity in our time are the ones offering such key ingredients as feasting, presents, jolliness, and masquerading. Armistice Day is not a contender.

Rejecting and revamping ritual

A second twentieth-century rejection of Victorianism followed. After the period in which Americans were thought to reject the rituals they had bequeathed, marrying themselves as a sunrise lark in the park and eschewing funerals as having no effect on the dead, a craving for ritual arose. This time it added the very un-Victorian caveat that ritual had to be authentic.

The truth is that neither of these much-touted trends was of statistical significance. All the while we were supposedly overcome with disdain for ritual, wedding and funeral processions were marching steadily on, in more or less recognizable form, to accompany the calendar and the life cycle. The spirit and emphasis might have changed, but the majority of the population was still celebrating personal, religious, and national holidays approximately as everyone remembered they always had been, right down to the traditional bickering over their being done "right," whatever that might mean to the various people exchanging accusations of ruining things.

This was no departure, because there are always alterations being made in the way rituals are conducted, some thoughtful, some expedient, and some whimsical, and there are always objections. Despite the slow transformations that resulted from this go-around, there were enough people participating in seriously meant rituals to give the lie to the claim that such set forms no longer spoke to modern emotions, and from now on, all behavior would be improvised. This would go against all we know about the human need, from the earliest traces of it in ritualized burials, to make life appear, if deceptively, to have meaning and continuity.

So it was not factual evidence that caused the belief to falter that a national rejection of ritual had taken place, but the announcement of the opposite trend, taken up by a similarly small number of conspicuous people. It was said that this sort were no longer baring their feet and thumbing their noses at their parents' dowdy wedding demands and dreary Thanksgivings. Rather, although they were continuing to sneer at their parents (which itself could be defined as a generational tradition), they were also reverently approaching their grandparents and other elders and experts on their families' history and racial, ethnic, and national affiliations, hoping to extract instructions for re-creating truly authentic rituals. The intention was to revive these deep expressions of culture as they had been from time immemorial until their own parents presumably messed them up.

The result was little more than the grafting of even more cultural odds and ends—a food, a song, an item of clothing, a "custom" or two (likely to be of vague provenance)—onto the basic Victorian routines. Their influence made minor contributions to the continual evolvement of American rituals, along with the countless other contributions accruing over the years, but the heralded return to authenticity never took place.

The authenticity test

It is not that the reformers failed to get definitive answers on their living history expeditions, even if sometimes only after being requested to stop brandishing their tape recorders in elderly faces. What they failed to discover, and would have found antithetical to their proud efforts, is that there is no such thing as an authentic ritual. Here are some of the problems in the concept of their quest:

As small differences and developments in the most familiar ritual make it vary according to time, place, and participants, when should such an event be frozen and deemed authentic? If such a time can be identified, how much leeway is allowed in adapting to individual circumstances or modern conditions without destroying the authenticity?

Do the origins of a ritual matter in judging whether or not it is authentic?

If so, should it have sprung up unaided, as a spontaneous response to an event in nature, such as whoopee marking the end of the annual harvest, or to an event in the human life cycle, such as achieving maturation, or to one in the society, such as the passing of political power from one ruler to the next?

What if it was deliberately invented, perhaps by a single person, or by an authoritative group whose other ideas have since been overtaken, if not discredited, or by a business for direct financial gain? In any of these cases, is the ritual tainted?

If it is invented by business for commercial purposes, as was Secretaries' Day, can it be authentic? If it is overtaken by commercial interests, as has Washington's birthday, does it forfeit its original authenticity?

If it was recently invented by one person, as Kwanzaa was by black studies professor Maulana Karenga in 1966, how many older elements does it require to be on its way to being considered authentic? If it has none, but its invention by one person took place before living memory and it is widely observed, for example Mother's Day, can it be considered authentic?

Should the original directions for a religion-related ritual have come from God, in which case how can any changes in it ever be made within the same faith without discrediting historical predecessors and present dissenters?

Testing American rituals for authenticity would be an even dicier undertaking than doing this elsewhere, because of the unusually large number of foreign cultural contributions and the peculiarity of dual loyalties. Not only do the older American rituals draw heavily on English and German ones, but newer ones have been identified as foreign—for example, Chinese, African, or Mexican—in spite of their being unrecognizable to the people who actually live in the place from which such rituals are supposedly imported.

In the former case, a custom may be deemed entirely American because it has been forgotten that the idea—white wedding dresses from England, or birthday cakes with candles from Germany—was imported, or because we feel entitled to claim ownership because we have so successfully exported these elsewhere under our own imprint. In the latter case, there is the opposite problem, a reluctance to acknowledge the transforming American influence on an imported ritual or on the thinking of the modern, hyphenated American (or hyphenated-American) who wants to launch a foreign ritual here.

Then there is the question of who, in a population descended from various combinations of separate immigrant groups, is entitled to claim possession of a custom traceable to a particular one of them. The American heritage is considered the property of all citizens, regardless of their time or place of emigration, so the privilege of speaking of the Founding Fathers or the Pilgrims as our forebears belongs to the most recent immigrant from any country, not just to those who were in America at the time.

America now also maintains a cultural boutique, where people can choose whatever customs they like, and create whatever mixture they prefer. In theory, for a ceremonial occasion, the choice of foods, dress, and excerpted customs will be explained as homage to different elements of a family's heritage—for example the bride wearing a red dress to honor her Chinese ancestry, while the bridegroom stomps on a glass to honor his Jewish ancestry—although in practice, such touches are selected when they are also philosophically and aesthetically pleasing to the people in question. Casual observation shows that if such is the case, an ancestral justification is not deemed necessary, while disliked customs are discarded no matter how strong their bloodline claims. The bride who insists that receiving cash at the reception is part of a heritage she must honor does not insist on the better-documented tradition by which her new mother-in-law should check the bridal sheets the next morning to verify that her son married a virgin.

Yet there are idiosyncratic prohibitions against some affiliations. The most infamous was the legal identity of people of mixed black and white heritage as black, regardless of the percentage of mixture or the resulting color; yet for anyone with such heritage not to identify himself as solely black now would carry the social stigma of self-hatred. On St. Patrick's Day, it is considered charming for anyone to "be" Irish by wearing an item of green clothing; but while it is also considered charming to wear an item of American Indian jewelry, it is considered insulting to wear items that would suggest an attempt to "be" a Native American without an ancestral claim.

In contrast, affinities for the food of different American sub-cultures are always laudable. One might say that the sign of a true American is a love not for apple pie but for sushi, pizza, enchiladas, and bagels.

Modern authenticity

A truly American ritual would reflect the historical development of its traditions over the centuries, and feature homegrown customs that have domesticated an imported ritual. It would have fancy meals and costume-like clothes, and allow individuals to collect praise and presents. To honor our predecessors, it would follow the tradition of involving the family. To honor our more remote ancestors, it would include their customs as well.

There is such an occasion in the life of nearly every modern American—high school graduation.

Think about it: In the most prized version, the graduate goes through an approximation of a centuries-old European ceremony, dressing up in traditional academic robe and mortar board. Family members attend, and there may also be a family party in the graduate's honor. Presents are certainly expected, the begging being done in the form of gift registry lists on the graduate's Web site. Mischief, in the form of a senior prank, precedes the ceremony, whooping and minor jokes continue even during it, and additional opportunities abound for the days of celebration afterward.

Another opportunity for costumed high jinks is the senior prom, loosely based on movie notions of high society in the 1920s, and of dating in the 1950s, and requiring evening clothes, corsages, and boutonnières, rented limousines, grand restaurant meals, and dancing in a ballroom, or a gymnasium got up to look like one.

This being clearly a masquerade, it has a time limit, concluding before the end of the evening, when there is a stylistic switch to the modern equivalent of the early American celebration, with its emphasis on free-form rollicking. Nobody pitches drunkenly into an open grave, but there is a tragic similarity in the cars that are drunkenly pitched from the open road. A senior trip, to a beach or other destination, can keep the celebration going for days.

Many of the same ingredients are what transformed Halloween, in only the last few years, from a children's holiday into a major adult holiday with a month-long marketing impact second only to that of Christmas. Costumes, mischief, and begging are even more blatantly featured, and misbehavior is sanctioned by the satirically satanic religious aura, making the climax a complete one-night carnival in itself.

Weddings

Where both graduation and Halloween fall short is that neither guarantees a starring role. One person might be valedictorian or, better, elected most popular, and someone will have the best costume, but the terms offered in advance are only the chance to compete. The greatest vehicle available to everyone, regardless of intellectual or artistic ability, is the wedding.

Considering how little practical difference marriage now makes in the lives of most people entering it, the burgeoning importance of the wedding ritual is extraordinary. The couple are likely to have been living together in effect, if they have not actually established a joint household. They may own property in common and may already have children. Many legal benefits and protections of the partnership are available to them without the marriage. The bride may choose not to change her name, and the couple may decide not to pool their finances. Whatever their hopes, they are clearly aware that they are not making a permanent and irrevocable change in their lives but an arrangement that either one of them can terminate pretty much at will, with minimal social consequences.

The perfect ritual

Yet the investment of emotion, money, and time into the wedding will be overwhelming. As bridal couples will often say, they expect this to be the happiest day of their lives. Alas, this could be only too true, even when the marriage itself is successful. With the squabbles that arise in producing such a huge undertaking, and the anticlimactic return to ordinary life afterward, creating a single perfect day should be as much as one could expect.

Even that will not materialize unless they happen to have a quirky and tolerant definition of perfection. First it is jinxed by the expectation of perfection—"perfect" is the term most associated with the dreams and merchandizing of weddings—creating an impossible goal that is bound to be disappointed. If perfection is obtainable on earth, the last place to find it would be at an event mixing families, friends, and champagne. Added to that is the strain of dealing with the unfamiliar. Before the Victorian invention of the splashy wedding, weddings were simple additions to the ordinary household routine, often held at home with no more elaborate accoutrements than any other pleasant occasion. As they got progressively fancier, so did social life in general, so that those who put on the next half-century's weddings—the key planners being not the bride but her presumably more experienced mother—had practice in handling formality and producing comparable events.

The inexperienced planners

Now bridegrooms may be more involved than previously, but the directions they used to be given—to offer no opinions but just to show up looking pleased—are issued to parents.

Brides with full professional workloads but no hostessing skills outside of restaurants and potluck suppers will think nothing of spending upwards of a year planning complex marathons involving dozens, perhaps hundreds, of people, numerous events, travel, and the purchase and use of clothing, correspondence, and customs that are stylistically alien from the way they or the bridegrooms have ever lived.

Beyond learning the lore and working the logistics, they assume the job of redoing it all, from the liturgy to the social forms, to their own particular taste. That these "personal" touches turn out to be pretty much the same (readings from *The Prophet,* hearts printed on the invitations, colored bowties coordinated with the bridesmaids' dresses) is not as odd as the choice of which customs are considered sacrosanct. "Giving the bride away" has survived despite female independence, the number of times she may have been previously donated, and the absence of a father or any other man who can reasonably be thought ever to have had jurisdiction over her. The white wedding dress survived the unseemly habit of speculating about whether it accurately symbolized bridal purity to emerge as the unapologetic choice of pregnant and previously married brides as well.

The power of performing a ritual so as to join the great stream of humanity in its repeated life cycles is still there, in spite of all the tinkering being done. It shows in the emotion people put into doing it "right," as if there were a single pattern for all time. The same people who won't follow the simple formulae that do exist—for example, the precise wording of formal invitations that has been standardized for longer than, for example, the white wedding dress—are mistakenly convinced that there must be precise instructions that they should follow on such minutiae as who dances with whom for the third dance of the reception.

Repeat performances

The devotion to this ritual is so strong that once is no longer enough. The same wedding might have more than one enactment, not because there are both civic and religious ceremonies but to bring it to different audiences—for example, a wedding on one coast, followed by one on the other, or one near the bride's relatives and one near the bridegroom's, with perhaps a third in the city in which they live, or at a location that has no family or residential ties for either but that they happen to like. Furthermore, the once minor and optional events in connection with weddings—showers, rehearsal dinners—have grown in solemnity, and new ones have been added, such as a brunch for guests the morning after. In the case of "destination" weddings at vacation spots, the entire honeymoon is also a social occasion.

Second and subsequent marriages, once done in a more subdued style that was presumably geared to the maturity of the bride and the tolerance of her friends, are generally given the same full treatment as the first. There the explanation is that this is the first "real" wedding, failed marriages no longer counting.

Even an enduring marriage is no barrier to continuing to have weddings. The reasoning might be that the actual wedding lacked the full treatment, either because the couple wished at the time to avoid it or because they couldn't afford it, so they are now "entitled to have a real wedding." Anniversaries are sometimes celebrated as imitation weddings, and religious institutions have cooperated in a new ritual of "renewing" wedding vows in later years, as if recognizing that the original vows were not binding but contained options about whether or not to continue.

Best roles, costumes, story line, profit potential

Weddings have a powerful hold because they have theatrical ingredients and enable the principals to be both the stars and the directors. They are even viewed as profitable because of the wedding presents (and sometimes direct fund-raising efforts), although only by a sort of Hollywood accounting system in which the stars get their percentages even if others, including the investors, do not.

There is costuming not only in the sense of dressing up far beyond the principals' other experience but in that the clothes indicate the roles. At most weddings, there will be at least three distinct styles of clothing worn: the most formal on the bride and bridegroom, a second degree of formality for the rest of the wedding party, outfitted identically like chorus lines, and a third, still less formal, style worn by the guests (and perhaps an even lower fourth level by those guests who refuse to dress as expected). Some frankly approach the costume angle by declaring "theme" weddings and having the wedding party dressed in "medieval" or "Victorian" style. There may also be lavish props, such as fancy cars or horse-drawn carriages.

Most of all, there is the sense of stardom. "It's your day," the couple is repeatedly told. In the spirit of generosity, or of fairness because they want a turn to do the same, people will tolerate self-aggrandizement at the expense of their own claims as relatives, friends, and guests.

Even beyond those attractions, a wedding has the power of narrative. This has only increased as the exciting plot once inherent in courtship has been severely curtailed. Fond as we all are of stories, especially love stories, the drama and suspense that helps make the possibility of romance so compelling has been cut out by the efficiency of modern society. If people meet through dating services and size each other up over coffee, they miss the excitement of spotting someone and wondering whether that person might be available or susceptible. If they consummate a mere spark, they miss the agonized yearning that fans erotic fevers. If they marry after maintaining a household together, they miss the thrill of danger in taking such a step. When the story runs backward—from lovemaking to becoming acquainted—the suspense is gone.

Whether couples are better off without it, suspense having led to many an injudicious leap, is not the question here; rather, it is what this does to the story line. There isn't much of one, so the wedding must supply one that is now likely to be fictional: The innocent young girl and the hitherto elusive bachelor, both being swept by pure emotion into a mysterious future of unending passion. Wedding photographers have become adept at presenting such a story in retrospect visuals, regardless of how the actual courtship was conducted.

Funerals

These spectacular shows are certainly more entertaining than funerals, which could explain why funerals seesawed down in importance as weddings shot up. At least it has been the modern view that funerals are a drag. In previous eras, the mystery connected with death held far more fascination than the more easily explained phenomenon of young people pairing off.

The dreary ritual

Once, funerals were unparalleled as an opportunity for the aggrandizement of the individual, but that was when it was thought not quite nice to aggrandize oneself, so it was necessary to wait for someone else to do it. Death is now considered too long to wait, even presuming that one could count on others to do this without being prodded and supervised by the person it would most benefit.

The motivation might have come more easily when death often struck the young, perhaps making the loss more deeply felt than when the individual has lived long enough to be a care, if not a nuisance, to his descendants. The habit of congratulating the bereaved ("It was all for the best"), while not exactly polite even yet, would have been unthinkable; but, then, the impetus for predating the bereavement ("We felt we lost her long ago") only came with the prevalence of Alzheimer's disease and the use of life-sustaining equipment.

It is interesting—and alarming—to note that children and teenagers who have known enough violent deaths among their classmates and neighbors to make it seem a normal hazard of their own lives also take a deep interest in the funeral ritual. In Washington, D.C., and other cities hit by spates of killing related to drug-dealing and miscellaneous armed anger, where bystanders may be in mortal danger even in their own homes or high schools, youngsters are used to attending funerals. When they are interviewed, they shock their elders by the unflinching way they face the possibility of being next, speculating about their own funerals to the extent of picking favorite clothes in which they would like to be buried.

In less dangerous circumstances, most people do flinch at death and its trappings, and rationales have developed for avoiding or minimizing the ritualistic duties it once entailed. One scathing argument was that funeral customs had grown so cumbersome that they went beyond their purposes of honoring the dead and protecting the grieving from public scrutiny, and had turned into a patently hypocritical charade. (Note: All societies have a horror of being thought hypocritical, and all are convinced that they are not but that all earlier societies were.)

Mr. Jefferson's example

Another of Thomas Jefferson's failed essays into etiquette was to make this point, as well as one about funerals being a financial drain on the poor. "Among other customs which he thought did more harm that good was the wearing mourning for deceased relatives and making very expensive funerals," reported his friend Margaret Bayard Smith, in her book *The First Forty Years of Washington Society*.

On this point, he enforced precept by example. When he lost his almost idolized daughter Mrs. E, keenly and deeply as he felt this bereavement, neither he nor any of his family put on mourning, neither did he make any change in his social habits, but continued his dinner parties and received company as usual, considering it as a portion of his public duty to receive and entertain members of Congress and other official characters. In this he went too far and miscalculated the common feelings of humanity.

He might only have been ahead of his time. Eventually, the concept of piety toward the dead was suspended on the grounds that they were too dead to care. They were not, however, exempt from posthumous criticism. Burgeoning health consciousness, of both the emotional and physical kinds, contributed to quashing previously mandated obligations. As people began to assume responsibility for their own health, deaths that were considered blameworthy—typically because the deceased had smoked, or weighed too much, or failed to have a positive attitude toward "battling" illness, but not because of a habit such as racing cars or jumping from airplanes—seemed to compel less response.

Long after generalized depression came to be treated with respect, at least in theory, sadness specifically resulting from a death was treated as a weakness on the part of anyone in whom it was protracted. The seclusion and trappings of mourning— veils, armbands, black-bordered writing paper, black-ribboned door wreaths, as well as the elaborate formula of somber clothing that specified periods for unrelieved black and later ones permitting touches of lavender—were eliminated as delaying recovery and spreading gloom. (The exception was black clothing, which came back to life as a chic color for happy occasions.)

Mourning reborn

When this reform movement had become so successful that considerate people were instructing their families not to hold services for them and more or less respectable people felt free to announce that they avoided funerals because funerals were so depressing, the reinvention of funeral customs got under way. A formal mourning period was reinstituted, only this time as a progression to acceptance, with the emotional steps to be followed being spelled out and recited as a guideline to mourners.

Then, on a number of occasions, national grief was expressed with an intensity of emotion that had faded from private life and a proliferation of new rituals. The dead-and-gone approach clearly did not apply to victims of violence or to celebrities, and piety toward them took the form of mounds of flowers and teddy bears, badges of ribbons (although these were not black but color-coded for the cause of death, such as red for AIDS, pink for breast cancer, and yellow for being missing and in mortal danger, if not already dead), and messages addressed to the dead that were left on walls and Web sites.

Meanwhile, attempts had been made to remedy deficiencies in the funeral rite, including ones that one would suppose to be inherent in the occasion. Eulogies by members of the clergy were not entertaining, especially when done by someone unacquainted with the deceased. The practice now is to have eulogies by relatives and friends, who followed a different tradition of speechmaking. Patterned on platform introductions, tributes, or roasts for the living, these make funerals more entertaining, with the addition of anecdotes, jokes, and perhaps a startling dash of bald truth, although perhaps not entertaining enough.

The boldest such experiment was the premature funeral, a substitute rite honoring the terminally ill and allowing that person to enjoy and, incidentally, monitor, what was said about him. Although this would seem to solve the most egregious charge against funerals, it has not yet caught on. No matter what the improvements, funerals are not the attraction that weddings are.

Birth

The social possibilities in the act of giving birth have been rediscovered only comparatively recently. With the advent of hospital birth, the centuries-old home birthing party at which the principal was both patient and hostess to her support system had disappeared, not just from use, but from the range of activities considered socially palatable.

Baptism, bris, and various christening ceremonies take place afterward, with everyone dressed, and they focus on the baby. What had been missing was the excitement, suspense, and bonding in a ritual in which women had rallied around the mother for the birth itself, combining practical help with feasting and partying. Fathers were missing, too, confined to the walk-on part of being summoned to admire the baby.

Sideshows

In the interim period, pallid substitutes arose for both of these rituals, with the serious contributions obviously being supplied professionally, and the mother reduced to a passive part. The father, being assigned a comic role, received as much admiration for delivering an entertaining account of being so flustered as to be barely capable of getting through his tasks of driving his wife to the hospital, pacing in the waiting room, hearing the news of the arrival from the doctor, and passing out cigars to his friends.

Banished from any participation, female friends invented the baby shower. Given before the actual birth, it enabled the expectant mother to participate as guest of honor, and the other women to impart their expertise about the enterprise. Like the bridal shower, this ritual harked back to community involvement in outfitting those embarking on new stages of life, and forward to the support group, where people from the wider community of the Internet exchange stories and advice with those in similar situations.

The shower has nevertheless remained a distinct event, growing from a simple gathering to an elaborate ritual no longer connected in people's minds to the need to advise someone achieving a milestone and in need of ordinary equipment for it. Brides now expect showers for every marriage, and mothers, for every child. Presents have increased in importance and expense, food and arrangements are apt to be elaborate, and the guest list has increased from the honoree's close female friends to include relatives, co-workers, and neighbors, the men often being expected to participate along with the women.

*Birth
as a
moral
test*

The idea that men, as well as women, should have a serious role in childbirth (suspendable in the case of single mothers) helped turn the event of birth into a drama of major proportions. How the parents acquit themselves during the event has come to be regarded as a test of character, for which they attend rehearsal-like classes during the pregnancy (which many claim also to share, as in "we are pregnant"). Home births underwent a small revival, but hospitals, too, made room for fathers as coaches and photographers. For the mother, success is measured in the amount of pain relief that is refused; for the father, it is the ability to maintain a doctor-like dependability and imperviousness to gore (although real doctors are not expected to be detached where their own relatives are concerned). Lapses by either are accorded nominal sympathy, but success inspires something akin to reverence.

Especially from the co-stars themselves. The evidence, the video, is considered of such prime importance that attempts to ban cameras from the delivery room have brought angry protests, with accusations that the doctors wish to protect themselves from malpractice suits. Hopes for a wider live audience have resulted in allowing other relatives and friends into the room to witness the event, an unwitting but faithful revival of the old ritual.

Birthdays

Birthday parties are another of those nineteenth-century rituals that became so widely observed that they seem to go back to the beginning of civilization. Yet those, too, grew over the last few decades. From being barely noticeable, to being family occasions, to being a combination of social treat and etiquette workshop for children, they have expanded indefinitely into adulthood and become another important emotional test, this one being of how much one is loved by others.

Again, the ritual thrives because it has the right ingredients for modern success: star-for-a-day status, presents, special foods, and indulgence for childlike behavior. Unlike the wedding and childbirth, it does not require a co-star, has no qualifying skills, and recurs with gratifying frequency.

Furthermore, there are superbirthdays every few years, with special maturation rites or parties, and these are soon followed by the ones that get special attention for the comic-pathos now associated with growing older. At thirteen, the Jewish boy or girl may have a bar or bat mitzvah of wedding-like splendor. At fifteen, the Mexican-American girl may have a debutante-like quinceañera. The debutante tradition, pretty much abandoned by its original practitioners when its purpose of bringing young women into their parents' social circles disappeared, survives in name (and curtsies) in showy balls in cities where the debutantes may not even reside, and in a more conservative form put on by African-American clubs. Other especially marked birthdays include the twenty-first, thirtieth, and every following decade, with the seventy-fifth marking the shift to every five years.

Honoring oneself

As it is the ritual now most familiar to everyone from childhood, the birthday's influence on other rituals is marked. The notion that one can throw oneself a party and at the same time be the guest of honor—the one role having the privilege to issue directions, and the other to be on the receiving end—has come to whitewash a kind of social slipperiness now often encountered:

The host's duty of providing the ingredients is thought to be canceled by the guest of honor's position as the beneficiary of generosity. The guest of honor's need to express gratitude is thought to be canceled by the host's being regarded as the provider of hospitality—even if the guests are directed to bring the refreshments or help pay the costs—who should receive thanks. The host's obligation to ensure that all his guests are looked after is thought to be canceled by the guest of honor's special status as the person due the most attention and care. One can find evidence of this double-edged reasoning in the conduct of bridal couples and others with expectations on such occasions as Valentine's Day, Mother's Day, Father's Day, and wedding anniversaries, with a gridlock of expectations converging on Christmas.

Theoretically, there would be rough fairness in indulging others in this temporary tyranny with the compensation of taking one's own turn. This is the rationale behind the common toleration of bridal neglect of the wishes of relatives, bridesmaids, and guests: "Well, it's her day, and she can do whatever she wants." In fact, the American sense of fairness, or possibly greed, has been violated by the uneven distribution of occasions. The enterprising have been busy thinking up new rituals at which to honor themselves so that they will not fall behind: "singles" showers for people who are not getting married, divorce parties, housewarmings for transient quarters, job promotion parties, and job loss parties.

Alternative holidays

A more general method of dealing with this unevenness has been the expansion or invention of holidays equivalent to—and occurring at approximately the same time as—major ones in which one does not participate. Most notably, Christmas, having coalesced from more general winter festivals, grew to where it was impossible for nonparticipating Americans to ignore. What with the days off from work and school, the ubiquitous music and decorations, and the vast merchandising, those who did not take the easy solution of regarding it as again being simply a winter festival whose Christian associations are optional had a lot of explaining to do to their children, who were feeling left out, and perhaps to themselves as well.

The formerly minor Jewish festival of Hanukah conveniently occurred in the winter and lasted over a week, topping even the Christmas-to-New-Year's week of celebrations. In the late nineteenth-century holiday boom, some American Jews started putting it forth as an alternative to Christmas. As this caught on, and the coins children received metamorphosed into eight days' worth of Christmas-equivalent presents, it was the Christian parents who might have some explaining to do to their children, especially if their Jewish friends' Hanukah celebration was followed by a nonsectarian Christmas.

Kwanzaa, newly minted for the purpose, could be deliberately timed to serve as a black alternative to a "white Christmas," and its observance, with seven days of candle lighting and reflection on moral principles, has grown with the years. It was not so easily separated from the habit of focused consumerism as its inventor had hoped. Some elements of American holidays are nonnegotiable.

National Holidays

The major American holidays, both because of their commemoration of significant historical events and because of their inclusiveness, are Independence Day and Thanksgiving, although neither of these qualifications is quite true. Native Americans naturally have a dissenting view of Thanksgiving, and African-Americans of an Independence that countenanced slavery.

Independence was declared on July 2, 1776, and although the Declaration is dated July 4, which is the date John Hancock affixed its most prominent signature, the official signing ceremony was held on August 2 and was not fully completed even then. The first celebration was held by the Continental Congress on July 8, although the monarch of whom they declared themselves independent was unaware of this action until late August. Thanksgiving was based on a single harvest-like festival week in 1621, without invoking God (as Pilgrims did not believe in mixing religion and fun) and probably without the blessing of a turkey dinner.

Both are products of the nineteenth-century holiday craze. The Fourth of July was rescued from partisan squabbles to become a national holiday in 1826, and Thanksgiving in 1863, after President Lincoln was lobbied to proclaim it by the editor of *Lady's Book* and *Godey's Magazine*, who then provided readers with instructions for the celebration.

However explicitly the instructions delineated a patriotic, family-oriented day, they were not universally followed. It is always difficult to detach people from the traditions they have known, especially if the earlier ones have inherent attractions, and it was some years before the populace was persuaded to celebrate these holidays in a decorous way, rather than with the old-fashioned customs of drunkenness, masquerading, and other such traditional pursuits.

Holiday dropouts

There may be some holdouts yet, and there are beginning to be dropouts as well. Fireworks, parades, and feasting are clear enticements, but for many, the family-oriented day is no great draw, and in some cases perhaps a repellent. Divorce has produced bitterness and divided loyalties; the lost habit of private entertaining makes hosting and even being a guest seem burdensome; and normal overscheduling makes a day without work, rest, or a favorite leisure pastime feel wasted.

Ensemble pieces don't work well now that the emphasis has shifted from the family to the individual, and people are as likely to consider themselves to have been psychologically damaged by family life as benefited. Valuing frankness above tact does its own damage. The manners needed to accompany such a day have given way to the idea that people should keep a running check to make sure they are not exploited, even over the short run; give freely of their opinions and advice, whatever effect this produces; and that how one dresses and eats affect only one's self. All that to put up with, and there are not even any presents to take home.

For similar reasons, the simpler nightly rituals of family meals at home are rare, and the more formal one of Sunday dinner, which had been observed up and down the economic scale, is gone. As far as we know, the shared meal has been a basic way of affirming kinship and friendship, as well as of marking special occasions, throughout the history of civilization.

Oh, well. The human craving for ritual and creativity in developing it has given us replacements that will be looked upon by future generations as eternal, and probably annoyingly old-fashioned as well. In place of Sunday dinner, we have Sunday brunch, as the marking of the Sabbath has its counterpart in Thank God It's Friday office parties. The family may not gather around the piano in the evening, but there are still communal gatherings to watch televised games or rented movies.

We have ceremonies that are shared across the nation, and serve as models for conducting other ceremonies and religious services: the Academy Awards and the Miss America Pageant. From that we learn that the ingredients for ritual should include not only spotlights, praise, and prizes but thanks and applause.

"MAYBE WE SHOULD RESCHEDULE FOR MONDAY."

Chapter 8

Costumes, Props, and Sets
The Designer Life

ONE OF THE unacknowledged but jealously prized American freedoms is the freedom to assume a misleading appearance through choice of clothing, dwelling, and possessions. The common exercise of this goes beyond the universal quest to look richer than one actually is to a mild form of fantasy through using artifacts associated with a way of life other than one's own.

An urban office worker may live in a scaled-down version of a southern plantation house. An artist may wear a diver's watch and cowboy boots. A statistician may drive a pickup truck.

Children may dress as adults, in revealing black outfits suitable for cocktail parties; adults may dress as children, wearing sweatsuits in primary colors suitable for the playground. Workers may dress as if they were at leisure, and those at leisure may dress for jobs they've never had.

Messages that are literally spelled out may be just as deceiving. Wearing a college's insignia does not necessarily indicate that the person inside received any education from that institution, even secondhand from a romance or a relative. A corporate logo may not mean that the bearer is an employee, an owner, or a customer. It would be an especially bad idea to believe the command "Kiss Me!" on the T-shirt of a stranger. The second line suggesting the incentive "I'm Italian" (or French or Iraqi) may not be true, either, even in the American usage of claiming ancestral dual or multiple citizenships.

Costume

The liberty to choose our own costumes, props, and sets is one we take for granted, not only because we are a freedom-loving people who like to play dress-up but because we have a hard time imagining how a society could have so little of importance to do as to fuss over what its citizens wear. Other than pleasure-hating monsters, such as the Taliban and school principals, who cares how other people present themselves? How you dress doesn't hurt anyone.

Freedom of wardrobe

Apparently, it does. All that laxity of dress belies the fact that Americans are always good for a fight about clothing. We started with sumptuary edicts, in the sixteenth century, and then moved to dress codes, which are within the realm of etiquette rather than law but are nonetheless binding in the venues over which they have jurisdiction, such as schools and clubs. That the life cycle for all attempts to impose clothing standards is short—1. they are declared; 2. they are defied; 3. they are dropped—has not discouraged the practice. There are reasons for this, some better than others.

The underlying problem is that some people look better than others, even aside from their physical attributes and inner beauty or the lack of it. Cinderella may be stunning and virtuous, but her fairy godmother, like any Hollywood image-maker packing a client off to the Oscars, recognized that enhancement from the wardrobe department and jewelry vaults was necessary to make her socially mobile.

The more respectable explanation of sumptuary laws was to hold back the rich from becoming unbearably dazzling, and thus relieve the poor from the expensive and doomed temptation to compete. Today this is a major argument used in favor of dress codes at schools. Youths having murdered one another for a coveted item of clothing, the idea of putting controls on competition no longer seems outlandish.

The less respectable explanation is the opposite: that the people backing these laws did not want to worry about being outdazzled by upstarts, and therefore put the best stuff on reserve. In the past, people had no compunctions about stating this. No self-respecting king would have been expected to tolerate ordinary people decking themselves out in crowns, purple, and ermine, and if high school students were able to bar the elementary school crowd—or their own parents—from wearing scaled-down versions of the styles they prize, they might not be so opposed to dress codes.

As long as they could, Americans who fancied themselves to be members of an oligarchy passed laws with the frank intent of putting others down. The nineteenth-century South Carolina legislators who decreed that slaves should not wear silks, satins, lace, and such (unless, of course, this was the household livery, in which case it was compulsory) because it might make them lose sight of their inferiority sounded remarkably like those seventeenth-century Massachusetts courts that repeatedly reproved "men and women of meane [*sic*] condition, education and calling" for wearing gold, silver, lace, silks, and other such refinements. Both groups made sure they had moral justification for maintaining their own political and social advantages in this obvious way, Massachusetts emphasizing the desire to protect people from the sin of pride, and South Carolinians from the temptation to steal.

Looking important

Making the ruling class look better than those whom it is protecting from the temptations to which it is, meanwhile, yielding is not the only reason for using clothing to distinguish elements of the population. In their official capacity, at least, persons of authority need to be identifiable and to inspire respect. The general should have an awesome appearance even if he is the least prepossessing physical specimen in the field. The police officer should look different from the thug, the doctor from the patient, the firefighter from the looter, and the judge from the defendant. As nature is not always accommodating, we cover its deficiencies with brass stars, blue uniforms, white coats, red hats, and black robes.

The citizens find this unobjectionable, although occasionally those who are entitled to such distinctions, yet not legally required to bear them, are stricken by the symbolic inequality. This has caused a division in the medical profession over whether employing an etiquette of status is beneficial to the patients, morally repugnant, or simply unnecessary because distinction radiates from their learned selves without such assistance. The dispute is somewhat generational, with older doctors generally valuing not only their white coats but the habit of using their patients' first names while expecting to be addressed as "doctor," and the younger doctors shedding both their coats and their own surnames.

Both are sabotaging the delicate way in which such differences can be reconciled using American principles. The conventional acknowledgment of earned rank through symbolic clothing and titles is inoffensive, presuming it is unaccompanied by extenuating swagger. It becomes insulting only when emphasized by the bearer's denying others their own dignity, as when the doctor insists on his own title but omits using any honorific for the patient. It is true that forgoing such symbols, as when the doctor sheds title and coat, eliminates the possibility of offense, but it is also true that undercutting the expected symbolism is worrisome to those who have hired the person for his or her credentials. Patients do not object to indications that their doctors are superior to them in medical knowledge. Anyway, doctors who feel that they should be on a symbolic level with their patients should not imagine that wearing street clothes will accomplish this. They should be wearing paper hospital gowns that open in the back.

Dress codes

Fooling with the symbolism of one's own wardrobe is not as dangerous as attempting to get others to look the part they are—or should be—playing. Anyone who makes the mildest suggestion proposing or upgrading a dress code had better stand back. Possibly because the disappearance of "Sunday best" means that many people have now grown up unfamiliar with using more than one clothing style, they have an extraordinary emotional investment in the belief that it is personally degrading to capitulate to any standardization of style.

Almost any, that is. There are those nightclub bouncers whose volatile codes are accorded respect and obedience. Relatives, employers, and hosts who venture suggestions, never mind demands, meet with righteous opposition based on charges that they are proponents of discomfort on the verge of torture, enemies of individuality and creativity, and, besides (the devastating blow), old-fashioned.

The first two charges are countenanced more than they deserve, because they can so easily be refuted by the irritating method of pointing to contradictions in the accuser's own habits. There is hardly anyone who will not undergo discomfort for the sake of fashion he or she admires in others. Being eloquent about the misery inflicted by wearing a tie or a skirt does not preclude eloquence on the pleasure of tattooing and the shame of not being able to keep up with one's peers.

The charge about being out of date, which is so facilely, falsely (and, for some reason, effectively) made about morally based manners, is a valid one in regard to symbols. Injunctions such as those requiring expressing gratitude and offering condolences are not subject to change, but symbols are intrinsically unrelated to what they symbolize and capable of quick change, so those who use or oppose them have to keep up with what they mean.

Changing symbols

We all agree that the flag is a symbol, and therefore that how it is treated reflects one's feeling about the country or its policies at the time. The difference in attitude between those who salute it and those who burn it is clear (although a worn flag is reverently burned as an honorable form of disposal). Yet fifty years ago, to wear a flag pin on the lapel symbolized political conservatism, while incorporating the design into clothing symbolized contempt. In the aftermath of the attacks of September 11, 2001, both came to symbolize mainline patriotism without reference to political opinion.

Anything perched on the head—hair, hats, wigs, tiaras, crowns (and, for that matter, lice, although they are not likely to symbolize any wish on the part of the wearer)—is loaded with meaning, although those meanings also change. Lice symbolized poverty and parental neglect until epidemics spread in private schools, at which time they quickly became a mere affliction with no symbolic content.

In colonial America, patently false wigs, such as the cottony curls even now plopped atop English judges, symbolized dignity and importance. They were "bigwigs," as we still say of the mighty, and naturally, this was enough to make everybody crazy to wear a wig, including derelicts and small children. Such popularity is a deadlier way of killing off a fashion than pastoral denunciations of vanity. That wily old trendsetter Benjamin Franklin, who had suffered an encounter in which a French wigmaker had the rare distinction of topping him in wit ("No, sir," he replied to the American minister's accusation, "the wig is not too small, but your head is too large"), helped change the symbolism of wiglessness from ignominy to independence, and by 1800, wigs had pretty much disappeared in America.

The meaning attached to hair length goes up and down, and its habit of frequent symbolic restyling did not dampen enthusiasm for interpreting morality from haircuts. For centuries, women who wore their hair short when custom decreed it should be long, or long when it should be short, were deemed hussies in addition to being sexless, which is an odd combination; men who did the same were deemed both defiant and effeminate. Now that the length argument seems exhausted, people who miss the reactions have had to go to greater lengths, in the way of employing odd colors and shapes, to provoke it.

That women's hats long served as a major outlet for their most fanciful and outrageous creativity did not protect hats from coming to symbolize conformity. Many black church women—whose stalwartness in preserving manners and morals when these were most under twentieth-century siege is comparable to medieval monks' preserving scholarship—kept the custom alive. For some years now, its general return has been predicted seasonally by the fashion industry. Men's hats used to symbolize maturity, and in a way, they continue to do so, while it is maturity that went out of fashion. More stylistically limited than women's, men's dress hats, too, came to symbolize lack of individuality, a characteristic despised by defiant modern men, who all wear baseball caps.

And so it goes. At the turn of this past century, clothing that had long been symbolic of recent immigration and failure to grasp or afford modern American ways, such as shawls, homespun, and hand-me-downs, became the chic choice of fashion-conscious New Yorkers, in the form of pashmina scarves, hand-loomed materials, and a style called "vintage." Pearls, once a sensual indulgence for languorously rich women, became the badge of timid ones. Watches went from being the temporal account-keepers for solemn grandfathers and stern supervisors to being flashy jewelry for high rollers. Dark glasses, signaling the pathos of blindness or the geekiness of beachside vacationing, became the insignia of hard-edged youth. The cigarettes of temptresses became associated with a different sort of villainy, the kind with bad breath.

Men's evening clothes suffer from mistaken symbolic identification, although they are now worn in a wide range of circumstances—by partygoers, waiters, musicians, statesmen, bridegrooms, and women. The form of it that is now considered "formal," the dinner jacket, also called "black tie," was never associated with the old robber barons and similar plutocrats because it had not yet been invented. When it was, it served only as an informal alternative to white tie and tails. Yet the symbolism of economic exploitation clings to it so severely than men who balk at wearing it consider that doing so is a virtuous act of humanitarianism, even at the expense of the feelings of their hosts and brides. Or perhaps because.

Protests against the symbolism of daytime ties are more egalitarian, because one can indulge in them without the prerequisite of being on guest lists for formal occasions. The symbolic (as opposed to comfort) case against ties is that they represent subservience to unwarranted expectations, a despised trait commonly called conformity, even though anti-tie nonconformists are now in the majority. For women, the equivalent is "little white gloves," a reference to the expectation that ladies should not leave their houses without wearing gloves, the summer version of which, in white cotton, being used as the symbol. That the custom fell into disuse some fifty years ago has not lessened the tones of horror and disbelief with which it is cited.

With all this confusion and anger, not to mention the history of disastrous conse-quences, why would any person or establish-ment be so foolhardy as to attempt issuing a dress code? What is in it for them?

They recognize what nobody will admit: That everyone who sincerely denies doing so is unknowingly reading dress for symbolic content anyway. They are spurred to mandate a code if they detect symbolic messages that are in conflict with the purpose of the establishments they run—sub-verting the seriousness of its purpose, for example, as bankers would if they wore mouse ears, or distracting attention from work, as when students wear revealing clothes (possibly even more than when they wear unrevealing clothes).

Arguments against codes are always framed in terms of prac-ticality, comfort, individuality, cost, and so on, but such matters could be settled by simple debates about the relative merits of this type of clothing or that. The emotion brought to bear is because the opponents, as much as the proponents, know what is at stake. The very anger with which dress codes are met is proof of the power of clothing to convey meaning.

Therefore, a business or school that uses a dress code to sym-bolize what it wants to encourage and convey is only in conflict when its people want to use their clothing to symbolize some-thing different. If they agree on their goals, there is no problem with dress codes. The club bouncers prevail because their clien-tele endorses the premise that only those with the right look should be admitted and concedes that the arbiter of this is the tough employee standing at the door. Those who join organiza-tions with which they deeply agree speak of their pride in "wearing the uniform." At a school where the student body may vehemently protest against minimal clothing regulations—banning bare midriffs, or requiring shoes—as denying their basic human rights, the football coach is not hearing complaints from the players about their having to wear uniforms.

In the usual work or school situation, the population is there because it has to be. At least that is the official line they must take: Young children who are too fond of school have trouble with their peers, and older people who remain in school when not in pursuit of a professional goal or a sideline hobby are considered failures. However much admired the work ethic is, employees who seem overly devoted to their jobs are regarded with either pity or suspicion. So when required to symbolize seriousness about work or study, even people who are serious get upset. Symbolism is their chief means of denying the fact that for several hours a day, they are not their own masters.

The numbers are against those making codes, and so is the rhetoric of liberty. Then there is the fact that code makers tend to be bad at their jobs. They rarely study symbolism carefully enough to avoid making mistakes, and so they condemn styles as symbolically subversive or lewd that turn out to be emblems of legitimate cultural affiliation or benign fashions that have been adopted by people of unquestioned respectability.

Casual Friday

Thus they make themselves easy targets for righteousness and ridicule. Small wonder that many of them have given up, exhausted with the struggle. Casual Friday in offices was not just a concession that workers could wear weekend clothes to work on Fridays. It was a surrender by which employers agreed to accept the fiction denying that clothing has any symbolic content. The deal was: Just do the work, and you can dress as you like.

Even this was a fiction, as the occasional rebel was able to prove by managing to go below the no-dress-code dress code by wearing undershirts or see-through blouses. Supervisors who at least thought the defeat relieved them of struggles over clothing found themselves asked to deal with employees who objected to the way their colleagues looked or smelled.

Whether dressing for leisure at work lessened attention and loyalty to the job by reminding people that they wished they were at leisure was impossible to determine, because it happened at a time that so many other concessions had been won—listening to the radio, playing computer games, and sending personal e-mail using work time and equipment—that it all coalesced into a business theory that the charade of not being at work actually increased efficiency. More dire predictions were not realized. The workers were not throwing off their shackles, just their jackets. It was a revolution against symbolism, after all, not a symbolic revolution against work.

Predicted benefits did not materialize, either. Life did not get easier for those who had been using the code to project and interpret information, and whatever the claims to the contrary, that means everybody. Just getting dressed in the morning was harder. People who had not previously paid attention to creating an impression with their clothes now had to, because under the new system, the suits that had always been a safe choice would make them look stuffy. Those who were in the habit of taking into account what others might think of the way they looked were newly confused. What do you wear to symbolize authority, competence, and relaxation all at once? Certainly not what they really wore on weekends at home. The only people who had expensive, authoritative-looking sports clothes were the top level of employees who had already been wearing them to weekend conferences and emergencies, to convey symbolically that their dedication came from knowing they were essential, not from having nothing else to do with their time.

Business now required three wardrobes for everyone: business clothes for Monday through Thursday, true leisure clothes for weekend, and faux leisure clothes for Friday. When Friday predictably expanded to cover the week, Monday to Thursday clothes might still be needed for dealing with clients and others outside the office, in case those people were operating under the old code.

Casual Friday was both a result and a harbinger of change. The danger of seeming uptight, bossy, and out of touch was creating a flurry of disclaimers and assurances. Hosts added the word "optional" to formal invitations ("ties optional," "black tie optional," "costumes optional," but not "casual optional"), as if their guests had not already been exercising their options no matter what instructions were sent out. Courts stopped requiring that jurors look as respectable as criminal defendants and lawyers. Opera companies hoping to attract the young advertised that blue jeans would be considered proper attire, as if their big donors were spoiling the atmosphere by dressing up.

Symbolic chaos

As the symbolic information system that Americans understood went down, we did not miraculously stop judging one another on superficial signs and pay attention only to innermost qualities. Many did not even become wary of acting on their assumptions in regard to appearances, although the possibility for error had soared. Explosive incidents continued to be set off by clothing symbolism, discounting the possibility that many formerly recognized symbols no longer corresponded to any identity or views but were being worn unintentionally or playfully. The particularly volatile areas in which these occurred were, naturally, religion, sex, and crime.

American tourists in Italy were attacked by religious toughs for wearing baseball caps in Catholic churches. Now, people who live in tourist destinations have always been annoyed by the very presence of tourists, however much their livelihood may depend upon them. Tourists crowd the most attractive areas, they have the effrontery to be on vacation while the locals have to work, and most of them are figuring that they can dress as they please because no one they know will see them. Nowadays, the locals may dress similarly for their own leisure, as American styles have modernized a great part of the world, but they grumble all the same. So do Americans who find that their hometown parking has been taken by out-of-towners so crude as to take trips for the purpose of admiring the locals' own habitat.

Here, however, was a clearly punishable offense. Obviously, these tourists intended to show their lack of respect for the church by failing to remove their hats according to well-known custom. In America, too, the custom of men removing their hats to show respect was just as widely practiced, and keeping one's hat on when conversing with a woman or when entering someone's house was rude, and keeping a hat on in church outstandingly rude. (Or failing to wear one in an orthodox synagogue: Symbols being arbitrary, the offense in this opposite gesture would be the same. For that matter, women entering

Catholic churches showed respect by covering, not uncovering, their heads, although that rule is now rarely observed.)

The trouble here was that the Americans involved were unaware of the custom, and therefore shocked at the reaction they provoked when they had had no intention of showing disrespect. Milder versions of such clashes occur every day in America, between those who know the hat symbolism and those who are caught by surprise because they grew up in the no-hat zone between the formal hat and the baseball cap and have never heard of the rules.

Culturally sensitive souls will point out that the tourists should have studied the local customs before they embarked, and done what was expected. In this case, that happens to be right, but the simplistic when-in-Rome mantra also leads to trouble when it, too, ignores the power of symbolism. It is a mistake to assume that customs may be different but are all equally benign, and that one can travel about trying them all. Some rituals, such as a man's removing his hat in church, are indications of respect only, and must be practiced by every man who enters a church wearing a hat; others, such as taking Communion, express so much more that an outsider who participated would be treating it with insulting nonchalance, as if this ceremony were no more significant than tasting the local food.

Symbolizing American values

At the same time, self-respecting Americans should be loyal to customs that come of deep American values. Those who think it charming to pay the obeisance of bows and curtsies to foreign potentates, especially ones from whom we won our independence, are going through the motions of disloyalty.

Benjamin Franklin's success at using appearance to symbolize emerging Americanism in Paris did not settle the matter for later American diplomats. Andrew Jackson, having had his own stylistic success at politics as the "common man," revived the idea when he abolished the court uniforms that American diplomats had continued to wear—white silk capes with gold embroidery, white silk knee breeches, gold shoe buckles and all—in favor of black coats.

The interim before the rest of the diplomatic world modernized was enlivened by stories of American ambassadors being mistaken for court servants. It would have been dangerous to venture abroad without a snappy comeback.

There was the one about the American minister who was asked by a lady at a reception they were both attending whether he was the butler. He replied, "No. Are you the chambermaid?"

Then there was the one about the ambassador at whom another guest, departing from a court gathering at the same time, barked, "Call me a cab!" The American came back with "Very well, sir, you are a cab." Ba-doom, ba-doom, and then he added, "At least you didn't ask me to call you a hansom cab."

Even yet, not every American institution understands that Americans abroad cannot afford to accommodate others by using symbolism to belie American principles. Only recently, and under pressure of a lawsuit, our air force rescinded a policy requiring its female personnel stationed in Saudi Arabia to wear the abaya (the long black covering and head scarf that is the local equivalent of the burqa, which was mandated in Afghanistan by the Taliban) when traveling off their air base. By going along with the locally observed custom, the American military was acquiescing, in symbolic language, in the belief that the mere sight of some of its own personnel, no matter how decently dressed by American standards, was a legitimate cause of offense.

This was no more a case of politeness requiring imitating the host country's restrictions than challenging it was an argument for total freedom from clothing restrictions, which military people do not have. What the pilot who brought the case recognized, in charging that it violated her own religious freedom and the freedom against discrimination that she was fighting to protect, was that symbolism is a language that officialdom cannot afford to use carelessly.

Symbolism gone wrong

The opposite error, that of claiming that clothing symbolism is even clearer and more binding than the spoken word, used to be put forth as a defense in rape cases. The argument would be made on behalf of the defendant that the victim had been wearing provocative clothing, and thus had symbolically agreed to make herself available to him even if she had attempted to deny this by using words and fists. As provocation is in the eye of the beholder, and the crime of rape is not mitigated by the allure of the victim, it is amazing that this was ever given a serious hearing, or needed to be rebutted by establishing that the clothing worn during the crime was within the conventional range of respectability. It was, however, a strange validation of the fact that people do interpret the symbolism of dress.

In the interests of elementary justice, we have agreed that clothing should not be allowed to contradict the testimony or impugn the character of its owner. Putting this to the test, fashion has been recycling more and more former vulgarities as legitimate styles, so that there is no longer a clear spectrum from the respectable to the daring to the sluttish. It seems tough on prostitutes that the items on which they depended to advertise their calling, such as microskirts, tight pants, fishnet stockings, see-through tops, necklines plunging to the navel, strategic cutouts, and visible underwear, have been co-opted by society matrons and little girls.

Other law breakers do not have to worry about identifying themselves as ready to commit a crime, so law-abiding teenaged boys who co-opt criminal styles only created social and legal problems for themselves. There was a dramatic such case in Washington, D. C., in 2000, when a fashion featuring pants worn below the underwear line, shirttails hanging below jacket hems, and untied shoelaces was in vogue among schoolboys.

Some of them found that when they got themselves all dressed up like that, empty taxicabs they were trying to hail went sailing right by them. Presumably up on their civics, they brought the matter to public attention as a case of racial profiling. (The boys were black, as were the drivers who ignored them and the taxicab commissioner who ruled on the case.) Washington has a history of taxi discrimination against black passengers, and the police have run checks that confirmed instances of drivers bypassing one passenger and stopping for a subsequent one when both prospects wore suits and carried briefcases, and the only obvious visible difference between them was their race.

It also has a history of drivers being murdered by thugs they picked up as passengers, and the drivers have been arguing the life-or-death necessity of guessing from a glance whether someone might be dangerous to pick up. Unlike race or other inherent characteristics, clothing choice is voluntary and can therefore reasonably be interpreted as a statement the wearer makes about himself, admittedly fallible but better than nothing for making a crude preliminary identification.

The commissioner ruled that avoiding ersatz thugs was not culpable as racial discrimination. The assumption that someone was a thug because he was black is abhorrent and, in this context, illegal, but the assumption that someone who had worked on getting himself up to look like a thug might actually be one did not seem unreasonable. Obviously, there should be no question of abrogating any citizen's rights for choosing to look sexy or scary. Patience only runs out when people who find it amusing to use symbols to lie about themselves—honest people who pose as sluts or thugs—get upset when they are believed.

Props

While the use of costuming is being denied, undercut, and practiced as much as ever, only with more confusion, the symbolism of props gets franker and more blatant. A question that is thought to reveal the complexities of an unknown individual, to the point where it is a pet probe used by people speculating about whether they should allow themselves to fall in love, is: "What kind of car do you drive?"

If there were one right answer to this that would impress everyone, we would have only one brand of car. Each type and each make of automobile is invested with such a mix of cultural associations that it would have to be matched to another's experience and taste. To one person, a red convertible symbolizes erotic adventure; to another, it symbolizes the middle-aged divorce.

*Status
symbols*

Still, there is a shared symbolic vocabulary. At any given time, Americans would probably agree on which car would be chosen by a ruthless young executive, a lawyer doing full-time child rearing, an academic who has just gotten tenure, a pampered child who has just gotten a sixteenth birthday present, or an aspiring country music singer. Pre-automotive Americans were no less adept at guessing what sort of carriage and horses would be kept by a country doctor, the young wife of a robber baron, a factory worker who was just made supervisor, or an opera star.

Depending less on family history and land ownership than more static societies, we place people by their choice of purchases, and we call it "taste." In judgment by possessions, cost is a factor, but not the overriding one that it may be assumed to be. A symbol that could be read so easily would not be pulling its symbolic weight. The same game used to be played with cigarette brands, when the cost was negligible. There is even a residual American sense of embarrassment about luxurious possessions—not that you would notice it. That blatant greed you may observe and that others are unkind enough to keep pointing out is merely people at an early stage of the universal process of laundering money to produce what is known as taste. It is a truism that you can tell a tycoon by the way he counts his pennies, and the rich are supposed to love a bargain even more than the poor.

*Money
and taste*

Our endorsement of social mobility gives us a special need for social markers at every stage of an individual's rise, the new owner producing them as proof, and others checking them out. As a result, the shopping forays of those overexcited by finally having large amounts of disposable income are widely exposed. Nevertheless, we know, from belief, experience, and example, that the generational process of acquiring money first and then aesthetic discernment can be accomplished in less than a single lifetime. Indeed, it must be. People are born with more or less aesthetic sense—artists rarely spring from old money, nurtured to genius by infant exposure to beautiful surroundings—but a consumer eye for good quality takes individual education. That rumor about its taking generations was started and perpetuated by heirs and heiresses.

World opinion was long stuck on an evaluation of American culture as being permanently at the first, brash stage of being happily dazzled by frippery. As our economy burgeoned past European countries', their compensatory rationalization was that this was at the expense of aesthetics. We could produce goods, and it had to be conceded that we were good at producing popular culture. High culture was said—and it was said in the same sort of unrefined terms that were used to declare that we were congenitally too crude ever to master subtle and refined manners—to remain beyond us. Only decades after the fact did the world began to notice that America had become an international center of excellence in the creation and exhibition of music, dance, art, and theater.

Before then, rich Americans would sweep through Europe acquiring the props of aristocracy—paintings, statuary, furniture, partial or entire houses to dismantle and rebuild in America—with a largesse that brought sneers from the sellers, who pronounced them materialistic as they pocketed their cash. That supposedly indiscriminate lavishness has now filled our museums and made them among the great depositories of art in the world.

At a less grand level, every age and every subset of society has its checklist of desirable props, subject to constant additions and subtractions with the individual's changing age and economic, social, and aesthetic level. In an academic circle that considers it not just vulgar but idiotic to buy jewels or expensive cars, vast sums may be spent on wines. People who decry the power of fashion to make its victims discard perfectly useful objects simply to own whatever is newest may be constantly abandoning their cellular telephones, personal organizers, and laptops in favor of the newest designs.

*Shopping
as
sport*

The American zest for shopping has never quite yielded to the notion that refined people only buy expensive things to have investments for the long run, for the sake of the children, or to help the economy. Acquisitiveness is not what makes Americans unique in this respect. Aside from having a fortunate number of people who have the money with which to indulge this, what is peculiarly American is the frank way in which possessions are acknowledged to be theatrical props to augment whatever drama in which the individual fancies himself.

There is a cheerful willingness to use fakes when these are handiest. It is almost a point of snobbery with the rich to point out that a certain string of pearls or a rickety cabinet they own is a clever fake. Money is no excuse for lacking the discernment to know whether a bargain will produce the desired effect.

There is more of a spirit of anticipation than of wrenching regret when it is time to clear the stage for the next show. Americans are no less sentimental than others, but rarely have the experience of having been in one place long enough to think of it as the only possible home. The process of change in itself becomes an attraction, so an interest in treasures from the past or a devotion to fixing up one's dwelling does not preclude getting things just right and then chucking it all and starting again with a different approach. That an individual's "collection" of art or antiques goes on the market is no longer an indication that the collector is dead and his heirs are turning his treasures into cash. It may be the collector himself who is selling the collection to finance collecting something else.

Finally, there is a peculiar devotion to useful things that will never be used but are saved as "good," meaning that they are deliberately acquired to be used only as props. Any bridal list will confirm this. Silver flatware, china dishes, and crystal glasses are eagerly sought by people who are not seriously thinking about giving dinner parties, who already consider these items too good for their own everyday use, and who will decide, each time they do have friends in for pot luck, that there are now perfectly nice disposable dishes which are so much easier to deal with after a party when it's too much trouble to load the dishwasher, much less to give delicate items the hand care they require.

When props are expensive, they are called status symbols, but the most powerful totem among them costs very little. This is the guest towel, the great prop of the powder room. Presuming that it is not intended to be used as a towel, the guest refrains from touching it, knowing that the host may take such defilement as an unwarranted liberty. Sometimes the mere risk of its being used will prompt the host to provide an inferior means of wiping the hands, such as paper towels or a bath towel. More usually, both guest and host have been trained to think of a small towel as strictly there to serve as a prop.

Sets

Even Americans of modest means have had a tradition of keeping an unused room as a carefully decorated stage set for a play that is rarely, perhaps never, performed. Depending on the circumstances of immigration, the family may have started its American life in a sparse shelter in the wilderness or a corner of a jammed tenement, but there was a shared ideal: to possess an unpopulated parlor, the splendor of which one could finally enjoy when laid out in one's coffin.

The front parlor was the pride of the American house and its proof of gentility. It was here that the props were showcased, and it proved that there was living space to spare. More importantly, it implied that important occasions were expected: weddings, funerals, and visits from distinguished people. To keep it unviolated, it was necessary to have an inferior back parlor for the use of family and ordinary visitors.

The parlor expands

This tradition has not only continued but expanded. In what is considered a comfortably appointed modern house, the front parlor, renamed the living room or the drawing room, depending on the value of the house, is even more pristine, now that weddings and funerals have been moved off the premises and important visitors are entertained at restaurants. There may be more than one back parlor: the recreation room, which became the den, which became the family room, and the TV room, which became the computer room and then the media center. Now there is a second grand, unused room, as the function of the dining room has been taken over by an enlarged kitchen, and the vestigial dining room can serve as another showcase for props.

The back parlor turned media center may also be rising to the status of the front parlor, if it is not eliminated entirely, because its function keeps being cut back. Communal space was never as much a sign of shared emotion as of shared equipment.

In its earliest manifestation, it was, indeed, associated with family warmth and the rosy glow of the hearth, because the hearth was the family's only heating system. By default, it served as the entertainment center, as the family and visitors were one another's only source of animated amusement. Entertainment in the way of storytelling, reading aloud, or playing parlor games required an audience, and successive forms required gathering around the family's only piano, radio, television set, VCR, or high-definition theater-sized screen.

One by one, these items have multiplied in the household and migrated to individual rooms, leaving even more communal space unused. A different source of fellowship is available to each, individually, through the Internet. As a symbolic confirmation of the parlor mentality, white rugs have become popular, along with warnings that they are not to be violated by shoes.

Until recently, the empty stage was a tradition that the rich, like the poor, could not afford to follow. Unlike the poor, they had space, but they also had a tradition of hospitality that kept it filled. Visits were long, house parties were frequent, and entertaining in commercial establishments was considered only grudgingly gracious long after it even became feasible.

Just when technology and social customs might have made it possible for the rich to forgo the upkeep of large houses, they went in for the use of unused space in a spectacular way. At upper-income levels, and among the truly rich, there will be an entire downstairs spread of rooms that hardly ever feel a footstep, while the inhabitants have their quarters above. The set is intended not for them but for the occasional audience provided by a business gathering, a house tour, or a charity party.

Modern architects guessed wrong, with their flowing open spaces. It has always been the number of parlors that counts, along with a suggestion that the owners are living a more traditional, supposedly graceful life than they are. That is why the typical new community is a version of Colonial, Federal, Tudor, Georgian, plantation, neoclassic, Italianate, Victorian, or even prefabricated Sears, Roebuck or ranch style, rather than a style, no matter how beautiful, that proclaims that contemporary life is being lived inside.

It is not that people want to exchange their lives for past ways, even past ways as glamorized by distance and ignorance. They just don't want to come home from their jobs as office workers or salespeople or factory workers to places that look like offices, stores, or factories. Even the hint of entering a stage set for another life is more imaginatively theatrical.

Out front and backstage

Americans are not, however, passively waiting for the play to begin. The stage set at home is merely a backstage area attached to a small and rarely used experimental theater compared to the vast multiplex theater available.

Restaurants have become theaters, with themes and characters and amusing flourishes, and the more successful ones keep up a semblance of auditioning their clients. Houses of worship have become theaters, with performances, lectures, and dramas of personal, rather than religious, falls and redemptions. Shops have become theaters, transforming their backstage services into dramas about designers.

As a theatrical people, we have always had an affinity for the backstage life. The people who are essential to putting on a show—those who design costumes or sets, who know how to dramatize a meal or select just the right prop—are admired. More than that, they have been uplifted to the category of artists and brought onto the stage. Indeed, they create the stages. If it were not for events given for designers and stores—their shows, their openings, the parties they sponsor—there would be few venues in which to display the upper-line products they sell us.

As a result, the demarcation between backstage and onstage is gone. Once it was a byword of crudeness to say that a woman went out in public wearing curlers or that a man touched up his hair. Now hairdressing establishments have picture windows on fashionable streets where their clients can have their hair cut or dyed in full public view. Commuters who might have hidden to sneak a breath mint now brush and floss their teeth on public buses and subways.

This can be interpreted as a breakdown in manners, but it can also be looked at as the extension of American frankness, unpretentiousness, and theatrical camaraderie. Or all of that.

Chapter 9

Publicity and Marketing

Pitching Your Persona

"Nothing national is exhibited for money, and no public officer is a showman."
In America?

Never mind what is going on now, here and elsewhere. To anyone who has a passing acquaintance with the genre of foreign commentary on American manners throughout our history, this observation, made by Charles Dickens in his *American Notes*, is startling.

The bash-America industry

By that time, a literary industry had already sprung up to declare exactly the opposite: that Americans were brash and materialistic. Made greedy by Mrs. Trollope's success, Victorian English tourists hit the shores, eavesdropping on strangers on steamships and quizzing chance acquaintances in boarding houses to provide material for volume after sardonic volume announcing that Americans cared nothing about the niceties but only about money.

There was no shortage of illustrative anecdotes to prove these contentions. All visitors had to do to provoke Americans into brash declarations of their own superiority was to treat one of them as an inferior. Visitors were remarkably willing to do this, following the time-honored customs of their own countries where they were able to insult with impunity those they could classify as their inferiors.

There is an obligatory scene in these travel books featuring a member of what the writer is pleased to call the lower classes, typically a servant or a farmer, who announces, with a flounce, "I'm just as good as anyone else." This is considered to be a comic gem, especially if enhanced through imitating the speaker's accent. Another staple is the reception the writer encounters when pointing out how American society compares unfavorably to his own and how much it would be improved by modifying or dropping all that nonsense about equality. In these instances, the visitor registers his astonishment at the prickliness of the citizens when their loyalty to their own nation and its principles is challenged.

Finding evidence of American materialism was even easier. There was little attempt here to disguise the interest people have in earning and spending money. To be sure, religious exhortations and injunctions against particular forms of luxury poured from the pulpits, but they were incidental to the main message of building and sustaining economically viable com-munities. Accordingly, ambition to make a fortune and pride in earning a living were laudable, rather than greedy, and taking pleasure in one's purchasing power was not thought to be an unreasonable response to financial success. The notion never really caught on in America that the exchange of labor for money and money for goods was too vulgar to mention.

Elsewhere, the poor had little to mention, even in the way of hopes, and the upper classes bolstered the propaganda that their ranks were impenetrable with a taboo against acknowledging the relationship between wealth and power. Losing money could not deprive an upper-class person of his status, they claimed (although it eventually did), and amassing money would not gain anyone else entry (although it eventually did). The frank enterprise of Americans (before many of them, too, acquired enough status to worry about risking it with the vicissitudes of their fortunes) forced the world to conclude that Americans simply lacked the subtlety to understand the gracefulness of inheriting money and the patina of inherited possessions. That must be why they kept exerting themselves to earn money and spend it on fresh goods—or, outrageously, on the heirlooms of finer people in straitened circumstances.

Charles Dickens also cited the "national love of trade" and the annoying frequency with which Americans asserted "their self-respect and their equality," and acknowledged in a letter that he could not live in America "on any consideration . . . I think it impossible, utterly impossible, for any Englishman to live here and be happy"; but he had contrary evidence to report. Many of those conceited citizens took a serious interest in justice and social reform, he discovered, and the pursuit of money was not so all-encompassing as to preclude the pursuit of culture, even among the humbly placed.

Contradictory discoveries

His travelogue, based on his 1842 speaking tour, went beyond the usual tourist, or celebrity-tourist, denunciation of hotels, newspapers, and tobacco-spitting to explore "the public institutions and charities" of

Boston, including courthouse, prison, factory, insane asylum, poorhouse, juvenile delinquent center, and university. It was in this context that he noticed that the show business potential of such attractions as trials was not being exploited for money, directly or indirectly via bribery, because "in every Public Institution, the right of the people to attend, and to have an interest in the proceedings, is most fully and distinctly recognized." (He also noted that "in all the public establishments of America, utmost courtesy prevails"—although that was before he got to Washington and observed "the many legislators of coarse threats; of words and blows, such as coalheavers deal upon each other when they forget their breeding" who served as Members of Congress.)

In regard to private citizens, commonplace evidence that money was not all-powerful came with his discovery that—at that time—Americans disdained tips as being beneath their dignity. Working people in China still do, to the bafflement of a visiting American president whose munificence was indignantly rejected. "The common men render you assistance in the streets, and would revolt from the offer of a piece of money," Charles Dickens reported in a letter.

He found deeper evidence that working people had something on their minds besides money—a revelation that he promised would amaze his English readers—when observing the leisure-time pursuits of the female factory workers of Lowell, Massachusetts:

Firstly, there is a joint-stock piano in a great many of the boarding-houses. Secondly, nearly all these young ladies subscribe to circulating libraries. Thirdly, they have got up among themselves a periodical called THE LOWELL OFFERING, "a repository of original articles, written exclusively by females actively employed in the mills,"—which is duly printed, published, and sold; and whereof I brought away from Lowell four hundred good solid pages, which I have read from beginning to end.

The large class of [English] readers, startled by these facts, will exclaim, with one voice, "How very preposterous!" On my deferentially inquiring why, they will answer, "These things are above their station." In reply to that objection, I would beg to ask what their station is.

It is their station to work. And they do work. They labor in these mills, upon an average, twelve hours a day, which is unquestionably work, and pretty tight work too. Perhaps it is above their station to indulge in such amusements on any terms. Are we quite sure that we in England have not formed our ideas of the "station" of working-people from accustoming ourselves to the contemplation of that class as they are, and not as they might be? I think that, if we examine our own feelings, we shall find that the pianos, and the circulating libraries, and even the Lowell Offering, startle us by their novelty, and not by their bearing upon any abstract question of right or wrong.

Forty years later, Oscar Wilde made a similar discovery on his lecture tour. In a newspaper interview, he gave the example of a railroad repair worker who "quoted Pope to me, analyzed his method, discussed my positions with me, understood me, and where he doubted, gave his reasons in homely phrases, but unmistakably and clearly. He took an interest in the best of life, was keen, kindly, receptive and pugnacious in need, withal—

altogether a charming fellow. Now in England, in men of his class, such a conversation would be simply impossible. Here I learn that a man is fairly representative of a myriad."

Mrs. Trollope's legacy

These discoveries on the part of British writers who were both eminent and popular at the time of their respective reports, and each of whom was, in his own way, keenly skilled in social criticism, made not a smidgeon of difference in the reputation of the American character. It was the appraisal by Fanny Trollope, who went on to produce formulaic novels and travel books that are now forgotten, that stuck.

Nor has this been significantly altered by anything that has been observed since. By now, Americans are so accustomed to being thought uncultured, greedy boors that many who are told by foreigners that they don't "seem American," respond by saying "thank you" rather than offering the otherwise universal response to being told that one has managed to escape being as dreadful as one's countrymen. No doubt that restraint is a tribute to American good manners, which can hardly now be characterized as prickly in this regard. One might rather question the manners of the critics, beginning with their idea that the way to evaluate a culture's behavior is to prod its citizens with direct personal and national insults.

Foreign interpretations of the American responses are also open to question. It is not personal vainglory alone that prompts unlikely individuals to claim social parity when the most basic national policy has promised them equality, even though absolute equality is ultimately unachievable. Where there is no objective social structure, how one is treated is of utmost importance in determining one's dignity. Yet how a society feels about wealth cannot be easily read by whether or not it has a convention of frankness or reticence in speaking of it. The delicacy of muting any enthusiasm for acquiring money and goods may be charming (and is more easily pulled off if one already has plenty of both), but it is not an indication of indifference to gain, any more than Victorian silence about sex sprang from a lack of interest in that activity.

Furthermore, the two traits identified as typically American are not infrequently contradictory. Laments over the highhandedness of menials, who are quick to quit when treated as such, fail to acknowledge that this act is proof of the triumph of pride over greed.

So how is one to account for that awful reputation? Transference, perhaps?

When Charles Dickens ran into other Englishmen, he reported:

> ... of all grades and kinds of men that jostle one in the public conveyances of the States, these are often the most intolerable and most insufferable companions. United to every disagreeable characteristic that the worst kind of American travellers possess, these countrymen of ours display an amount of insolent conceit and cool assumption of superiority, quite monstrous to behold. In the coarse familiarity of their approach, and the effrontery of their inquisitiveness (which they are in great haste to assert, as if they panted to revenge themselves upon the decent old restraints of home), they surpass any native specimens that came within my range of observation: and I often grew so patriotic when I saw and

heard them, that I would cheerfully have submitted to a reasonable fine, if I could have given any other country in the whole world, the honour of claiming them for its children.

As English superiority toward American manners has still not let up, it would be amusing to think that our acerbic critics have been mistakenly targeting their own roaming soccer fans and the marauders who preceded them. There is, however, too much past and present evidence of Americans' exceeding the limits of even American tolerance for self-assertion and greed to dismiss the charges.

Growing greed

For example, haughtiness about accepting tips is as foreign a concept in America now as if it had never existed here. What? Pass up a chance to pick up some change?

On the contrary, schemes are rampant for increasing the opportunities and amounts. Businesses where tips are expected make the size of their expectations clear to their customers by issuing "guidelines" with the excuse of anticipating and relieving the customers' anxiety. Service people put out containers seeded with generous sample tips, even in situations, such as catered parties in private premises, where they are paid to act as the staff of the host, who also tips them. Door-to-door workers provide self-addressed envelopes to encourage Christmas tips. People who are in positions still defined as being too dignified to accept tips—typically, the proprietors of restaurants and hairdressing establishments—are at pains to reassure customers that they observe no such silly delicacy, and that crossing their palms would not hurt their feelings in the least.

The concept has leaped beyond the bounds of business into

social life, where demands for handouts have transformed invitations and announcements into frank solicitations. These may be framed as shopping lists, through gift registry selections mailed to guests or posted on Web sites, or as outright instructions for contributing money to a fund (typically for a bridal couple's mortgage, a baby's bank account, a student's tuition, a married couple's anniversary trip). As people find themselves writing checks to mark weddings, births, graduations, anniversaries, and deaths, the response to receiving social news is less "How nice" than "How much?"

*Signs
of
selfishness*

In everyday life, social equality has been taking the form of everyone's claiming first place and preparing to fight it out. Objective standards for establishing order among equals, such as who arrived first, who is older, or who is in greater need no longer command general acquiescence, as people shove, wheedle, exaggerate, bribe, or intimidate to obtain an advantage for themselves.

We have seen the concept of equality misused to damage such basic American concepts as sportsmanship and meritocracy. These are accomplished from opposite premises: the taunting of losers in sports presumes that success justifies ruffling the feelings of others, while the taunting of those who triumph in academics as being "elitist" presumes that ruffling the feelings of others does not justify success.

If the contradiction does not appear to bother anyone, Americans are increasingly bothered by the cantankerous atmosphere arising from the materialism and brashness that we detect among ourselves. Not bothered enough to stop practicing it, of course, but bothered enough to be hurt that this belief could be used to characterize people who, whatever else was said about them, take pride in thinking of themselves as both generous and fair.

The usual explanations are offered—that people have grown selfish and that the times are stressful. The historically minded offer examples of bad behavior from the past to show that nothing has changed, and observers of the present offer examples of good behavior to show that nothing has changed. Certainly, brashness and materialism have always been present in human character, without contaminating all of humanity or particularly afflicting Americans. Still, the general feeling persists that there is something driving modern American behavior in the directions identified by its critics. Only the seriously disgruntled are satisfied to ascribe it to unprecedented moral disintegration.

A theatrical analysis

A less damning explanation can be found in the society-as-show-business model. The rewards of stardom have become enormous, the qualifications more varied, and the opportunities more numerous. Celebrityhood is now itself an American career, perhaps *the* American career, to which every other career should ideally lead. The prototype for this is moviestardom, but the realization of it has spread far beyond the entertainment industry.

Money and respect barely describe the remuneration of being an American celebrity. Auxiliary incomes could include vast fees for lecturing, serving on boards of directors, retailing one's life story, and endorsing commercial products. Free services and goods, even to the clothes on one's back, may be offered. Exhortations to support one's chosen charity or politician can make it possible to command the use of other people's money. Respect comes not only in the form of the much-cited good-table-at-a-restaurant but in opportunities to air one's views on subjects other than one's own field of expertise. Such sober fora as editorial page commentary and congressional testimony are as welcoming to celebrities as television shows and magazine interviews. The formal congratulatory system of awards, testimonials, retrospectives, and grants, complete with dinners, statuettes, checks, certificates, and other souvenirs, rotates them as recipients, judges, and awarders.

Naturally, interest in and knowledge about the mechanics of achieving celebrityhood have increased accordingly, and its techniques are commonly incorporated into the lives of aspirants—whose number is approaching that of the population. Without disrespect to the great Schwab's Drugstore legend, it is not producing results commensurate with the demand. Combining the hopes it offers with the spurt of enterprise delineated in the Coca-Cola legend is thought to increase an individual's odds. The numbers are still bad, but there is a clearly defined career path for those who can get themselves to the starting point.

The qualifications

It is no longer necessary to be an actor (or a photogenic high school girl) to aspire to celebrityhood. Any career or accident has the potential. Performers and politicians predominate among the successful, by the very fact that they must already have captured enough notice to sustain being in such a profession, but one may also begin as a lawyer, an academic, a business executive, a writer, a member of the clergy, or a scientist, or hold almost any other job that happens to bring one into the spotlight or can be maneuvered into doing so.

In such areas, the actual qualifications need not be superior. Excellence at the celebrity level is presumed by those not in the field, and disparagement from those who are is put down to envy of success. In other positions that might equally well lead to celebrityhood, excellence is not an issue; such callings as grand-scale embezzler, hostage, kidnapper, or leading lady in a sex scandal can serve to hoist one into a career more like that of the respectable celebrity than of one's former colleagues, just as diplomats' or congressmen's lives more resemble one another's than those of their fellow citizens back home.

Self-promotion

This is not a career in which virtue has any particular bearing. If anything, bad behavior is supposed to have the edge, although the attention-getting ability of the shocking may have been so overused by now as to have lost its value. The key skills needed are the ability to sustain public interest beyond that first notice, and the acumen to turn this into a paying career. To that end, Americans working toward celebrityhood become their own business managers and publicity agents. It is the services offered in those professions—maximizing the client's income and public exposure—that have been deemed vulgar when openly applied to private life.

Yet the concept of celebritydom has done away with private life and given that name to something that is conducted in public. The basic deal is that the person becomes a character in the national theogony, providing occasional dramatic adventures involving romance, parenthood, crime, addiction, or life-threatening illness, while at the same time offering a running commentary on all this, bolstered by insights and details garnered from the mundane part of the celebrity's life.

Done successfully, this is a two-character play co-starring the celebrity's "image" and the celebrity's life as a "real person," and keeping the audience on the alert to discover and reconcile apparent contradictions between the two. The image is glamorous, while the real person makes a show of being ordinary. The image acts graciously (or dramatically ungraciously) weary of attention, while the real person confesses his secrets to the public, the chief such secret being that he is "a very private person."

The more a celebrity has been photographed, the greater is the demand to see that person "in person"; the more a celebrity has repeated ideas and stories on television, the more eager audiences are to hear the real person say the same thing "live"; the more a celebrity's life has been open to view, the more people puzzle over what he is "really like."

To this end, there are no inhibitions on curiosity, nothing that is considered too personal or too insignificant. Typical questions posed on behalf of the public, and therefore presumably corresponding to areas of public curiosity, are: What do you eat? How do you exercise? What's it like to make love to your lover? Do you worry about your diet? How do you explain your jail time to your children? Where do you buy your clothes? How much plastic surgery have you had? Who cuts your hair? What kind of underwear do you wear? How do you furnish your house? Do you sleep naked? Are you attached to any pets? Are you upset that your spouse earns more money than you do? Where do you go on vacation? and so on.

The truly successful celebrity is one who has the acting ability to project "naturalness" under such scrutiny, to appear "relaxed" and to win the highest praise of seeming "very human." It is by such tests that our political contests are decided.

Eventually, people who live under this attention find it does not always result in undiluted admiration, and that it can be decidedly inconvenient. Disillusionment sets in when the discovery is made that it is impossible to participate selectively. Politicians, especially, who welcome examination of their domestic lives as a form of character reference are outraged when the connection they declared is extended into an examination of their extramarital behavior.

It does not seem to suggest to them, however, that instead of appealing to the public as personalities, complete with their admiring spouses and pets, they might put themselves forward simply as advocates for views that might match the voters' own. As everyone knows, this would be boring theater. Oddly, the only challenge to the truism that the public can never get enough of personalities and gossip, preferably of the salacious variety, came when this appetite was bountifully fed. Surfeited with gossip about former President William Clinton's extramarital affairs, an ungrateful public astonished political theorists by begging for less, not more.

Self-protection

Yet those who have not experienced public exposure do not seem to be able to credit the desire for privacy. A celebrity who tires of the public gaze is considered to be either a mentally unstable "recluse" or a canny type hoping to increase interest through mystery. Normal people are thought to welcome the attention for its own sake as well as for its contribution to the other rewards of celebrityhood. As a result, the boundaries of private life have been knocked over by the very people they were set up to protect.

Considering how hard-won privacy has been over the centuries, it is strange that living in public view should now be considered desirable. Government and religion, not to mention nosy neighbors, have traditionally taken a deep interest in how people conduct the most intimate aspects of their lives. American legal history and the evolution of American etiquette reflect years of desperate struggle to be free of public judgment of the citizens' love lives, their family conflicts, their living arrangements, their political opinions, their religious beliefs, their wardrobes, their vocabularies, their spending habits—the very things that people are now eager to discuss and display on television.

The authority to bludgeon people into revealing such things, which was stripped from governmental and religious institutions, has returned under the aegis of mental health. Those who may be reticent about disclosing their living arrangements and their very thoughts and feelings to the now-casual probes of acquaintances, colleagues, and strangers are diagnosed by the same people they hardly know as emotionally unhealthy. From social bullying to job-mandated activities, the pressure for self-revelation can be intense. In the theatrical context the coyness of resisting publicity is condemned as counterproductive.

The rise and fall of privacy

Time was when the poor were all crowded in together, and the rich lived under the gaze of their not-always-benign subordinates and dependents. Technological and logistical problems—meaning poor and unreliable lighting, no bathrooms, no central heating—forced people to live in clumps. Beds were shared for the least erotic of reasons—there were fewer beds than people.

Yet space was used whenever possible to separate the backstage areas where mundane upkeep, including household work and personal care, was performed. A premium was put on protective devices, such as back staircases, where people could come and go undetected by those in the front rooms.

Poverty and romance are now the only excuses for shared bedrooms, much less beds, and proliferating bathrooms are a high priority. Yet the idea that personal renovations should be performed out of public sight has been abandoned. It is not only the press of time that has encouraged people to brush their teeth on city buses and shave or apply makeup in cars while clearly visible to others on the road. Once-secret procedures such as abortions and hair transplants are openly admitted. There is a sort of glorying in the frankness. Grown-out dyeing—hair purposely left one color in its length and another at the roots—became fashionable. Plastic surgery is admitted to, even announced, by the patient, and seems on the verge of having its recovery stages brought into the open.

This amounts to a daily personal demonstration of the burgeoning interest we have in the behind-the-scenes mechanics of all kinds of performances. Partly in reaction to the suspicion of being manipulated, the public has become more engrossed with explanations of how the world contrives to present itself than with the surface picture presumed to be manipulated for its benefit. In the style of movies about moviemaking and books about writing books (and the inevitable speech that begins "When I was wondering what I was going to say today"), we want our leaders to explain to us how they manipulate us. We don't hold it against them, because we are in the business our-selves, and can admire those who do it well.

To professionals, backstage is more interesting than what is happening onstage. Looked at another way, there is no back-stage area any longer. The concept that there is a difference between readying oneself for public view and being in the pub-lic view is disappearing, and the concept of certain aspects of human life being unfit to be displayed may soon follow.

This change has been welcomed as affording relief from the fear of being caught unprepared in public, the presumption being that nudists must be free of that classic nightmare about finding oneself naked in public. There is a great boon, in that the habit of disclosure has sabotaged the social shock and per-sonal guilt previously associated with common failings.

It is less of a boon to society that it seems to be working on sabotaging the social shock and personal guilt associated with uncommon failings as well. The more one hears of crime, the less deviant it appears. What remains scandalous is a refusal to package being caught into the accepted expiation of confession, therapy, and renewal, which experts can accomplish with amaz-ing skill. Pairing self-condemnation with positive spin is surely one of the great triumphs of the public relations field, and rejecting the opportunity to use this amounts to a betrayal of the business of self-promotion.

At the same time, never being offstage can be wearing, and that is why people went to great lengths to establish places of refuge from the judgment of the world. The Victorian idealiza-tion of the home, in which members were protected not only from outside view but by a code of loyalty within the house-hold, provided a form of relief that has become elusive.

Symbolically closing the door on the outside world has been suspect since the invention of the telephone. Before that, the fiction of "not being at home" to callers was respected, but the telephone was permitted to barge in at any time. When the answering machine finally came along to challenge the idea that no one has the right to remain beyond reach, it was met with enormous hostility. "Screening calls" was commonly denounced on egalitarian grounds that anyone who dialed ought to be equally welcomed, as if it were snobbish to decide whom one wanted to chat with in one's own home, and when one might be available. Finally, the answering machine became acceptable, but then along came a succession of other devices—the pager, the fax machine, e-mail, the cellular telephone—again making it seem antisocial to place oneself out of touch from the world.

Broadcasting from within has also intensified. The destruction of the code by which family members did not speak ill of one another has exposed hidden worlds of crime and cruelty, but it has also left the innocent vulnerable to spite and ridicule from privileged eyewitnesses. Home no longer being a reliably safe haven from the vicissitudes of work, its personal functions may be parceled out to strangers and hired professionals. Confidences offered to airplane seatmates or cyberspace addresses may seem safer than those uttered to family; advice may seem more objective from someone trained in general principles rather than someone with only a lifelong knowledge of the person. The professionalization of personal care is what housewives predicted when, insulted at being undervalued, they announced that if not for them, their families would have to pay counselors, nutritionists, cooks, cleaning services, car services, per-

sonal shoppers, therapists, personal trainers, and so on. Now
they do, and hire life style managers besides.

Even more dire consequences have resulted from applying
sensible business techniques to the private realm, where the
objectives are not efficiency and profitability but community
and compassion. Circulating job descriptions to recruit lovers,
holding performance evaluations to determine whether marriage partners should be replaced and to inform children how
they are holding up against the competition, and hiring outside
experts to provide such personal services as emotional support,
advice giving, and nagging have not produced the happy results
promised, although they may have succeeded in making the
workplace seem cozy by comparison. With everyone at work,
the playboy has no one with whom to play and the society lady
no one with whom to socialize, so, they, too, have turned businesslike. Thus we have such innovations as the no-frills seduction, from which the candy, flowers, diamonds, and sweet talk
have been trimmed and the time reduced to its minimum, and
the pay-as-you go party, where what is requested is not just the
pleasure of a guest's company but his contribution of food, cash,
or goods.

It is not only the abdication of women that created this situation but the conception of the home as business management
office for career building. The job of analyzing all expenditures
to maximize profit and cut unprofitable activity—to be business
manager to the star—must be performed for the aspiring star by
himself.

This is the thinking that has people figuring how much time
to invest sizing up a romantic prospect, and how to combine

charitable donations with public exposure. It has given rise to the astonishing belief that a formula exists in the annals of etiquette that requires wedding guests to bring presents equal in value to the cost of their entertainment at the reception, and that a person who directs others to bring cooked food to his house or to pay their own way in a restaurant at his initiative is dispensing hospitality.

Marketing private life

Most of all, it has ignited the notion that personal life can be packaged and sold in the form of product endorsements and sponsored events, even by the unknown. From the "product party," where the salesperson uses personal ties to embarrass guests into being customers, to the "opportunity" a bridal couple may present to a business to provide free services in return for being touted to their demographically appealing wedding guests, business schemes are popping up everywhere. Hardly anyone is left who would question the ethics or taste of accepting a fee in return for selling one's name and likeness for commercial use. The argument would be made that everybody involved gains by these activities—businesses get effective advertising, individuals get public exposure as well as fees, and the public is not fooled because the scheme is done out in the open. Cultural institutions, schools, and "worthy causes" make the eloquent argument that this is the only method by which they are able to exist.

Brash and materialistic beyond the wildest accusations of young America's critics, all this springs from basic American virtues: frankness about money, personal ambition, willingness to work, ingenuity in combining entertainment with profit, and the rejection of false coyness about how the world works.

To a thorough American, and increasingly to the American-influenced world, these methods are surely preferable to the glorification of indolence and the pretense of despising money. As with many American problems, there is no ill intent, but good ideas have taken an exaggerated turn.

It can no longer be said that nothing national is exhibited for money, and no public officer is a showman. Nearly everything national, or private, is offered for exhibit for money, and not only is every public officer a showman but every private citizen seems to aspire to be one.

Yet there are signs of a possible reaction. The old privacy rules having been forgotten or condemned as old-fashioned, people are hesitatingly beginning to speak up against what they presume that etiquette requires or permits—responding to nosy questions, buying merchandise they don't want from their acquaintances or, worse, their acquaintances' children, meeting payments sent as social announcements, and being force-fed other people's intimacies. This time around, it might be Americans who are growing uneasy about the country's brashness and materialism.

Chapter 10

A Critique

To Achieve an Even More Nearly Perfect Etiquette

THE CRITICS AGREE: American manners are bad.

Even the criticized agree, which is a violation of theatrical tradition. Everyone in show business knows that the way to deal with bad reviews is to claim not to have read them and to point out that they were written by uninformed and uncreative people who failed to understand what is being attempted and are filled with envy (because they lack the talent to produce such a thing themselves) and bile (because their dinners do not agree with them, and neither do their spouses).

Competitive criticism

Across the north and west, big cities compete about which is our second rudest. New York is conceded to have a proud hold on the championship, so when Boston and Los Angeles claim to have the rudest drivers in the country, they are presuming that New York, with its taxi, truck, and "limo" drivers, in their permanent state of feisty gridlock, is not in the running.

Any city with a downtown parking garage also considers

itself a contender in the Rude Drivers' Division. Any in which merchants don't greet their customers by name and anticipate their orders feels ready for the Rude Clerks', Waiters', and Repairmen's Division. Density doesn't matter when it comes to the Rude Teenagers' Division, for which every town declares its eligibility—while the local teenagers take this as evidence of its pokiness, and fix their sights on more excitingly rude places.

Miami aside, southerners are latecomers to this competition, having so long anointed themselves winners of the competition for Most Polite. If that were not disorienting enough, their old challengers, New York and Boston as well as Philadelphia and San Francisco, now proclaim themselves bastions of rudeness. So do the midwestern cities that had been steadily doing well in the lower division of the Most Polite Contest—its less sophisticated Just Plain Nice Division. Visitors who remark on how nice everyone seems are less likely to produce civic pride than denials and counter-examples, although those, too, spring from pride.

It adds up to something being wrong pretty much everywhere. People feel that famous American openness has turned brusque or oily. Our easy accessibility to friendship has become a parody: Gestures of intimacy are much more pronounced and promiscuously distributed, but a commercial motive is lurking shamelessly nearby. Traditionally, Americans neither hugged strangers nor dunned their friends.

With an occasional truce for however long it takes to clean up after a natural or unnatural disaster, we have been living in a state of low-grade mutual suspicion, subject to sudden outbreaks of hostility. The yearning to reduce this strife to a more bearable level has made civility a major item in the national discourse. For the last few elections, politicians on all sides have been promising to bring it back, just as soon as they knocked off their rivals by whatever means it took.

That the problem is just "modern life," meaning a combination of work-related stress and family-produced trauma, is a thoughtless explanation, hopelessly offered. We have no reason to suppose that life was more relaxing before the technological and humanitarian advances we are otherwise so proud and relieved to have achieved, or that family relationships were warmer when there was less choice and little escape. If this were the case, however, it would still not excuse abandoning the quest to make the society more civil. That disease, poverty, and cruelty have always characterized human existence does not make us refrain from attempting to understand the causes of these ills and mitigate the results.

Foreign theories

The original foreign view was that America was populated by riffraff, and one could hardly expect refinement from a bunch of religious crazies, criminals, and savages. This is not constructive criticism. It may not be the obligation of the critic to supply the solution to the problem he is able to identify, but being of low birth is not something one can be expected to fix.

Until the American Revolution, that is. With a few strokes of the quill, we abolished the idea of low birth, high birth, or anything in between. Birth was just birth, and whether the baby would eventually rise to the heights or sink to the depths was yet to be determined.

The audacious declaration that there is no such thing as gentle birth goaded foreign gentility to pounce afresh. Now there is your problem right there, they would explain: that business about being equal. As soon as you let the lower orders get ideas about themselves, they are going to be insolent and disruptive.

Leaving aside the question of their own peasant uprisings (or tell-all books) against aristocratic arrogance, notice that we seemed to be going up in their estimation. That reference to the lower orders implied that there were at least some Americans whom they deemed to be of a higher order. This was a step up from earlier assessments. Americans had not produced a noble class, but it was producing a rich class that was becoming too attractive to dismiss.

The birth of the nation was also a rare period of American pride in regard to manners, occurring between the time when colonials felt their cultural inferiority to the Old World and the time when independent Americans felt their cultural inferiority to the Old World. Apart from the ranks of would-be aristocrats and whatever lackeys or slaves they could coerce or command, there was a burgeoning population of disparate immigrants in small towns and rural areas that was developing its own etiquette. Typically American manners were coming to be recognized, although not necessarily admired, as helpfulness in place of standoffishness, frankness in place of pretension, and pride in place of obsequiousness. Whether one found these qualities delightful and dignified or stifling and stuck-up was another matter.

Even so, the argument that equality ruins manners continued to be made nonstop, even into the modern era. As other countries adopted representative forms of government or were pressured to do so, it was no longer made with the bland confidence

Mrs. Trollope had in attempting to correct American political theory. The tone became either more subdued or more vicious.

Where majority rule has triumphed, her view survives in the disgruntled murmurings of the displaced (possibly augmented by the secret regrets of those who took their places and found the distinctions diminished) and the frustrations of everyone who is exhausted by the constant clash of opinions that our form of government produces. Hampered from targeting equality, those critics have revived and adapted the riffraff argument: It is no longer individuals whose faulty ancestry is deemed responsible but, in their harsh opinion, the whole country's. America is simply too young a country to be expected to know how to behave, it is still being said, long after it passed its two hundredth birthday and dozens of younger nations have declared their independence.

In countries where a distaste for equality is not inhibited by liberty, criticism of etiquette turned virulent, a harbinger of the violence with which political and social change would be resisted. Of all the crimes attributed to America by its serious detractors (as opposed to its carping friends), poor etiquette skills may be the hardest to explain as constituting an offense to societies half a world away, as economic or military power are interpreted as doing. Perhaps that point is overlooked in view of the fact that misbehavior, especially of the kind one considers decadent, is so much more engrossing to observe. Our reputation as being brashly materialistic seems impervious to change, while we give away money, produce artists and intellectuals, and educate the children of foreigners who can afford to send them to our schools.

Americans have been alternating theories about why Americans (other than each of ourselves) behave badly. When everyone is bored with one theory, we take up the other, until that, too, is given up and we go back to the discarded one. We have just undergone one of those switches.

The theory that dominated the second half of the twentieth century was that the problem was not a lack of etiquette but etiquette itself. When pinpointing etiquette as the problem, we sometimes tend to speak of a surplus of etiquette, but now and then we blame the very existence of etiquette. The case is made that it inhibits natural human behavior, which would have been fine on its own if allowed to proceed unimpeded.

We will never know if this is true, because there is no way of testing the wolf-boy theory of how people would behave toward one another if they burst into society from total isolation and had to improvise every aspect of their behavior. What we do know is that whenever the restraints of etiquette are loosened to the extent that people have an imperfect knowledge of the rules governing their own society or are encouraged to defy them, they begin to find one another unbearable.

When we approach that stage, we switch to the other theory. That one is that things used to "work," and would work again if only we went back in our history to the place where we took a wrong turn. The back-to-the-good-old-days proposal is as impossible to execute as the back-to-innocence one. Not only can we not go back into time, but we have no idea of where (or, rather, to when) we would go if we could. When did we— or any other people—get it right? Advocates will cite a period such as the 1950s or the Victorian Age or a favorite Heroic Age, all of which come enticingly packaged in historic and personal fantasy kits. The horrors of such a time that we have overcome, such as slavery and plagues, are omitted, as are the evil effects such things had on manners. People who believe life was better in the old days also have a way of casting themselves in the top positions, dreaming of being knights or their ladies, rather than the statistically more likely possibility of being these people's serfs.

Natural behavior and historic behavior, insofar as we can imagine either one, seem glamorous from a distance, but even the path between their existence and ours is obscured to us. The progress of civilization, whether from the simple, if not natural, to the complicated, or, alternatively, from the virtuous to the degenerate, is not that orderly. Anthropologists keep pointing out that rituals such as the etiquette of eating are often much more elaborate and strictly enforced among so-called primitive peoples than in our own highly advanced, snack-ridden society. Historians keep pointing out that the strictures of straitlaced societies of the past sprang up in reaction to loosely laced societies of the past. None of this dampens the fun in imagining that people were more charmingly or more laughably guileless in the past than we sophisticates.

Flawed as are these explanations of the state of our manners, with their naïve reasoning and unfeasible solutions, they have some use as social tools. The naturally good theory also produced the explanation that social ills (other than etiquette) are the cause of misbehavior, some focusing on slum crime and others on the corporate kind, so it has had the beneficial effect of bolstering society's interest in bettering the conditions of its citizens. The good-old-days theory, even if it does not correspond to reality, provides an inspiring standard of behavior at which to aim.

Forgotten virtues

Ricocheting between these accounts of our failings and distracted by sniping from the sidelines, we lose sight of the glory of American etiquette. If we ditch the delusions that we can return to some perfect historical past or, even more laughably, revert to a state of natural goodness, we can still take enough modest pride in our historical achievement and national character to provide hope for the future.

Equal respect for all human beings is not an etiquette premise in need of improvement. For America's founders to have examined the hierarchal systems that seemed inevitable to lord and peasant alike, and to ditch that idea to introduce a measure of simplicity into ceremony and fairness into daily life, was extraordinary.

Human behavior can certainly stand improvement, but that is why etiquette systems are promulgated. Left to their own devices, people put their own interests first and are disappointed and puzzled that others do not either enter their service or stay out of their way, those others being too selfish to surrender their own interests. This is as close as we can guess natural behavior to be. All of us try it upon birth, most of us find that it actually works for the first few weeks, and all of us are shocked that it never fully works again, not even on the most devoted of sleep-deprived parents.

To be sure, our etiquette system does not fully work, either. Scofflaws abound, polite people have lapses, and a complicated and changing world provides endless opportunities for mishaps and misunderstandings. That the only way to prevent other people from being offensive is to agree to accept limitations on oneself is difficult for any former infant to accept.

Surrender on that point does not require merely making the effort to memorize the rules and practice them. It leads to the burden of assessing countless situations and sifting through a complexity of rules to determine which is the correct one to apply. Conflicts between one's own interests and others' recur, but so do unselfish conflicts about how best to be kind to others.

If a colleague's child asks you to buy something you don't want because it benefits a charity, is it more polite to acquiesce so as not to rebuff the child and antagonize the parents, or to decline so as to discourage emotionally pressured solicitations and to use the money for what you consider to be a worthier cause?

Many situations have a moral element with demands that must be weighed against etiquette's moral demand of being respectful of others' legitimately made choices. Does truth telling require that you tell your son-in-law that he is lazy or your neighbor that her smoking is going to kill her? Does the likelihood of the person's reforming figure into this, and, if so, how great do the chances have to be? This leads to the unpleasant question of enforcement. If one person always spoils the party with his antics, is it rude to exclude him? Does one have to claim it is done to encourage him to reform, or is it enough to protect others from annoyance?

None of this constant weighing is easy on people who do want to be polite, the existence of whom domestic and foreign critics of American manners will not grant.

All the same, most Americans believe that we are a warm and generous people who have proven ourselves in both national and neighborly ways. Those who believe no such thing nevertheless believe strongly enough in American fair-mindedness that they cherish the hope that the greediness and warmongering they identify will cease once these attributes are forcibly called to Americans' attention.

Even our etiquette failings come out of our virtues. Friendliness carried too far produces nosiness. The desire to be helpful easily leads to invasions of privacy. Individualism unhampered by communal concerns becomes as burdensome to other individuals as is community spirit unhampered by respect for the individual. Compassion that offers fresh starts to transgressors has to stop short of endangering others and destroying the distinction between good and bad so as to make positive efforts meaningless.

Americans who condemn etiquette may mistakenly believe that it is etiquette itself that is unbalanced. Anyone who thinks politeness would require him to buy cookies he hates from a child he doesn't much like, anyone who feels that the only way to shut up nosy intruders is to blast them back, and anyone who feels inhibited by manners from banishing the obnoxious will conclude that etiquette renders people helpless. It is not well known that politeness is perfectly compatible with firmness, and ranks of the kindly disposed thin quickly when they think they are being played for suckers.

That manners must sometimes yield to morals, so that pointing, screaming, and grabbing someone is the right thing to do to prevent him from being run over, is easily understood. That morals must sometimes yield to manners, so that freelance harassing of adults about the choices they make is wrong, is not. Yet seeking balance between individual rights and community needs is as necessary—and as difficult—in our etiquette as in our law.

With the declaration of social, as well as legal, equality, the architects of America proclaimed a noble basis for its etiquette. They jump-started the implementation of the new etiquette by putting down pretensions to which they as its leaders might have been tempted, and by lifting the dignity of the masses.

Then they left it to future generations to develop.

Now more than ever

It is surely time to get back to work on this project. That Americans are unhappy with the state of American etiquette is surely enough reason to improve it, as we strive to improve other circumstances of our lives. Besides that, we owe it to our Founders not to let the fine work they did be wasted.

Perhaps we also owe it to the rest of the world, not just to make them sorry for being so snippy to us all these years, but because—dangerously characteristic as this desire is—we can set an example and provide overseas aid. During all those years that American etiquette inspired only criticism and rebellion and neglect, some of the conditions for which it was created have been showing up in other areas of the world. The problems we have yet to solve by coming to terms with a workable daily etiquette are popping up elsewhere, sometimes in a more volatile form.

Word has gotten around about equality, freedom, and moving on to improve one's living conditions, and it is not only on

America that people focus their dreams of a better life. A restless world has deposited immigrants around the globe, and the clashes associated with dual or multiple populations accompany them. Having been schooled in a different etiquette makes the transition even more difficult for newcomers than speaking a different language. When we refer to conflicting cultures, we do not mean exposure to different music and films, which are more likely nowadays to have international audiences, but ways of dressing, eating, ranking importance, offering compliments, taking offense, making friends, entertaining, courting, celebrating, and mourning, all of them rife with subtle distinctions and fraught with emotion.

That people want to assimilate to the culture of the country in which they choose to live is by no means the natural consequence of changing nationalities, as Americans once naively thought. That people can do so if they want and find full acceptance—that an immigrant can come to be truly English or Japanese, for example—is even less believed, and attempts have ended in such bitterness that this is thought to be a futile exercise in self-abasement. Many countries have elements of their citizenry that claim, or are viewed by others as having, identities unassociated with their legal or residential status.

Economic dreams have similarly spread. Where poverty was once thought to be as much of an inheritance as aristocracy, the concept of fairness is taking hold, sometimes very gradually, sometimes all in a rush. Public exposure has made it hard for the rich to hide their advantages and luxuries even if they have the self-control to attempt doing so, and viewed up close, their antics have a way of grating on the nerves of people with less disposable income. No one could still believe that those who lack the jobs and resources to have a stake in the economic system, or who occupy its lowest level, accept what used to be called their station; even the unsympathetic are aware that the poor consider themselves misused.

Despite America's commitment to perpetual change, which has us defining social progress as going only in the direction of improvement (as opposed to acknowledging the possibility that things could equally well be progressing toward a worse state), there are anguished Americans for whom the world is moving too fast. We tend to dismiss them as nuts, it being a given that they are just slow at recognizing the benefits of change, and will either understand eventually (and buy a cellular telephone themselves) or be marginalized (and at the mercy of their children to keep them functioning), or, now that we are increasingly familiar with violent resistance to progress, are so seriously nuts that they require emotional treatment rather than rational argument.

*Progress
so
far*

Examples of these conflicts have found their way into our courts, but we also have etiquette experience to offer. Sometimes we have been able to recognize that the main issue among the discontented is the question of dignity. People who feel culturally disoriented, unaccepted, cheated, looked down upon, or left behind are pursuing dignity, perhaps even more than justice.

Grudgingly and imperfectly, Americans have learned to concede that being what used to be called "one hundred percent American" is not incompatible with affiliations with religions other than Christianity, ties to countries of personal or family origin, and identification with international communities based on occupations, interests, or beliefs. Some have noticed that unlike in other countries, where the most characteristic people are those of the "oldest" families, the most characteristic dream-pursuing Americans are apt to be the newest ones.

Awkwardly and haltingly, Americans have been broken of the habit of casual, although not of serious, bigotry. Only the occasional public figure committing career suicide remembers the once popular pastimes of ethnic joking, belittling women, and taunting menials. People who remain unconvinced that these expressions are wrong nevertheless recognize that they are socially dangerous.

From a slow start in developing stylistic simplicity among its leadership, America has raced into a universal informality that cuts the obvious distinctions in private life between rich and poor. As the English language and American folksiness in the way of first names and embraces became the international standard for diplomacy and T-shirts and tennis shoes acquired an internationally recognized chic, social barriers were lowered.

For all that, none of the problems these changes addressed has been solved, and now we have new ones. Respect for cultural subgroups of the society and for foreign or specialized customs has vastly increased the number of ways the population can give and take insult. If all customs that exist anywhere in the world are recognized as prevailing wherever anyone who practices them happens to take them, no one can know them all and thus be safe from inadvertently causing offense. Possibilities for innocent misunderstandings have multiplied, while the amount of tolerance for such errors has evaporated.

As the old bigotry was condemned, new forms sprang up to take its place. We now have insider bigotry, in which members of a targeted group claim the privilege of aiming the old bigotry at one another; majority bigotry, which deems bigotry acceptable if directed at groups whose numbers previously protected them; shock-value bigotry, which takes advantage of a fresh way to break social rules; and, most prominently, bigotry against anti-bigots, who are accused of being prickly people determined to quash both liberty and humor by misinterpreting innocent remarks.

Stylistic compression has not served to squelch competition but has spread it to include such previously humble articles as tennis shoes and drinking water, and introduced a pure form of competing with names on labels, where intrinsic value may not be a factor. Meanwhile, the demise of formality has destroyed useful forms that once provided some pleasant variety, such as the touches that distinguished important occasions from ordinary ones, age from youth, and degrees of relationship, from intimate to acquaintance to telemarketer. For a people who profess to despise phoniness, we have locked ourselves into the charade of being forever young and on terms of friendship with everyone.

The hard part

It is not some sort of perverse law of nature that keeps these problems multiplying. We get into trouble because we keep dealing with them, one by one, at a superficial level, without tackling the underlying conflicts.

Our etiquette is rich with paradoxical aims. We want liberty and order, liberty and equality, equality and special respect, openness and privacy, spontaneity and tradition, continuity and change.

And why not? This should not be beyond people who were

clever and audacious enough to pair equality and etiquette in the first place. However, it takes work and trade-offs and being willing to face the concessions and compromises.

The first great task on the agenda is to acknowledge a standardized national etiquette that is firmly enough fixed to allow people to learn and practice it in the security that they will then be credited with good will and able to interpret the intentions of others. As it is, the assumption that people know and follow the simplest methods for annoyance control is wildly optimistic. Instructions have to be announced every time we participate in the most ordinary activities of the society: Don't talk during the movie, bus your trash, answer this invitation, wait your turn, turn off your pager during the ceremony, let the donor know that the present arrived and is appreciated, leave your message after the beep.

The restriction on liberty involved in agreeing to perform such functions without prompting is not crippling. Surely that amount of freedom is worth trading for freedom from being coerced and annoyed by others' claiming the freedom to break into line and leave their trash for you.

The harder job is to make the system porous without shooting it full of holes. There will be plenty of people attempting that.

Standardization

A righteous challenge, commonly made, is that any choice of rules is exclusive. So it is, in the sense of not including everything, but not in the sense of devaluing what is excluded. On the contrary, Americans are fascinated by the etiquette of others, whether they are foreigners, celebrities, rich people, poor people, or teenagers.

American etiquette is drawn from such sources, and continues to absorb elements wherever it finds something of use or charm. We have rich people who cultivate foreign accents, teenagers who try to look poor, and an entire population trying to look like teenagers, except for those who are. We have adopted so many gestures of greeting from different sources in recent decades—air kisses, hugs, bows and curtsies, high-fives, namaste, shoulder-thumping, knuckle-thumping, to name a few, each with its variations—that people are dancing at one another in all directions just in the course of saying hello. If such gestures are obviously well intentioned, even if unknown and unexpected, they are not likely to cause trouble. If they leave room for suspicion, they do. Someone who greeted people by slapping their bottoms would not be likely to get away with claiming it was the custom of his culture.

Standardization only means that at any given time, there should be an overriding body of rules that everyone can interpret and handle. Otherwise, there are daily disconnections that wear people out: the mangling of names as people try to guess the informal versions strangers prefer, the insistence on literal interpretations of conventions that produces hostile responses to such thoughtless pleasantries as "Have a good one" or "How do I look?"

Beyond that, people are free to practice other forms of etiquette among themselves or for interested outsiders, which is to say people who know or want to learn how to interpret and perform them. It is comparable to speaking a foreign language or slang, which is a wonderful skill, but no substitute for being able to make oneself understood to one's fellow citizens.

That is not, however, to say that all customs are acceptable in

America, even ones with ancient credentials. When there is compelling philosophical or religious meaning attached, an extra warning is out to grant leeway and respect for its practice, unless the meaning violates American notions of freedom, decency (such of that as is left), or—the value in high ascendancy at the moment—hygiene. We have lots of tolerance for strange wedding customs and none for arranged marriages, great enthusiasm for new dishes and horror at shared utensils.

Respect

Respect is a huge issue to Americans, and it is a tall order. We are always checking querulously if we are getting enough, and there are so many kinds we require. We demand respect for our origins, respect for our professional and romantic situations, respect for our opinions, respect for our privacy, respect for our feelings, respect for our talents, respect for our achievements, and respect for something called "who I am," which can mean anything, including the demand for noninterference when your child wants to have his tongue pierced.

Respect for age has been challenged, however, on the grounds that it is no sign of merit. The demand for it, an elderly equivalent of respect-for-who-I-am, ceased when we decided that it was embarrassing to grow old. Nobody still says things such as, "How dare you talk to me like that, young lady—I'm old enough to be your father." On the contrary, it is respectful treatment that would be countered with a reproof: "Oh, don't call me Mr. That was my father. You make me feel old."

Respect for family is no longer in effect, even though respect for family origins is of high concern. The idea seems to be: Watch what you say about my people, but let me tell you why I hate my parents.

In regard to romance, what is sought is approval, rather than respect, although that is the term that is used. It is similarly unsatisfactory to be told that someone respects your opinions but has not been swayed by them. In matters of choice, respect for privacy is the best hope of protection. People who fail to respect their own privacy to the extent of promiscuously issuing confidences and seeking validation are asking to be judged, rather than respected, and probably will be. Only parents seeking to extract information from their children are desperate enough to promise that they can listen to their confessions without passing judgment—yet if they could surrender such a basic parental function, they would only be rubber-stamping the child's standards.

Respect in regard to the job one holds is a particularly touchy matter, since the answer to "What do you do?" has become the point of identity most used for adults—and since hardly anyone feels placed according to his deserts. Parceling respect according to job ranking sounds an awful lot like the system American etiquette was invented to avoid. It does not take more than the ability of one person to reply, "I'm a landowner," and the other, "I'm a serf," to impose a class system. Egalitarian etiquette accords respect to everyone just for being a human being, with extra helpings awarded for age, hardship, and merit.

Care was taken that respect should be accorded to the highest office, the presidency, but some of those who eventually became president had vehemently opposed this allowing significantly more respect than that to which any citizen was entitled. Now the distinction between the presidency and the person who holds that office has shrunk, and political opponents no longer say, "I despise the man but I respect the office."

We were left instructions on how to amend the Constitution, so we have the principle of making changes in accordance with developments in human enlighten-ment and other conditions. Our etiquette follows the same principle, but the instructions were missing. We have the exam-ple of change being a slow and deliberate process, so as not to be swayed by fleeting fads and sentiments. We know it requires the consent of the governed, and that it should work for every-one. We know we have to give weight to tradition, preserving beloved old habits yet jettisoning troublesome ones, and to be open to modernization, learning practical new ways.

These should be our guidelines for changing etiquette. The reality is that everybody jumps in to declare or combat change without authority, without a consensus, and without considera-tion of how it might affect anyone but himself. Whatever peo-ple no longer feel like doing, such as offering apologies or thanks or condolences or responses to hospitality, they declare no longer has to be done; it is only when they are the ones who are injured or generous or bereaved or issuing invitations, they reverse themselves.

There have also been those who labored tirelessly to wrest increased politeness on behalf of people who had not received a fair share. A few such campaigns were actually conducted politely. This is a less dramatic approach than most reformers prefer, but one that speaks directly to the sense of fairness of the society. It is to the credit of American society that rude tactics—shocking public sensibility in irrelevant ways (usually meaning combining idealism with indecency), attacking or embarrassing bystanders, and leaving trash on the streets—are forgiven if the cause is perceived as just.

As things change, there should be a grace period when those who have trouble reprogramming themselves are helped along with gentle and tolerant guidance. The grandfather clause, we used to call it, before the grandfathers abused it by decades of denying having gotten the word about treating women with the same respect they expected to receive and keeping their hands to themselves. The time is long since up for them—as it is for grandmothers who address their granddaughters by their husbands' surnames no matter how many times they have been told that they did not change their names at marriage.

Enforcement

Finally, there is the enforcement problem. As the practice of etiquette is, by definition, voluntary, how can it be required, much less reconciled with our respect for the sovereignty of others who may dissent from it, and our faith in reform that entitles transgressors to obtain clean slates? In addition to the aforementioned grandfather clause, allowances are made for those who cannot be expected to have mastered the system, such as newcomers and small children. Medical excuses and religious requirements are accepted at face value.

Does that excuse everybody? How much toleration do we have to have for violations? Do we have to forgive everyone who apologizes no matter how often he repeats the fault?

As a good etiquette system should be porous enough to absorb valid changes, whether imported or invented; flexible enough to permit other practices for compelling reasons or for emotional satisfaction within subgroups of the society; tolerant

312 Judith Martin

enough to grant leeway to laggards and eccentrics who seem to
be of good faith; and generous enough to forgive the penitent,
will there be anything left to call a system?

Failed
techniques

This difficulty has divided reformers into
two opposing camps: There is the nonjudg-
mental approach, which has given up trying
to enforce etiquette but believes it can coax
people into making fundamental changes in
their attitudes and aspirations that will result in untutored kindness amounting to the same thing. Then there is the draconian
approach, which also cultivates a lack of judgment. This is evidence in what are called "zero tolerance" policies, where etiquette is policed without consideration of motivation or other
circumstances that we acknowledge to be necessary in applying
law to achieve justice in particular cases.

Neither the therapeutic nor the police-state method of
enforcing etiquette has proved effective, and neither is harmless.
They are both rife with the very outrages that have been falsely
ascribed to etiquette—seriously interfering with liberty and
applying rules mindlessly. Popular psychology and vigilantism
have made their own contributions to turning society intrusive
and inconsiderate. Etiquette only attempts to control people's
behavior, not their psyches, and is meticulous about giving violators the benefit of the doubt.

Hardest of all to perform with a straight face is etiquette's
requirement that the presumption of innocence be granted to
those who look guilty—as a technique, if nothing else. "I'm
sure you didn't intend to offend anyone" is as broad an offering
of peace as can be made in the hope of inspiring a retreat from
rudeness. Apologies, groveling, and sending flowers are other

forms of disarmament. When such offers are ignored and offenses cannot be passed off as accidents, the violator can still be declared an eccentric whose failure to meet common standards is harmless.

However, all of these peacemaking offers have been so thoroughly abused that the ability to imagine good will behind bad behavior is exhausted. When newcomers don't bother to learn and children are not taught, offenders are brash and offenses are serious, and apologies are unrelated to reform, those escape routes must be narrowed.

Polite punishment

It is in desperation over this state of affairs that the victims of rudeness have considered every remedy except traditional methods of polite punishment. It may have been forgotten that the only weapons recognized for legitimate self-defense against willful and unrepentant rudeness are shame and exclusion.

As these are some of the same weapons employed by diplomacy against the transgressions of sovereign nations, we are aware that they do not always work. Still, the condemnation of other nations and exclusion from international organizations and rites can be surprisingly effective, and sensible governments refrain from skipping that approach in order to proceed directly to warfare. These techniques are also surprisingly effective at the etiquette level as an alternative to proceeding directly to bullying and bashing.

It is odd that just when the use of shame is being suggested in America to augment the law's more concrete methods of dealing with violators, polite people have become too timid to use it as an informal method of self-protection. A society that forces public confessions and thinks of posting signs on the houses of convicted sex offenders and the cars of convicted drunk drivers nevertheless shrinks from expressing disapproval of the rude by rebuffing their slights and refusing their company. That leaves the choice of either swallowing insults, intrusions, and outrageous demands, which is falsely deemed to be polite, or adopting the very behavior being condemned.

For the etiquette leaders of the world to be caught in this pointless exercise—futilely flailing away at the same pesky irritations with the same pointless instruments instead of advancing the cause—is pitiful. All it would take to solve our own problem is a commitment to obey our own etiquette code, which is minimally restrictive, to adjust it where deemed necessary by achieving consensus and practicing patience during transitions, to teach it to our children, and to marginalize people who defy it. Then we could get on with the more interesting task of translating the concepts of fairness and compassion into everyday behavior for a complicated and volatile world.

Concentrating

What is distracting us? Could it be—entertainment? Is there possibly something wrong with that youthful insistence that it is perfectly possible to concentrate on serious work and enjoy a favorite show at the same time?

There is, if the standards of one activity seep into the other when their objectives happen to be antithetical. The purpose of the entertainment industry is to entertain. The purpose of etiquette is to provide an atmosphere where people can seek their own entertainment—the pursuit of happiness, as we say—without being gratuitously thwarted by other such pursuers.

This is where our show business orientation, which has dramatized our dreams and provided us with wonderful flair and frills, is counterproductive. People are now complaining that we are learning our own history from filmmakers' interpretations, and therefore getting our past distorted by the selectivity and simplifications necessary to turn raw life into a coherent ninety-minute story—but we have always gotten our social history from fictional versions. The difference is that we are now knowingly sacrificing what truth we can learn to enhance dramatic values.

As Harriet Beecher Stowe pointed out in her complaint that English literature continued to present the master-servant relationship in feudal terms centuries after feudalism, the arts often lag behind social change in the interests of supplying a clear class structure as background to a story. In the American theatrical tradition, the rich are heartless (with the exception of beautiful and rebellious heiresses and an occasional conscience-stricken tycoon) and worshipful of etiquette, by which they mean only the most formal forms, which they execute stiffly and humorlessly; while the poor are goodhearted and behave "naturally," which is to say that they are full of generous impulses and madcap fun.

Dramatically, we would not want it otherwise. Depicting the poor as loutish and the rich as charming would offend our sense of fairness, and be no more true. In real-life America, unlike countries that had insulated, self-perpetuating aristocracies, exhibiting good manners was as likely to be a solace for the poor and a tool for advancement for the upwardly mobile as an inherited habit of the rich.

Theatrically, outward behavior has to provide clues to inner morality, but when we apply the convention that manners are a sign of bad character, we distort our sense of what makes society work. It is as if the convention of the car chase, with its thrilling maneuvers and miraculous escapes, were taken literally as a guide to how traffic works.

The simplest television fan surely knows that what looks real is usually staged, but the habit of using its perspective to interpret reality takes hold all the same. Dramatic tension and exaggeration, as well as the relief of tension through jokes and personal confessions, have been introduced into such institutions as politics, religion, art, education, and museums with the compelling argument that their first job is to get people's attention.

We know the difference between political opponents and real enemies, but elections have become more entertaining as candidates cast themselves as good guys rescuing us from bad. When they offer up their personal stories, we judge them on their ability to appear concerned about us, to be relaxed on television, to make fun of themselves, and to redeem themselves from their mistakes—which is why the ultimate sin is to refuse to confide in us totally. We figure that no harm is done in skipping tiresome debates, because few of our officials are ideologues, anyway: They get their positions from polling us, so it would only be telling us what we told them.

Similarly, the argument that television dictates our behavior is belied by its worthy effort to picture a society in which the races have achieved full social and professional parity. Show business does not originate social ideas, it merely exaggerates them for dramatic effect. The changes it wreaks on institutions is to dizzy them with visions of achieving the scale of success enjoyed by popular entertainment, and thus lure them to copy its lowest common denominator approach and its willingness to jettison the unpopular.

Sacrificing standards

For individuals, casting ourselves as potential stars has given us heartbreaking requirements that may be necessary in show business but handicap us unnecessarily in life.

Actors must deal with the professional disadvantage that audiences like to watch people who are young and beautiful, but societies have been able to operate on the opposite, more humane system, of honoring the elderly most and setting a much lower standard for attractiveness. By making the same requirements of life as we do of show business, we doom everyone, including the temporarily beautiful, to failure.

Even the moment when stardom seems most graspable contains this doom. The love story is a perennially satisfactory plot device, and we have now dressed the wedding in such lavishness as to make starring in a huge production number available to all. The trouble is that then it is over. A love story requires suspense, which marriage is supposed to lack, and therefore it disappoints those who feel they will never again capture such a starring role. Little wonder that people want to do remakes, with new love stories and new weddings, rather than be relegated to the vague character parts we have available in the post-wedding life.

Adventure stories more easily lend themselves to repeated episodes, but their attractions—problem and solution, clearly presented and resolved in thirty minutes—play havoc with our expectations and sense of timing. The notion that every problem even has a solution, let alone a fast one, has led us to the angry conclusion that all tragedies, including death, can be traced to human error, and that someone ought to be held responsible.

The mixing of culture and commerce has skewered social relationships so that there is no refuge from being financially dunned, and the frank exercise of our critical faculties has robbed us of whatever comfort might be left. Everyone has become a critic of everyone else, but we have no such standards in regard to our own responsibility. There, the dramatic message is that a flop was just bad luck and there is no use dwelling on it. Continuity is so little expected that it is treated as unfair to bring up any past failures someone may have had; reputation has dissolved into image.

Finally, we have taken our sense of privacy from celebrities whose professional value can be estimated and enhanced by the extent to which it is fed by garnering attention as a public character. Not only has this led to the voluntary surrender of privacy, but it has subverted taste and dignity to marketability. The plain virtues stand no chance against the shock value of the obscene and the wicked, including criminal behavior, because they attract no attention. The saddest consequence is that fame and fortune, the advantages for which so many people have sacrificed living less dramatic but pleasanter lives, rarely follow.

Time to turn it off

None of these consequences is the fault of the entertainment industry, which has been unfairly blamed for failing to teach and embody the very attributes we have dropped from the society in hopes of achieving its glamour and success. If entertainers dropped the requirements of their own profession to become our models and instructors, that glamour and success would disappear overnight.

American drama has made enormous contributions to our cultural life by illuminating American character, dramatizing our legends and hopes, brightening our lives with humor and suspense and spectacle, and occasionally providing actual insights. It employs techniques, such as the symbolic use of costume, that we would do well to study.

However, people who mistake the stage for the world have botched or neglected an even more fascinating and certainly nobler task: that of studying the Socratic question of how they, and how we all, should best live our lives. The quest could continue to be, as it was in the past, one of America's greatest contributions to the world.